M000014575

The Psych 101 Series

James C. Kaufman, PhD, Series Editor

Director, Learning Research Institute
California State University at San Bernardino

Dr. Michael D. Mumford is the George Lynn Cross Distinguished Research Professor of Psychology at the University of Oklahoma, where he directs the Center for Applied Social Research. He received his doctoral degree from the University of Georgia in 1983 in the fields of industrial and organizational psychology and psychometrics. Dr. Mumford is a fellow of the American Psychological Association (Divisions 3, 5, and 14), the Society for Industrial and Organizational Psychology, and the American Psychological Society. He has written more than 250 articles on creativity, innovation, planning, leadership, and ethics. He serves as senior editor of the *Leadership Quarterly* and is on the editorial boards of the *Creativity Research Journal*, the *Journal of Creative Behavior*, *IEEE Transactions on Engineering Management*, and the *Journal of Business Ethics*. Dr. Mumford has served as principal investigator on grants totaling more than $30 million from the National Science Foundation, the National Institutes of Health, the Department of Defense, the Department of Labor, and the Department of State. He is a recipient of the Society for Industrial and Organizational Psychology's M. Scott Myers Award for Applied Research in the Workplace. Dr. Mumford's professional interests lie in the assessment and development of high-level talent. His current research focuses on four specific areas: the identification and measurement of creative thinking skills, successful leadership skills in dynamic organizational settings, the relationship between workplace structure and skill growth and development, and the application of life history as a tool for understanding career development.

Leadership

101

Edited by
Michael D. Mumford, PhD

SPRINGER PUBLISHING COMPANY

Springer Publishing Company, LLC
11 West 42nd Street
New York, NY 10036
www.springerpub.com

Acquisitions Editor: Philip Laughlin
Project Manager: Mark Frazier
Cover Design: Mimi Flow
Composition: Apex CoVantage, LLC

09 10 11 12/ 5 4 3 2 1

Library of Congress Cataloging-in-Publication Data
Ebook ISBN: 978-0-8261-1135-7
Leadership 101 / edited by Michael D. Mumford.
     p. cm. — (The Psych 101 series)
  Includes bibliographical references and index.
  ISBN 978-0-8261-1134-0 (alk. paper)
 1. Leadership—Research.   2. Leadership.   I. Mumford, Michael D.
II. Title: Leadership one oh one.   III. Title: Leader one hundred one.
  HM1261.L4145   2009
    303.3'4—dc22   2009029257

Printed in the United States of America by Hamilton Printing

We would like to dedicate *Leadership 101* to the graduate program in industrial and organizational psychology at the University of Oklahoma. We thank you all for your support throughout the production of this book.

Contents

CONTENTS

Contributors

Alison L. Antes, PhD Candidate, Department of Industry and Organizational Psychology, the University of Oklahoma, Norman, Oklahoma

Jamie D. Barrett, BA, Department of Industry and Organizational Psychology, the University of Oklahoma, Norman, Oklahoma

Cheryl K. Beeler, PhD Candidate, Department of Industry and Organizational Psychology, the University of Oklahoma, Norman, Oklahoma

Cristina L. Byrne, MS, Department of Industry and Organizational Psychology, the University of Oklahoma, Norman, Oklahoma

Jay J. Caughron, PhD Candidate, Department of Industry and Organizational Psychology, the University of Oklahoma, Norman, Oklahoma

Tamara L. Friedrich, PhD Candidate, Department of Industry and Organizational Psychology, the University of Oklahoma, Norman, Oklahoma

Amanda S. Shipman, MS, Department of Industry and Organizational Psychology, the University of Oklahoma, Norman, Oklahoma

William B. Vessey, BA, Department of Industry and Organizational Psychology, the University of Oklahoma, Norman, Oklahoma

Preface

Leadership is a topic that has piqued the interest of many—across a variety of scholarly areas and levels of study. Those interested in political science, business, philosophy, history, and psychology, among others, have each taken unique approaches to understanding this quite important phenomenon. Leadership is a popular topic of study because nearly everyone has been affected by a leader or has been one themselves, and the outcomes of leadership are particularly critical. In this book, we hope to help those with an interest in leadership achieve a level of understanding beyond common assumptions made about leaders and leadership. In this vein, this book is geared toward novice leadership scholars or those who seek a summary of the current status of the field. Example populations that may benefit from this book are individuals in secondary and collegiate education who are not otherwise familiar with scholarly approaches to understanding leadership or individuals that study related topics but need a comprehensive review of leadership.

Because so many seek to understand leadership, we have sought to provide a road map for individuals to continue on to more in-depth study. In doing so, we have addressed what leadership is and the assumptions that are often made about it, so that novice leadership scholars will have an adequate foundation upon which to build their understanding of leadership concepts. We present this information from both a psychological and a business perspective and use research on relevant leadership topics to help readers separate fact from fiction and assumptions from empirical evidence. After reading *Leadership 101*, individuals should understand what leadership is, how it operates in the wider social system, and its important causes and outcomes.

Given the introductory nature of the book, we describe leadership topics in such a way that individuals could obtain a general understanding of specific leadership topics. Then, should they want to, they could delve deeper into specific areas. In addition to reviewing general information about a given topic (e.g., leadership traits), we also review important research findings on that topic, along with why it is an important consideration within real-world organizations. We felt it critical to take both a research and an applied focus, so that readers would understand not only how we know what we know about leadership, but also why it is important that we spend time researching these topics and what we can do with what we find.

The layout of the book consists of three general sections—the first three chapters provide important introductory information, the next four chapters focus on specific leadership topic areas, and the final chapter provides a peek into the future of leadership research. Within each chapter we have provided plenty of real-world examples to illustrate the concepts presented. Additionally, at the end of each chapter we have included key terms and phrases, review questions, supplemental readings, and activities that can be done as individuals or as groups to further develop an understanding of the information.

In chapter 1, we review ways of defining leadership and provide a chronological overview of the approaches that have been taken to studying leadership. In chapter 2, we specifically address many of the assumptions that have been made about leadership and some of the important questions that come up in discussions about leadership. Providing a context for these questions and addressing these assumptions is important in order to help novice scholars understand leadership on a deeper level. In chapter 3, we provide a summary of important information with regard to research methods. Because we review important leadership research throughout the book, it is critical that readers have a general understanding of how leadership research is conducted. Chapters 4 through 7 focus on specific areas of leadership research—leader traits, skills, and behaviors in chapter 4; follower and situational factors in chapter 5; how leaders think in chapter 6; and outstanding leadership in chapter 7. Finally, in chapter 8, we review some of the important emerging topics in the study of leadership.

Leadership is a very important topic, and as you read through this book we hope to not only address your questions about leadership but also continually inspire new ones for which this book can serve as a road map for future exploration.

Michael D. Mumford, PhD
University of Oklahoma
Department of Psychology
Norman, Oklahoma

We would like to acknowledge the editorial board members of the *Leadership Quarterly*, not only for their support and contribution to this book, but also for their continued commitment to the advancement of leadership research.

1

The History of Leadership Research

Tamara L. Friedrich

> He who has never learned to obey cannot be a good commander.
>
> —*Aristotle*
>
> There is nothing more difficult to take in hand, more perilous to conduct, or more uncertain in its success, than to take the lead in the introduction of a new order of things.
>
> —*Niccolò Machiavelli*

Leadership is a topic that has garnered the attention of both novice and notable scholars for centuries. As demonstrated by Aristotle's observations in the 350 BC work *Politics*, and Niccolò Machiavelli's 1532 work *The Prince*, it was as popular a topic among notable historic scholars as it is today. Where some research topics may only affect a subsection of the population, nearly *everyone* is exposed to leaders and leadership at some point in their lives. Also contributing to this consistent interest in leadership is the abundance of questions—questions that may very well have led you to this book. What makes a leader successful or unsuccessful? Are certain people more likely to become leaders? How do I become a better leader? Or, more generally, what is leadership, exactly? Leadership researchers have sought to address these questions, and many others, and we hope you will find the answers to your questions as you read through the following chapters. We also hope, however, to inspire further questioning and critical thinking about the topic of leadership.

With regard to the format of this text, we will begin by providing the necessary background knowledge of leadership in the initial three chapters. Specifically, we will focus on the history of leadership theories, reviewing past assumptions made about leadership and how research has addressed these assumptions, and describing the general methods that leadership researchers have used to study leadership. Following the first three chapters, we will shift our focus to several emerging, or hot, topics with regard to leadership research; and finally, in the last chapter, we will take a look at the future of leadership research. Within each chapter we have integrated case studies, information on critical research, biographies and speeches of real-world leaders, discussion questions, and activities to supplement the content discussed within the chapter. In addition, the important concepts within each chapter have been highlighted and defined in the margin and further readings are provided at the end of each chapter.

The study of leadership, aside from being popular, is important because it also has quite serious implications. In recent years, it has become clear that errors in leadership have dramatic repercussions. Consider the effects of the unethical behaviors of the leaders of Enron, or the fumbling of response efforts following Hurricane Katrina. Leaders' actions often carry more weight than the actions of others within an organization, both because they have greater responsibility but also because they are in more visible positions. Leaders are the ones who can set the tone, create the plan, and demonstrate to their followers the appropriate (or inappropriate) way to behave. They are the ones held accountable, and the critical decisions fall onto their laps.

Thus, understanding the characteristics and behaviors of leaders, both successful and unsuccessful, can provide the foundation for identifying and promoting good leadership and preventing leadership that may go awry. At a more basic level, we, ourselves, can take the findings of leadership researchers and apply them in our own lives, whether we are leaders or followers.

To begin our review of leadership research we now start, in chapter one, with a review of the history of leadership research. There are several important learning objectives for this chapter that are highlighted here.

Learning Objectives
- Understand the array of questions faced by leadership researchers
- Understand the different ways in which leadership can be defined
- Understand the shifts in focus of research efforts over the years
- Understand the implications of leadership research

DEFINING LEADERSHIP

As mentioned previously, leadership has long been of interest to scholars in many different areas of study, including psychology, management, history, and political science. However, leadership, as an area of research, did not really take off until the 20th century, but it made particularly great strides in the second half of the century. Although this may seem like a relatively short period, significant progress was made in this short time. The questions of leadership are quite compelling, and interest in the field continues to grow at a rapid pace. The first and most frequently asked, yet rarely agreed upon, question is—What is leadership? We turn now to the many definitions of leadership.

Leadership has been defined in many ways. It is very likely that you believe you have a clear idea of what leadership is, given that you have likely been exposed to many leaders in your lifetime.

Consider this, however: We can probably all agree that the president of the United States is a leader—but would you consider your teacher or professor a leader? What about a manager? Is there a difference between a leader and a manager? Can leadership be exhibited by someone who is not in a formal leadership position? Can more than one person fulfill the leadership role? Clearly, the concept of leadership is quite complex, and questions about leadership can be framed in several ways.

The main question that seems to emerge, when formulating a definition of leadership, is whether we are defining a person, a role, or a process. If you were asked to define leadership, do you first think of a person who epitomizes certain characteristics? Or do you think of a position in an organization in which you are a member? Perhaps you may have even thought of what happens in the exchange between a manager and a subordinate. A **person-focused definition of leadership** would specify a given set of traits or skills that would identify a person as a leader. A **role-focused definition of leadership** would focus on a set of behaviors or actions leaders must engage in to do their job. The person focus and the role focus may seem similar; however, by defining leadership as a role, it is possible to consider that it may be occupied by more than one person. Finally, a **process-focused definition of leadership** focuses on how leaders interact with followers regardless of role.

The questions that researchers seek to answer about leadership are often

Person-focused definition of leadership—a mind-set that defines leadership by the traits or skills that make someone a leader

Role-focused definition of leadership—a mind-set that defines leadership as a set of behaviors or actions that someone acting as a leader engages in

Process-focused definition of leadership—a mind-set that defines leadership as an influence process that occurs between individuals

directly related to the definitions with which they are operating. For instance, taking a person-focused view might lead to questions about what type of person is likely to emerge as a leader, who is likely to be more successful as a leader, what cognitive or decision-making processes a leader undergoes, and so on. A role-focused definition might lead to questions regarding the behaviors a person in a leadership position engages in, whether elements of the role can be shared, or whether there are differences between the management role and the leadership role. Finally, a process approach may result in questions with regard to the relationship between a leader and a follower, or whether the process of leadership is influenced by changes in a situation. For the purpose of the current effort we will define leadership generally as to encompass all three concepts: **leadership** is the influence of others toward a collective goal.

In addition to defining leadership, it is critical to also identify some of the terms that will be used as we discuss leadership, and leadership research in particular. The persons subject to a leader's influence are called many things—followers, subordinates, and constituencies, among others. For the purpose of our efforts we will use the most general of these terms—followers. Thus, **followers** are those individuals a leader influences for the purpose of achieving a collective goal. A second important term, which has already been used several times, is **influence**. According to Yukl (2006), influencing others involves altering the motives or perceptions of another to accomplish a given goal. There are many ways in which influence may be exerted, and these specific methods will be reviewed in chapter 5. Along similar

> **Leadership**—the influence of others toward a collective goal
> **Followers**—those individuals on whom a leader exerts influence for the purpose of achieving a collective goal
> **Influence**—altering the motives or perceptions of another to accomplish a given goal

> **Power**—the capacity of one person to influence the behavior or attitudes of others

lines, another term often used in conjunction with, or in the place of, leadership is **power**. It has been established that there are many different types of power a leader may possess (see chapter 5), but as a general definition, we use Northouse's (2007) description of power as the capacity or potential to influence others. The concepts of power and influence are discussed further in chapter 5, a chapter focused on relational and situational theories of leadership.

Finally, an important distinction that we must address is the distinction between leadership and management—two terms that are often used interchangeably. In the 2008 Republican presidential primaries, Senator John McCain made the point in several speeches that the country "did not need a manager, it needed a leader." He was arguing against Governor Mitt Romney's assertion that the executive roles he had held as a governor and as a business leader would help him serve as the nation's highest executive. It is likely that Senator McCain was hoping to invoke the positive qualities that are more stereotypically associated with a leader—inspiration, motivation, a guide out of troubled times—and devalue the image of a manager as a more sterile figure. But when it comes down to it, is there really that stark a difference between leaders and managers?

As Yukl (2006) pointed out, it is possible for a leader to not be a manager, and for a manager to not be a leader, but there is a great deal more overlap possible between the two than some may think. This assumption will be discussed in greater detail in chapter 2, but for now it is important to note that the research on these two titles typically focuses on some differences. According to Kotter (1990), who devoted an entire book to addressing the differences between leaders and managers, the distinctions between the two can be drawn with regard to their outcomes. He asserts that management is intended to produce organization, structure, clear problem solving, and action, whereas leadership focuses more on initiating change by communicating a vision or goals and seeking to inspire others into action. It is easy to see, however, that many of the behaviors managers engage in could also be undertaken by leaders and vice versa.

APPROACHES TO LEADERSHIP RESEARCH

As mentioned earlier in the chapter, the study of leadership has been ongoing for hundreds of years. The initial work, however, focused more on general observations and discussing one's own experiences. For instance, several ancient scholars documented their observations of the rise and fall of leaders or their theories of how leaders should rule. The most notable example of this is Niccolò Machiavelli's *The Prince,* in which he describes the ways an aspiring prince could attain leadership, or how a prince already in a position of power could rule effectively. Additionally, the lives of leaders have been documented by authors for centuries for the benefit of posterity, but also for future leaders to learn from leaders in the past. Even religious documents are sources of observation and guidance on effective leadership. Machiavelli's very early work on understanding leadership is incredibly important and often serves as a foundation on which research is built. The focus of this current book, however, is on the scientific research of leadership, which is a much more modern occurrence—beginning in earnest over the last half century.

As researchers over the last 50 years or so have sought to answer the many questions of leadership, there have been several broad changes in the way in which they have approached these questions. In the beginning of the century, leadership scholars were interested in finding specific traits or characteristics that differentiated leaders from others. A lack of conclusive findings, however, led to a shift in which researchers began to focus more on the behaviors that managers and leaders exhibited and under what conditions they engaged in certain actions. It became apparent, however, that there was more to leadership than just leader behavior, and scholars sought to understand the relational and situational dynamics involved, particularly the relationship between leaders and their followers. More recently, the field of leadership has focused more on the decision-making patterns of leaders, and what differentiates outstanding leadership from general leadership. Several leadership frontiers remain to be explored, and in the last chapter we will discuss a few areas that are likely to be the focus of future scholars. Figure 1.1 provides the chronology of these shifts in the focus of leadership research. In this chapter, we will briefly review each of these approaches to leadership research, and each of them will be discussed in greater detail in the following chapters. It is important to note that, although we discuss the different times to which these approaches correspond, a particular approach was not the only one used during that time. In fact, these approaches have all been used by researchers throughout the years, but we will discuss the predominant approach taken during each time period.

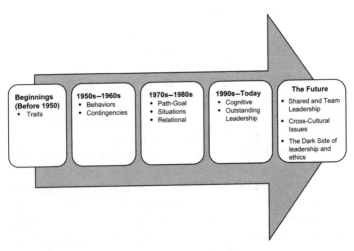

Figure 1.1 Timeline of leadership research.

BEGINNINGS: BEFORE 1950

The Trait Approach

Before the start of the information age, and with it the onslaught of sound bites that expose every error and transgression of individuals in leadership positions, the idea of leadership was highly romanticized. Leaders were extraordinary individuals exhibiting exceptional qualities that set them apart from others. More specifically, it was believed that there was a set of characteristics, or traits, that made someone a leader. Imbedded in this approach was an overall positive spin on the characteristics of leaders. Thus, early leadership researchers sought to identify these exceptional characteristics. The theories applied have often been referred to as "great man" theories as a result of the positive approach taken to leadership.

Studies that took this approach to research used what is called the trait approach, which means researchers focused on identifying the personal attributes leaders possessed that set them apart. It was believed that the presence of these particular traits could cause individuals to emerge as leaders or make them more effective as leaders than others who did not possess these traits. For instance, in an early review of research using the trait approach, Stogdill (1948) found that group leaders were different from group members with regard to characteristics such as intelligence, alertness, sociability, and self-confidence. Other studies over the years have identified different traits, along with situational factors that may influence whether these traits truly impact leadership. However, the traditional trait approach focuses solely on the leader—a characteristic of this approach that some view as a weakness. This perceived weakness, and the generally inconclusive findings of early trait studies, resulted in a gradual shift by leadership researchers away from the trait approach. A more detailed review of the trait approach, including research findings, strengths, weaknesses, and applications, can be found in chapter 4.

1950s–1960s

The Behavioral Approach

Following the frustration of the inconclusive findings that emerged from these early trait studies, leadership researchers turned to evaluating what leaders *do* rather than their personal characteristics. For instance, rather than study if a leader's personality characteristics could predict whether they would succeed as a leader, a researcher taking the behavioral approach may be interested in what goal-setting behaviors the leader engaged in with his or her followers and if those behaviors led to the desired outcomes. Two universities, Ohio State University and the University of Michigan, engaged in significant behavioral research efforts during this time that are considered the foundation of the behavioral approach.

The researchers involved in the Ohio State studies administered questionnaires to individuals about the behaviors of their supervisors. They found that the behavior of the leaders fell into two broad categories—behaviors related to initiating structure (e.g., "my supervisor assigns people under him to particular tasks"), and behaviors related to consideration (e.g., "my supervisor treats all of his subordinates equally") (Fleishman, 1953). The researchers involved in the University of Michigan studies used interviews and questionnaires given to real-world leaders to evaluate leader behaviors, and they examined the relationship of these behaviors to group-level indicators of effective leadership (e.g., group productivity). They found that leaders could be classified as effective or ineffective based on three types of behaviors—task-oriented behaviors, relations-oriented behaviors, and participative leadership behaviors (Katz, Maccoby, Gurin, & Floor, 1951; Likert, 1967). Although their findings have been subject to criticism over the years, the general categories of "task focused," or "initiating structure," and "relationship focused," or "consideration," are still used in leadership studies to this day.

Following these two initial efforts, which are discussed in more detail in chapter 4, the behavioral approach increased in popularity, which led to one of the major criticisms of this approach—that there were far too many categorizations of leader behaviors. Additionally, many of the studies relied on the observations of followers, who would respond to surveys about their leaders' behaviors. This approach is limiting because it assumes that those reporting on the leaders' behaviors are witnessing *everything* the leader does, which is unlikely. Further, much of the behavioral approach work made generalized predictions about the effects of leader behaviors on desired outcomes. Similarly to researchers utilizing the trait approach, the impact of other variables, such as follower motivation, was not often considered by those using the behavioral approach. Thus, leadership scholars began to question whether the success of leaders with certain traits, or engaged in certain types of behaviors, was contingent on these other variables. This led to a shift toward research that considered more situational variables in the leadership equation, the first of which was the contingency approach.

The Contingency Approach

The first concerted effort to consider situational variables in leadership studies was initiated by a model of leadership called the LPC contingency model (Fiedler, 1967). Fielder, using the LPC contingency model, sought to explore the interaction between a leader's motivational tendencies and the characteristics of a situation in predicting a group's ultimate performance. The leader's motivational tendency was determined by asking them questions about the co-worker that they had the most difficult time working with—or their least preferred co-worker (LPC). Based on their LPC score, they were categorized as either task motivated or relationship motivated (remind of you any other approaches we have learned about so far?). Fiedler and his colleagues then classified the leader's situation based on leader-member relations, the leader's position of power, and the level of structure of the group's task. They found that either a high

LPC leader or a low LPC would be better suited under different types of situations (e.g., good leader-member relations, structured task, and strong position of power). Thus, they found that a situation could, in fact, have an impact on whether different leader traits or behaviors were more appropriate.

The strengths and weakness of this approach will be discussed in greater detail in chapter 5; however, it is important to note that a major criticism of the contingency approach is that it did not address the *how* or *why*. Although a relationship between certain leader traits and group performance was found, we do not understand the mechanism of this effect. For instance, we are still unable to determine *why* a leader that scores high on the LPC scale is better in a situation with poor leader-member relations. The next shift in focus saw leadership researchers attempting to expand on the contingency approach method of considering the situation, but also making a greater effort to answer the *how* and *why* questions.

1970s–1980s

The Path-Goal Approach

As you will recall, leadership is defined as the influence of others toward a collective goal. The path-goal theory of leadership expands on the contingency theory by explaining *how* a leader responds to given situations and influences his or her subordinates' paths toward that collective goal—specifically influencing their job satisfaction and performance. House (1971), and later House and Mitchell (1974), outlined four leader behaviors—supportive leadership, directive leadership, participative leadership, and achievement-oriented leadership—that a leader could employ, depending on the situation and the subordinates' motivational needs, to maximize performance and satisfaction. For example, in a situation that is particularly stressful, a leader may engage in supportive behavior to make his or her subordinates feel they are capable of accomplishing the task and thus reduce anxiety and increase performance and satisfaction.

A particularly valuable contribution of this approach was that, if it was found that certain leader behaviors operated effectively to maintain or improve subordinate satisfaction and performance in various types of situations, leaders could be trained to respond appropriately in similar situations. Follow-up studies, however, have resulted in inconclusive findings, which some researchers attribute to the fact that leader behaviors are considered separately, such that each leader would be classified into a behavioral type. It is more likely, however, that leaders engage in different mixtures of behaviors, and this interaction between different kinds of behaviors at any given time may cause effects that are harder to interpret. Along these lines, Hersey and Blanchard (1993) proposed the situational leadership theory, which evaluated the interaction of two types of leadership behaviors in different situations.

The Situational Approach

The premise of Hersey and Blanchard's (1993) situational leadership theory is that different situations call for different combinations of leader behaviors. Specifically, they proposed that different combinations of supportive and directive leadership behaviors would be appropriate depending on the development level of the followers involved. Where the path-goal theory looked at supportive and directive behaviors separately, the situational theory evaluated combinations of different levels of each type of behavior. For instance, leaders who were engaging in low levels of supportive behavior and low levels of directive behavior were considered to be delegating, whereas leaders who were engaging in low levels of supportive behavior but high levels of directive behavior were considered to be directing. Delegating and directing, along with coaching and supporting, were four leadership styles proposed to be differentially appropriate depending on the level of development of the followers.

Central to this theory is the concept that the levels of development are not static, and, thus, a leader must know which combination of behaviors to engage in for different situations.

As with the contingency and path-goal theories, the situational theory can be used for leader training programs because leaders could be instructed on how and when to engage in these different leadership styles. For instance, the coaching style is considered to be high on both supportive and directive behaviors and would be advisable for leading subordinates who fall into the moderate developmental range—indicating some competence and marginal commitment. A leader could be instructed to provide both the emotional support to increase a subordinate's commitment, as well as the directing behaviors needed to compensate for a subordinate's lack of experience on the task. Although practical, the contingency, path-goal, and situational theories all suffer from a similar criticism in that they seem to address how the leader should respond to *group* situations (e.g., the developmental level of the group of followers); however, individual members of the group may have very different needs or present different situational variables. The relational approach to leadership sought to address the situation at the dyadic, or leader-follower, level.

The Relational Approach

The relational approach to leadership research focuses in on the one-on-one, or dyadic, relationships between leaders and followers. While the prior approaches to the study of leadership typically assumed that leaders treat all followers the same, the dyadic approach examines the differences in the relationships a leader has with each of his or her followers. Consider a situation in which you were in a work group. Did the leader provide an equal amount of attention to all members? Did the leader seem to trust some members more than others, giving them more responsibility or more challenging tasks? Did some members interact with the leader beyond what was required of the task? The predominant theory related to these exchange relationships, originally referred to as the vertical dyad theory, is the leader-member exchange (LMX) theory.

The basic premise of the LMX theory of leadership is that, over time, a relationship develops between a leader and each follower based on the history of each individual's contributions and gains from the exchange. Graen and Uhl-Bien (1995) outlined several stages an exchange relationship may go through. In the beginning of the relationship, both the leader and follower make assessments of one another's potential contributions to the exchange, perhaps including skills or resources. As expectations are met or exceeded, the exchange relationship may develop further. Those relationships that are based solely on the exchange of formal job requirements are considered low-exchange or out-group relationships. Relationships that develop beyond these formal requirements, in which there is a sense of trust or loyalty between the two parties, are considered high-exchange or in-group relationships. Finally, some relationships may develop to a third stage, referred to as a mature relationship, in which there is an equal commitment to each other and to the ultimate goal of the effort.

Hundreds of studies have been conducted examining how different variables may be related to the different exchange relationships established between leaders and followers. For instance, leadership scholars have evaluated how a follower's type of relationship with a leader may impact the follower's motivation, job satisfaction, or job performance. The findings of LMX research, however, are often plagued by criticisms with regard to the measurement of the exchange relationship. It is difficult to discern what constitutes whether a relationship between a leader and follower is high or low, and whether two followers that are in the in-group are there for the same reasons. For instance, one follower may have a high-exchange relationship because they put extra time into the group task, while another individual has a high-exchange relationship because he or she has a strong interpersonal relationship with the leader. Both are categorized as high-exchange relationships, but would they have the same outcomes? Questions such as this one, along with others regarding the strengths and weaknesses of the LMX theory and the relational approach in general, will be discussed in chapter 5.

1990s–TODAY

The Cognitive Approach

The cognitive approach to understanding leadership essentially refers to research that seeks to understand leadership by examining how leaders think, how others think about leaders, or how their thought processes change in specific situations (e.g., crisis, creative problems). This may include research on the cognitive resources of leaders or followers, such as intelligence or problem-solving skills (which overlap somewhat with the trait approach); research on the cognitive steps involved in actions associated with leadership, such as planning, evaluating problem situations, monitoring social interactions, or developing a mission or vision; or research on perceptions related to leaders and leadership.

Cognitive traits, particularly general cognitive ability, or intelligence, have been studied in the area of leadership for decades; however, a specific focus on developing a theory related to the cognitive abilities of leaders was not undertaken until the late 1980s and early 1990s with the development of the cognitive resources theory (Fiedler, 1986). This theory proposed that the stress leaders undergo affects how they utilize their cognitive resources—intelligence and experience—when making decisions.

A second body of research related to cognition and leadership is that of implicit leadership theories. Implicit leadership theories make propositions about how a person's implicit beliefs or assumptions of what a leader is, and how an effective leader performs, relate to the leadership process (Lord & Maher, 1991). For example, a follower's reactions to a leader's behavior may be more a factor of their perception of what a successful leader is than whether that leader is actually performing effectively. Consider your idea of what the prototypical leader is. If your mental image of an effective leader is a charismatic speaker motivating followers from a podium, you may be more critical of a leader who is not as good a speaker but still influences others toward the ultimate team goal. Whereas a follower that assumes problem solving and decision making to be more critical to leadership may rate the same leader higher.

More recently, leadership scholars have made attempts at understanding the cognitive steps that occur as leaders work through typical leadership activities. For instance, both theoretical and experimental efforts have been made to gain insight into the cognitive processes that leaders undergo to solve creative problems (Mumford, Connelly, & Gaddis, 2003), develop visions (Strange & Mumford, 2002), react to crises (Mumford, Friedrich, Caughron, & Byrne, 2007), and engage in planning (Marta, Lertiz, & Mumford, 2005), among other actions.

Clearly, understanding the complex cognitive processes of leaders is a daunting task; however, most of these efforts evaluate leader cognition within a specific domain (e.g., crises or innovation), making the processes somewhat easier to evaluate. Understanding the processes, however, is critical to understanding exactly *how* other variables (e.g., employee criticisms) influence the ultimate outcomes of leadership. For instance, previous research indicated that there was a positive relationship between a leader's creative thinking skills and a group's performance; however, the exact reason was for the positive relationship was unclear. Further evaluation of the cognitive processes of leaders during creative problem solving provided a more detailed view of the points at which a leader's creative-thinking skills proved most critical (Mumford, et al., 2003). Although significant preliminary steps have been taken in researching cognition and leadership, the future likely holds significant expansion of this area of research. Chapter 6 will evaluate these leader cognition theories and more, along with their implications, strengths, and weaknesses.

Outstanding Leadership

The final approach to studying leadership that has been quite dominant in recent years is the focus on instances of outstanding or exceptional leadership. You may be asking yourself how this is different from the "great man" theories of leadership developed in the first half of the century. The important difference is that not all outstanding leadership is effective or good, whereas under the "great man" theories it is assumed that all leadership is good. Rather, the classification of leadership as outstanding refers to the breadth of a leader's impact, rather than whether that impact was positive or negative. For instance, although Adolf Hitler had a quite negative impact on the world, he still had a significant impact nonetheless—making him an outstanding leader. Prior research may have shied away from evaluating outstanding leadership because it is more rare than standard instances of leadership, and it is quite difficult to contact and study outstanding leaders. It is important, however, to evaluate these most exemplary instances of leadership if we are to gain a complete understanding of the leadership phenomenon. Additionally, it is important to understand these particular leaders given the *outstanding* impact these individuals have on individuals, groups, and organizations.

Most research on outstanding leadership has revolved around theories of charismatic or transformational leadership (Burns, 1978), picking up particular steam following Bass and Avolio's (1990) development of a measure of transformational leadership. Both charismatic and transformational leadership are held to be based on the vision-defining behaviors of a leader—a quite powerful behavior that leaders use to motivate followers toward a change. Vision-defining behaviors refers to behaviors that a leader engages in to define a vision, or desired outcome, for his or her followers. The imagery of an impassioned leader conveying a vision can be quite powerful, and theories that sought to evaluate the effects of transformational and charismatic leadership easily found popularity among both leadership scholars and the general public.

Studies evaluating the differences in development, emergence, and performance of transformational leaders (leaders that engage in more vision definition, inspirational motivation, intellectual stimulation, and individual consideration of their followers) compared to transactional leaders (leaders that exchange rewards for performance and that respond to specific critical instances or mistakes) have dominated leadership literature in the last 10–15 years. This trend, however, may be shifting as it becomes clear that these two categorizations of leadership may be somewhat limiting. As Mumford (2006) notes, there are other leaders that have had a significant impact on the world but are not necessarily transformational or charismatic.

Consider the impact that Bill Gates has had on the course of the modern world. Clearly, in his direction of Microsoft, he would qualify as an outstanding leader. He is not, however, particularly charismatic. Thus, Mumford (2006) proposes three types of outstanding leadership—charismatic, ideological, and pragmatic. The differences in these three types of outstanding leaders lie in their developmental patterns, the way in which they view the world, and how they interact with their followers and seek to accomplish their goals. For instance, both charismatic and ideological leadership are considered vision based; however, charismatic leaders have visions oriented toward an idealized future, whereas ideological leaders have visions oriented toward an idealized past. The leadership behavior of pragmatic leaders, on the other hand, is based more on problem solving than vision. The specific differences outlined in this taxonomy, among other theories of outstanding leadership, are discussed further in chapter 7.

THE FUTURE

It is likely clear at this point that there is a multitude of questions researchers have attempted to address with regard to leadership, but it should also be noted that there is certainly no shortage of new questions. As organizations, or the nature of work, change over time, so will the nature of leadership and the types of questions that will need to be addressed. For example, organizations are becoming flatter, with fewer levels in the leadership hierarchy; in addition, the use of work teams is becoming more prevalent.

These two changes will require the advancement of research on the leadership of groups and teams, as well as groups made up of leaders or instances of shared leadership.

Globalization will also play a critical role in driving the direction of leadership research in the future. Significant work has been done comparing workforces in different countries, but as organizations begin to span several countries, it will be critical to understand the differences, if there are differences, between leadership across cultures. For instance, it may be important to examine what the implications are for U.S. companies that seek to expand into other countries, with Americans filling the management roles in the foreign country. A significant effort in understanding the relationship between leadership and culture has already begun with the GLOBE (Global Leadership and Organizational Behavior Effectiveness) research program, which has established a network of over 180 researchers around the world for the purpose of evaluating leadership and organizational practices across cultures (House, Hanges, & Ruiz-Quintanila, 2004).

A third, and quite important, trend in leadership research is toward understanding the dark side of leadership. As was discussed previously, the general approach to leadership has been one that considers most leadership in a positive light. It is often the case, however, that leadership results in negative outcomes. This can be a result of leadership with the intention of causing harm (e.g., violent, ideological leaders of terrorist groups), unethical decision making that leads to negative outcomes (e.g., unethical behaviors of Enron executives), or unintentional leader errors (e.g., making the wrong prediction about the potential success of a new product). To hopefully prevent, or at least learn from, instances in which leadership goes awry, leadership researchers will likely focus more on evaluating the trait, behavioral, situational, relationship, and cognitive factors that play into the dark side of leadership. For instance, research that evaluates the situations in which leader errors are likely to occur (e.g., highly stressful or novel situations) may provide valuable tools for preventing these situations. This potential avenue of future leadership research, along with those mentioned previously, will be discussed in greater detail in chapter 9.

CHAPTER SUMMARY

Leadership has been a popular topic of study in a number of fields for many years. The most significant developments, however, have been made more recently, with most happening after the middle of the 20th century. Not only is the topic popular, but the implications of leadership research are quite important, as leaders have the potential to significantly impact our lives. There is not always agreement among scholars about how to define leadership; however, general definitions indicate it involves a process of influencing others toward a collective goal. Just as there is not complete agreement in how to define leadership, there are also many approaches to studying leadership. Several large shifts in how researchers typically approach the study of leadership have occurred over the years. Prior to the 1950s, researchers focused on identifying specific traits or attributes that distinguished leaders from nonleaders. Inconclusive findings, however, led researchers to focus on what leaders *do*—their behaviors, rather than their characteristics. This behavioral approach was dominant in the 1950s and 1960s, along with the contingency approach, which began to take situational characteristics into account when examining leader behaviors. The 1970s and 1980s saw another shift in research focus, where situational variables and the interactions between leaders and individual followers were of greater interest. More recent research, in the 1990s and today, has looked closer at instances of exceptional or outstanding leadership, as well as examined the cognitive aspects of leadership. The future of leadership research will likely be affected by changes in how work and organizations are structured, such that team leadership and shared leadership will be of critical concern, along with determining whether differences exist in leadership across cultures. Finally, in light of recent instances of severe leader errors (e.g., Enron, Hurricane Katrina), there is an increasing interest in the "dark side" of leadership, or when leaders act badly, whether intentionally or unintentionally.

KEY TERMS AND PHRASES

- Followers
- Influence
- Leadership
- Person-focused definition of leadership
- Power
- Process-focused definition of leadership
- Role-focused definition of leadership

REVIEW QUESTIONS

1. What is the definition of leadership that will be used in this book?
2. What was the main research approach used in the 1950's and 1960s?
3. What is meant when we refer to the "great man" theories of leadership?
4. What is the difference between person-focused, role-focused, and process-focused definitions of leadership?
5. Which approach focuses on the one-on-one relationship between leaders and followers?
6. What are some of the emerging topics that researchers are focusing on now and in the future?
7. What is the basic argument of the situational approach?

DISCUSSION QUESTIONS

1. Why are you interested in studying leadership?
2. Why is it important to study leadership?
3. Why is it important to have one definition of leadership?
4. Why have researchers taken different approaches to studying leadership?
5. What do you think are the most important things about leadership that we need to understand?

INDIVIDUAL ACTIVITIES

INDIVIDUAL ACTIVITY 1

Leader Spotlight

The excerpt below is from President Franklin D. Roosevelt's first inaugural speech, in which he addresses the current state of the country, which was in the midst of the Great Depression, and his plans to help the nation. As you read it, take the perspective of an early leadership scholar—what characteristics of President Roosevelt might you identify that are indicative of leadership?

> President Hoover, Mr. Chief Justice, my friends: This is a day of national consecration, and I am certain that my fellow Americans expect that on my induction into the presidency I will address them with a candor and a decision which the present situation of our nation impels. This is pre-eminently the time to speak the truth, the whole truth, frankly and boldly. Nor need we shrink from honestly facing conditions in our country today. This great nation will endure as it has endured, will revive and will prosper.
>
> So first of all let me assert my firm belief that the only thing we have to fear . . . is fear itself . . . nameless, unreasoning, unjustified terror which paralyzes needed efforts to convert retreat into advance. In every dark hour of our national life a leadership of frankness and vigor has met with that understanding and support of the people themselves, which is

essential to victory. I am convinced that you will again give that support to leadership in these critical days. In such a spirit on my part and on yours we face our common difficulties. . . . Yet our distress comes from no failure of substance. We are stricken by no plague of locusts. Compared with the perils which our forefathers conquered because they believed and were not afraid, we have still much to be thankful for. Nature still offers her bounty and human efforts have multiplied it. Plenty is at our doorstep, but a generous use of it languishes in the very sight of the supply. Primarily, this is because the rulers of the exchange of mankind's goods have failed through their own stubbornness and their own incompetence, have admitted their failures and abdicated. Practices of the unscrupulous money changers stand indicted in the court of public opinion, rejected by the hearts and minds of men. True, they have tried, but their efforts have been cast in the pattern of an outworn tradition. Faced by failure of credit, they have proposed only the lending of more money. Stripped of the lure of profit by which to induce our people to follow their false leadership, they have resorted to exhortations, pleading tearfully for restored conditions. They know only the rules of a generation of self-seekers. They have no vision, and when there is no vision the people perish. The money changers have fled their high seats in the temple of our civilization. We may now restore that temple to the ancient truths. The measure of the restoration lies in the extent to which we apply social values more noble than mere monetary profit. Happiness lies not in the mere possession of money, it lies in the joy of achievement, in the thrill of creative effort. The joy and moral stimulation of work no longer must be forgotten in the mad chase of evanescent profits. These dark days will be worth all they cost us if they teach us that our true destiny is not to be ministered unto but to minister to ourselves and to our fellow-men. . . . We are, I know, ready and willing to submit our lives and property to such discipline because it makes possible a leadership which aims at a larger good. This I propose to offer, pledging that the larger purposes will hind upon us all as a sacred obligation with a unity of duty hitherto evoked only in time of armed strife. With this pledge taken, I assume unhesitatingly the leadership of this great army of our people, dedicated to a disciplined attack upon our common problems. Action in this image and to this end is feasible under the form of government which we have inherited from our ancestors. . . . For the trust reposed in me I will return the courage and the devotion that befit the time. I can do no less. We face the arduous days that lie before us in the warm courage of national unity, with the clear consciousness of seeking old and pre-

cious moral values, with the clean satisfaction that comes from the stern performance of duty by old and young alike. We aim at the assurance of a rounded and permanent national life. We do not distrust the future of essential democracy. The people of the United States have not failed. In their need they have registered a mandate that they want direct, vigorous action. They have asked for discipline and direction under leadership. They have made me the present instrument of their wishes. In the spirit of the gift I will take it. In this dedication of a nation we humbly ask the blessing of God. May He protect each and every one of us! May He guide me in the days to come!

INDIVIDUAL ACTIVITY 2

Think about a real leader from your own life who you consider a good leader and someone who you consider a bad leader.

1. What is it that makes the good leader good?
2. What is it that makes the bad leader bad?
3. Look at what you wrote and determine whether you were focusing on them as a person, their role, or the process of leadership.

GROUP ACTIVITIES

GROUP ACTIVITY 1

Get into groups or engage in a discussion as a class.

Everyone in the group or class should answer the following question and write down their response: How do you define leadership?

Discuss the definitions and identify some common themes among them.

Use the common themes to come up with a group definition of leadership

GROUP ACTIVITY 2

Get into small groups.

As a group you must come up with a plan to develop a new club. As you develop the club, you must define your general purpose (e.g., student government, service), the requirements for membership, what the club's name will be, your goals for the first year, and how you will raise money for your club.

After the group has finished the task, think about who emerged in the group as the leader.

1. Was there more than one person that served in a leadership role?
2. Why are you saying that this person is the leader? What behaviors did they engage in?
3. Why do you think this particular person became the leader?

SUGGESTED READINGS

Bass, B. M. (1990). Part I: Introduction to concepts and theories of leadership. In B. M. Bass (Ed.), *Bass & Stogdill's handbook of leadership: Theory, research, and managerial applications* (pp. 3–58). New York: The Free Press.

Hackman, J. R., & Wagerman, R. (2007). Asking the right questions about leadership: Discussion and conclusions. *American Psychologist, 62*, 43–47.

Northouse, P. G. (2007). Introduction. In P. G. Northouse (Ed.), *Leadership: Theory and practice* (pp. 1–14). Thousand Oaks, CA: Sage Publications.

Yukl, G. (2006). The nature of leadership. In G. Yukl (Ed.), *Leadership in organizations* (pp. 1–24). Upper Saddle River, NJ: Prentice Hall.

Perspectives on Leadership Research

Jay J. Caughron

> Anyone can hold the helm when the sea is calm.
>
> —*Publilius Syrus*
>
> If your actions inspire others to dream more, learn more, do more, and become more, you are a leader.
>
> —*John Quincy Adams*

Now that you have been introduced to the major leadership theories and their historical context, we will now examine what they tell us about some of the most fundamental questions about leadership. As mentioned earlier, leadership is a topic that has interested not only scholars but people in general for thousands of years. This inherent interest in leadership is most likely because we all have seen leaders in action or maybe have even been in a leadership role. However, because people have a variety of beliefs, values, and experiences with regard to leadership, a wide variety of opinions, myths, assumptions, and misconceptions about leadership have developed. Here, we will examine those myths and opinions to see what the different theories of leadership can tell us about them.

This chapter will be organized around a set of six controversial statements commonly discussed with regard to leadership. Each of these comments will be examined in light of what leadership research has revealed over the course of the last century or more of study. This will help you to begin thinking about leadership as a complex topic and let you get more familiar with the current research and theories of leadership before jumping into the nuts and bolts in subsequent chapters.

Learning Objectives
- Begin to understand the questions asked about leadership
- Become familiar with the debates and controversies in leadership research
- Begin to identify and question assumptions people make about leadership
- Recognize that there are many myths surrounding leadership
- Begin to think about leadership as complex in theory as well as in practice

Before jumping directly into the major topics of this chapter, one myth should be dispelled right away. This myth is that leadership only occurs at the top. It is easy to see high-positioned leaders such as presidents or chief executive officers; however, leadership occurs all around us every day. Chief executives lead their companies, but they could not be successful if the managers under their guidance did not lead the groups of employees that make up companies. Similarly, a president can only be effective at marshaling the armed forces because of the generals, colonels, and squad leaders directing the followers under their care and direction. Leadership in organizations occurs not just at the top of the organization, but rather at multiple levels, and it should be examined at each of those levels. While some theories focus on leadership as it occurs in the higher positions of an organization, many theories focus on the leadership people demonstrate when they are not at the head of an organization. Leadership at all levels is important. Organizations could not function without leadership occurring at multiple levels, and, thus, leadership at multiple levels will be examined here.

ARE LEADERS BORN OR MADE?

This question is one you hear often in discussions of leadership, and it was the driving force behind early theories of leadership. As you recall from chapter 1, some of the earliest leadership theories were called the **trait theories of leadership** (or "great man" theories). According to this line of research, leaders have unique traits that enable them to be leaders. Thus, if you were to ask a trait theorist whether leaders are born or made, they would likely argue that they are born. According to trait theories of leadership, people who are smart, self-confident, and sociable tend to be effective leaders. People without these certain traits may try to lead, and may perform well in leadership roles, but they will never be as good at leading as someone who has leadership-oriented traits.

The **behavioral theories of leadership** offer a stark contrast to trait theories. As interest in trait theories began to wane after WWII, researchers began to question whether leadership could only be displayed by special people with certain attributes. Researchers began looking into whether leadership was more about how a person acted rather than their personality, intelligence, motivation, or other characteristics. Researchers at Ohio State University and the University of Michigan suggested that leadership

> **Trait theory of leadership**—a theory that says leaders have unique traits that enable them to be leaders
> **Behavioral theory of leadership**—a theory that describes leaders in terms of the actions they take rather than the traits they possess

behaviors tended to fall into two categories. Behaviors that involved organizing people's work and giving them direction were called **task-oriented behaviors** (or initiating structure). Behaviors that revolved around building relationships and motivating followers were called **relations-oriented behaviors** (or considering others) (Fleishman, 1951, 1953, 1973; Halpin & Winer, 1957). For behavioral theorists, leadership was much more about what people did rather than the traits they were born with. It follows, then, that even if someone was not born with a certain set of traits that would make him or her a good leader, that person could learn the behaviors associated with effective leadership. Thus, if you were to ask a behavioral leadership theorist whether leaders are born or made, they would probably argue that they can be made if they take on actions that are leadership oriented.

To summarize, early theories of leadership tended to emphasize the characteristics of individuals who became leaders, suggesting that leaders are born rather than made. Indeed, some traits, such as intelligence, were shown to have an influence on how well a leader performs. However, as leadership research continued to unfold, it became apparent that being a leader is far more complicated than being intelligent, sociable, and self-confident. As researchers at Ohio State University and the University of Michigan demonstrated, a great deal of leadership is about the actions one takes. Specifically, behaving in such a way as to structure the tasks and goals that a group is working on and acting to demonstrate consideration of one's followers are two fundamental aspects of leadership.

Relations-oriented behaviors—behaviors that revolve around building relationships and motivating followers
Task-oriented behaviors—behaviors that involve a leader planning and organizing a work group's activity

So, which theory is right? The answer to this question is that *both* theories provide answers about leadership. There are some traits that are related to leadership and will help a leader perform well, but that is not the entire story. Leadership also involves action. The types of actions taken by a leader can have a strong influence on whether or not that leader is successful. Chapter 4 provides more details about what traits and behaviors in particular are related to effective leadership. Although there are traits and behaviors associated with effective leadership, considering only these factors is not enough to understand leadership. Rather, the situation a leader is in has a strong influence on the effectiveness of any given leader trait or behavior. This takes us to our next major topic of discussion: leadership situations.

IS LEADERSHIP ONLY ABOUT THE LEADER?

As psychological research has advanced over the course of the last century, it is interesting, and somewhat ironic, that one of the most fundamental conclusions psychologists have uncovered is not really about the mind as much as it is about what goes on outside of the mind. More specifically, psychologists have concluded, over the course of countless studies, that the situation a person is in can have a very profound impact on his or her behavior. When we remember that leaders are people, too, it becomes clear that the situation a leader is in will not only have a strong influence on what a given leader will do, but also on how successful that leader's behavior will be. There are countless instances in which a leader who has flourished at one organization leaves to take on a different leadership position and fails miserably. It is not that the leader has suddenly lost all ability to lead; it is that the situation the leader is facing has changed, and this has hindered his or her ability to be successful. This begs the question: How much of leadership is really about the leader?

There are two theories regarding the influence of a situation on a leader. Both agree that a situation has a large influence on

Contingency theory of leadership—a theory suggesting that leaders are well suited to lead in some circumstances, but that they may be ill equipped to lead in other circumstances

Situational theory of leadership—a theory of leadership suggesting that leaders should be able to recognize the circumstances they are facing and adjust their leadership style to match that situation

leaders, but they differ about how a leader should handle outside influences. Those who espouse the **contingency theory of leadership** would argue that leaders tend to have a certain style of leadership and that it is best for them not to stray from this style when they are leading. However, the **situational theory of leadership** suggests that leaders should be able to adapt their style to fit with the challenges of their circumstances.

Fred Fiedler, whose research was introduced in the previous chapter, developed the most widely accepted and applied contingency theory of leadership. Based on work done by previous researchers, Fiedler and his colleagues borrowed the task-oriented and relations-oriented leadership styles but then went on to suggest that the situations leaders face can be classified in one of three ways: (a) highly favorable for the leader, (b) moderately favorable for the leader, and (c) highly unfavorable for the leader (Fiedler, 1967, 1970). Furthermore, these researchers suggested that leaders who are task oriented tend to perform well in two conditions: (a) when the situation is highly favorable (i.e., when a leader has plenty of resources to accomplish a clear goal), or (b) when the situation is highly unfavorable (i.e., when a leader's group has a difficult task and lacks resources). In highly favorable situations, a leader does not need to waste time building relationships or being supportive of his or her followers. In fact, if a leader does this it will likely distract the followers from performing their assigned task. On the other hand, in highly unfavorable situations, a leader does not have time to spend building relationships and must focus on directing followers and dealing with problems. Relationship-oriented leaders were expected to perform better in situations that were moderately favorable. This is because leaders in this type of situation have the time and energy to devote to building relationships with their followers, and the followers become more productive by experiencing this support from their leader.

The most widespread of the situational theories of leadership is Hersey and Blanchard's life-cycle theory of leadership (Hersey & Blanchard, 1969, 1972). These researchers suggested that leaders should change their leadership style depending on the maturity of their followers. Experienced, or mature, followers are described as having relevant job experience, appropriate levels of motivation, and a willingness to accept responsibility. Hersey and Blanchard suggested that leaders who have less experienced followers should focus on task-oriented behaviors and de-emphasize relationship building. As his or her followers gain experience, the leader can focus less and less on task-oriented behaviors. However, the situation is more complex with relationship-oriented behaviors. As the group matures, the leader should focus more on relationship building, but only to a point. Once the group is fairly mature and the relationship between the leader and his or her followers is well established, the leader should start focusing less and less on relationship-oriented behaviors. This line of reasoning suggests that when followers are mature, they know what they are doing and do it efficiently, and that focusing on relationship building becomes a distraction for them; thus, the leader should essentially leave them alone to do their work (Hersey & Blanchard, 1969, 1993).

Another factor that has an influence on a leader's performance is the opinions of his or her followers. **Implicit theories of leadership** examine the effect of followers' opinions and expectations

> **Implicit theories of leadership**—theories that examine how peoples' beliefs and assumptions about leadership influence their perceptions of and behavior toward leadership

with regard to what a leader is and how a leader should behave (Anderson, 1966; Eden & Leviatan, 1975; Lord & Maher, 1991). These beliefs, opinions, and expectations followers have about their leaders can have an important impact on how effective a leader can be, especially if he or she does not live up to those expectations. The proponents of these theories suggest that followers tend to respond more positively to leaders who meet their expectations for what a leader should be. The implication here is not that leaders should do what their followers think they should. Rather, leaders should be mindful of the opinions and expectations their followers may have. By being mindful of these factors, the leader can be more cautious about violating those assumptions or can use the opinions others have to help facilitate team performance.

In conclusion, research into how leaders are influenced by their situation has revealed many interesting and important points. First and foremost is that leadership may not be entirely about the person leading. Some people may be well suited to lead in one set of circumstances but ill equipped to lead in another. There are many factors outside the leader's control that have a profound impact on their performance as a leader. The type of task or goal a group is working toward, the amount of resources a leader has at his or her disposal, the type of followers being led, and these followers' opinions about leadership are all important factors that may make or break a leader—even one with exceptional leadership experience and skill. So now a new question arises: If a leader's performance is determined by the situation he or she is in, or outside factors, are we sure we even need a leader?

DO WE REALLY NEED A LEADER?

Before tackling this question directly, let's consider another theory that discusses what leaders actually do for their groups. **Path-goal theory** suggests that leaders are primarily responsible for two types of activities: (a) goal-oriented activities, and

(b) path-oriented activities. **Goal-oriented activities** include setting, changing, defining, or revising goals. **Path-oriented activities** involve doing things that shape the way a group pursues its goals. This includes obtaining materials, finding new group members, providing rewards for helping the group, and providing guidance to group members (House, 1971).

Like other contingency theories and situational theories, the path-goal theory acknowledges the influence of a leader's situation. Specifically, this theory suggests that leaders can be categorized into four different groups:

(a) supportive leadership—leader actively encourages followers
(b) directive leadership—leader focuses on providing direction and instructions
(c) participative leadership—leader allows the followers to participate in decision making
(d) achievement-oriented leadership—leader focuses on setting goals and challenging followers

Which style of leadership will work the best in a given situation depends on the type of task a group is doing and the type of followers in the group (House & Mitchell, 1974). Interestingly, inspired by path-goal theory, some researchers began to question the need for a leader at all. They suggested that if a group has enough experience to set their own goals, enough resources to clear their own

> **Path-goal theory**—a theory that emphasizes the role of a leader as setting, defining, and clarifying goals; motivating followers to achieve those goals; and helping followers see a clear path toward goal attainment
>
> **Goal-oriented activities**—actions taken by a leader to set, change, clarify, or define group goals
>
> **Path-oriented activities**—actions taken by a leader to shape the way a group pursues its goals, such as providing guidance or obtaining materials

path, and if the task is interesting enough to keep the group motivated to do it, then a leader is not necessary (Howell, Dorfman, & Kerr, 1986). This is called **leader substitutes theory.** According to this theory, if a group is given the right set of circumstances, they will be able to perform as well, if not better, than a group with a leader (Kerr, 1977; Kerr & Jermier, 1978). Basically, this theory suggests that if the path- and goal-oriented duties associated with a leader can be resolved without a leader, then the group should be able to function without a leader.

> **Leader substitutes theory**—a theory that suggests that in some circumstances, groups do not need a leader to function effectively

To summarize this section, it would appear that, indeed, in some instances, groups can function with a minimal amount of leadership. However, it should be noted that a leaderless group cannot be expected to function well in all circumstances. While it is possible for a group to function without a leader, it may not be the optimal setup in many, if not most, situations. Additionally, coordination between group members, and between the group and the larger organization, may become more difficult if the group does not have a leader (Bass, 1990). At some point, someone has to be responsible for communicating information between the group and the organization the group is embedded within. In most circumstances, someone must be responsible for making decisions and giving the group a direction; that person is a leader, whether or not they are recognized as one by an organization.

HOW DO LEADERS MAKE THE TOUGH DECISIONS?

Leaders often find themselves in situations requiring them to make decisions. This may include giving advice to a follower or colleague, deciding how to direct others to act, or merely giving followers permission to pursue a certain course of action. Leader decision making is a very broad topic and current research has only begun to scratch the surface. The research methods that study this topic are called **cognitive theories of leadership.** Although this is a relatively new area of leadership research, there are a few tidbits of knowledge that can be passed along regarding how leaders make decisions, the difficulties of making decisions as a leader, and what to consider when you are facing tough decisions as a leader.

> **Cognitive theories of leadership**—theories that emphasize how leaders think and make decisions in determining leader effectiveness

To begin, let's consider some of the challenges leaders face when making decisions. As we discussed above, there are many factors in a leader's environment (what psychologists call *situational factors*) that can influence a leader. These may include the leader's followers, the type of task or goals the leader's group is working to accomplish, or the amount of resources at the leader's disposal. Another important factor to consider, especially when it comes to leader decision making, is time.

Leaders often have to manage multiple sources of information and deal with constant demands for their time and attention. These may be information from followers who are giving a report or the demands of a group of stockholders. The number of requests that a leader receives and must respond to can be very draining and can end up putting a great deal of stress on the leader. This stress, which is the result of having limited time to respond to multiple demands and having to make an unending flow of decisions, can have a strong influence on leader decision making.

Cognitive resources leadership theory was developed as an attempt to define *how* leaders make decisions in complex and stressful

> **Cognitive resources leadership theory**—a theory that emphasizes the type of intelligence a leader uses when dealing with problems or making decisions

circumstances. It was originally thought that leaders who were more intelligent would make better decisions, but this was not always the case (Fiedler, Potter, Zais, & Knowlton, 1979). Rather, it appears that leaders with high intelligence perform better when their situation is not very stressful. However, a leader's experience becomes more important in stressful situations. The reasons for these findings are still being investigated, but it appears that intelligent leaders who lack experience tend to focus on issues that are not directly tied to the problem at hand when they are stressed. Basically, they get distracted; the amount of information a leader attempts to think about overloads his or her system. That is, the leader's cognitive resources get used up, resulting in intelligence becoming a less important factor than it normally would be.

The reverse is true for leaders with a great deal of experience. Experienced leaders are able to fall back on their experience in stressful conditions. This allows them to chart a course of action that leads their group out of their troubling circumstances and back onto steady ground. Thus, the situation a leader faces may go a long way toward determining how successful a leader will be, given his or her individual attributes and stylistic preferences (Fiedler, 1986).

While it is useful to know that a situation can influence how effective a leader's thinking style may be, it still leaves us with a question—How do leaders go about making hard decisions? When you consider the different types of decisions leaders must make, the number of different situations leaders face, and the fact that there are multiple groups of people often depending on leaders to make good decisions, it becomes clear that this is a very complex question to answer. However, researchers are beginning to examine exactly how leaders make decisions; that is, how leaders go about solving the problems they are faced with on a day-to-day basis. These are called **leader problem-solving theories.**

Although work on leader problem solving is only in its earliest stages, researchers are finding that

Leader problem-solving theories—theories that explain leader performance in terms of how well a leader can solve problems and make decisions

leaders progress through a predictable set of steps when they attempt to solve problems. It is likely that this set of steps is not the same for all leaders in all situations, but Mumford and colleagues have proposed a model of leadership problem solving. Work to verify and elaborate on the model is ongoing, but overall research has been supportive of the model (Mumford, Friedrich, et al., 2007). A detailed discussion of this and the other leadership cognition models is provided in chapter 6. However, as the model indicates, leader problem solving is complex and involves many different processes that interact with and influence each other. Leaders not only need to identify important pieces of information and integrate them in a meaningful way, but they must also consider the potential outcomes for themselves, their group, and other relevant groups of people that may be affected by their decision.

In conclusion, is leadership about making tough decisions? It would appear that a leader's performance is influenced by how they think and solve problems. Given the complexity of most leadership situations, being able to think through a complex, ambiguous set of circumstances and then make a decision is an important element of being an effective leader. However, while decision making is an important part of leadership, other factors such as influencing others and building relationships are also important.

IS IT REALLY LONELY AT THE TOP?

It is no secret that some leaders keep their followers at a distance, while others attempt to form strong bonds with their followers. Theories of leadership that emphasize the leader's relationship with his or her followers are called **relational leadership theories.**

> **Relational leadership theories**—theories that emphasize relationship building as the main method of a leader exerting influence on his or her followers

Leader-member exchange theory—theory that suggests leaders establish an in-group of followers and an out-group of followers and that they influence these two different groups of followers in different ways

Leader-member exchange theory, or LMX, examines questions related to the relationships between leaders and followers. In essence, this theory holds that leaders develop special, unique relationships with each one of their followers. A leader's relationship with some followers is better than with others. Some followers have a high-quality relationship with the leader, and others have a low-quality relationship with the leader (Graen, 1976; Graen & Cashman, 1975). The result of these high- and low-quality relationships is the development of an in-group and an out-group. Those with high-quality relationships with the leader are in the in-group. Those with low-quality relationships are in the out-group.

Those in the in-group have many advantages over those in the out-group. Generally speaking, the leader likes the people in the in-group better than those in the out-group and thinks the in-group members are more competent than the out-group members. People in the in-group get better assignments and more attention from the leader. Those in the out-group get less desirable tasks, are more likely to be blamed if something goes wrong, and do not get as much support from the leader. While followers in the in-group do get special treatment, being a part of the in-group does have its disadvantages. Followers in the in-group are also expected to work harder, pull a greater part of the load for the group, and take care of emergencies or last-minute problems that come up in the work group.

In summary, while leaders are usually the most central figures in any group they lead, it is worth noting that leaders usually cannot do it all on their own. Leaders will typically draw in a small group of core followers from the group or groups they lead. These core followers represent those the leader can lean on to execute duties. This would suggest that a leader cannot shoulder the burden of leadership alone—a leader must rely on those around him or her to enable a group to perform at its highest capacity. This emphasis on relationships between leaders and followers suggests that leaders can have a tremendous influence over their followers, which brings us to our sixth and final topic of discussion.

ARE YOU ONLY AN EFFECTIVE LEADER IF YOUR FOLLOWERS LOVE AND ADMIRE YOU?

Most of the theories we have discussed up to this point do not explicitly focus on high-level leadership. These leaders (often called exceptional leaders) are people like chief executive officers of corporations or presidents and prime ministers of countries. Leaders in these types of positions make decisions that can affect millions of people, and, thus, it is important to study them as well as leaders who have a small circle of impact.

Transformational leadership theory addresses the issue of how leaders influence their followers. According to this theory, some leaders are able to form an intense bond with their followers, resulting in the followers changing how they view themselves and the issues they are facing. On the other hand, some leaders merely direct their followers' actions without creating a great deal of change within the followers themselves. Leaders who create this change in their followers are called *transformational leaders,* while those who direct their followers

> **Transformational leadership theory**—a theory that attempts to explain leader effectiveness by how a leader is able to mold and shape the way his or her followers perceive themselves, their world, and their place in the world

without creating change within their followers are called *transactional leaders* and are often described more as managers than leaders (Bass, 1990). Those who support this theory would suggest that transactional leaders can be effective managers and may be good leaders in some situations; however, transformational leaders will be more effective than transactional leaders most of the time. Additionally, proponents of this theory would probably tend to agree with the proposition posed above—leaders who do not engender the love and admiration of their followers will be less effective than the leaders who do.

However, other researchers would be likely to disagree with the statement that successful leaders must be loved and admired by their followers. According to **Mumford's theory of outstanding leadership**, there are leaders who are loved and admired by their followers, but this is not the only way to be a successful leader. As noted in chapter 1, Mumford and his colleagues have identified three primary leader types that have proven to be highly effective: charismatic, ideological, and pragmatic (Mumford, Antes, Caughron, & Friedrich, 2008; Mumford, Scott, & Hunter, 2006; Mumford, Strange, & Bedell, 2006). Leaders who use **charismatic leadership** typically fit the description of transformational leaders. They tend to create a close bond with their followers and are able to bring a wide variety of people together because they encourage others to change how they see their problems. Charismatic leaders, in particular, have

Mumford's theory of outstanding leadership—a theory that suggests leaders can be classified as charismatic, ideological, or pragmatic as defined by the way they approach leading their group

Charismatic leadership—a leadership style in which a leader tends to express a positive vision of the future, is highly self-confident, appears honest and generous, and attracts a wide variety of followers who are loyal to the leader rather than the leader's agenda or organization

received a great deal of attention from scholars during the course of the 20th century. Leaders who follow **ideological leadership** also tend to form close bonds with their followers, but only with those who share their ideological beliefs. Those who use **pragmatic leadership** are very different from charismatic or ideological. They tend to emphasize a practical path of solving the problems they are facing. Pragmatic leaders do not tend to focus on forming close bonds with followers as much as building relationships with people who can help them resolve the issues their followers are confronting.

To conclude, while many of the theories discussed thus far focus on leadership as it occurs on a day-to-day level at the middle levels of an organization, some theories—such as Bass's transformational leadership theory and Mumford's outstanding leadership theory—focus explicitly on leadership as it occurs at the highest levels of an organization. Those who support transformational theories of leadership tend to believe that truly effective leaders create intense bonds with their followers that result in follower transformation. However, supporters of Mumford's outstanding leadership theory would suggest this is only one way to be an effective leader. These researchers would point to leaders who have been effective without cultivating an intense bond with their followers or without encouraging their followers to change much at all. Thus, the question remains: Do you need to engender love and admiration from

Ideological leadership—a leadership style in which a leader tends to express the desire to return to an idealized past state and attracts a small group of highly devoted followers with a value system similar to that of the leader

Pragmatic leadership—a leadership style in which a leader emphasizes knowledge management, expertise, problem solving, and consensus building rather than a loyal following or adherence to an ideological stance

your followers to be a highly effective leader? It may depend on who you ask, but it is likely this is only one way to be an effective leader.

CHAPTER SUMMARY

Leadership research has made great progress over the last 50 years. Although much of trait theory has fallen by the wayside, the identification of intelligence and social skill as important elements of leader effectiveness were important findings. Behavioral theories highlighted the fact that leadership is as much about what leaders do as it is about who they are. It also suggested that at least some aspects of leadership can be learned, and that leadership is not only for individuals with certain traits. Contingency and situational approaches to leadership brought attention to the fact that the circumstances a leader faces often have a great deal to do with how effective he or she can be.

Building upon trait, behavioral, contingency, and situational theories of leadership, path-goal theory demonstrated the important role goals play in motivating followers. It also challenged the notion that groups need leaders by emphasizing the role of followers and the characteristics of a group's task. The importance of managing the relationships between a leader and his or her followers was highlighted by the relationship approaches to leadership research. Cognitive theories demonstrated that a leader's intelligence and experience are important predictors of their performance. Similarly, scholars have begun examining the steps and processes leaders engage in when they go about solving complex problems. Although this approach is still young, it suggests that understanding how leaders think is an important consideration to bear in mind when studying this complex phenomenon. Lastly, theories of exceptional leadership returned the attention of leadership researchers to leaders with the ability and position to motivate large groups to unify and pursue a common cause.

The future of leadership research is bright, and methods of conducting research advance as more people begin to realize that leadership is not just about being a civil rights leader or an elected official. Instead, leadership is something we encounter every day as we go to work, take classes, or participate in recreational activities. Hopefully this chapter has provided you with a clear overview of some of the fundamental issues and questions in leadership research, and provided you with a framework for thinking about leadership as you experience it in your daily life.

LEADER SPOTLIGHT: ABRAHAM LINCOLN

It is a common misconception that Abraham Lincoln freed slaves in the United States when he sent out the Emancipation Proclamation. However, a careful reading of the document (included here) reveals he declared slavery illegal only in areas of the South that were at war with the North. Lincoln gave an exception to areas of the South that were already in the North's control and to slave-holding states that remained loyal to the North. Lincoln made several speeches prior to becoming president in which he stated he opposed slavery. So, why would Lincoln provide an exemption for slave-holding states that remained loyal to the North rather than abolish slavery altogether? As you read the Emancipation Proclamation, consider the following: What situational forces was Lincoln facing as he created this document? Could Lincoln have been an effective commander-in-chief without the leadership of those on the battlefield? What factors did Lincoln have to consider when he made a decision of this magnitude? Was Lincoln being more charismatic, ideological, or pragmatic when he wrote this document?

THE EMANCIPATION PROCLAMATION

BY THE PRESIDENT OF THE UNITED STATES OF AMERICA: A PROCLAMATION

Whereas, on the twenty-second day of September, in the year of our Lord one thousand eight hundred and sixty-two, a proclamation was issued by the President of the United States, containing, among other things, the following, to wit:

That on the first day of January, in the year of our Lord one thousand eight hundred and sixty-three, all persons held as slaves within any state of designated part of a State, the people whereof shall then be in rebellion against the United States, shall be then, thenceforward, and forever free; and the Executive Government of the United States, including the military and naval authority therof, will recognize and maintain the freedom of such persons, and will do no act or acts to repress such persons, or any of them, in any efforts they may make for the actual freedom.

That the executive will, on the first day of January aforesaid, by proclamation, designate the States and parts of States, if any, in which the people thereof, respectively, shall then be in rebellion against the United States; and the fact that any State, or the people thereof, shall on that day be, in good faith, represented in the Congress of the United States by members chosen thereto at elections wherein a majority of the qualified voters of such State shall have participated, shall, in the absence of strong countervailing testimony, be deemed conclusive evidence that such State, and the people thereof, are not then in rebellion against the United States.

Now, therefore I, Abraham Lincoln, President of the United States, by virtue of the power in be vested as Commander-in-Chief, of the Army and Navy of the United States, and as a fit and necessary war measure for suppressing said rebellion, do, on this first day of January, in the year of our Lord one thousand eight hundred and sixty-three, and in accordance with my purpose so to do publicly proclaimed for the full period of one hundred days, from the day first above mentioned, order and designate the States and parts of States wherein the people thereof respectively, are this day in rebellion against the United States, the following, to wit:

Arkansas, Texas, Louisiana (except the Parishes of St. Bernard, Plaquemines, Jefferson, St. John, St. Charles, St. James Ascension, Assumption, Terrebonne, Lafourche, St. Mary, St. Martin, and Orleans, including the City of New Orleans), Mississippi, Alabama, Florida, Georgia, South Carolina, North Carolina, and Virginia (except the forty-eight counties designated as West Virginia, and also counties of Berkley, Accomac, Northampton, Elizabeth City, York, Princess Ann, and Norfolk, including the cities of Norfolk and Portsmouth), and which excepted parts are for the present, left precisely as if this proclamation were not issued.

And by virtue of the power, and for the propose aforesaid, I do order and declare that all persons held as slaves within said designated States, and parts of States, are, and henceforward shall be free; and that the Executive government of the United States, including the military and naval authorities thereof, will recognize and maintain the freedom of said persons.

And I hereby enjoin upon the people so declared to be free to abstain from all violence, unless in necessary self-defence; and I recommend to them that in all cases when allowed, they labor faithfully for reasonable wages.

And I further declare and make known, that such persons of suitable condition, will be received into the armed service of the United States to garrison forts, positions, stations, and other places, and to man vessels of all sorts in said service.

(continued)

47

And upon this act, sincerely believed to be an act of justice, warranted by the constitution, upon military necessity, I invoke the considerate judgment of mankind, and the gracious favor of Almighty God.

In witness whereof, I have hereunto set my hand and causes the seal of the United States to be affixed.

Done at the City of Washington, this first day of January, in the year of our Lord one thousand eight hundred and sixty three, and of the Independence of the United States of America the eighty-seventh.

KEY TERMS AND PHRASES

- Behavioral theory of leadership
- Charismatic leadership
- Cognitive resources leadership theory
- Cognitive theories of leadership
- Contingency theory of leadership
- Goal-oriented activities
- Ideological leadership
- Implicit theories of leadership
- Leader-member exchange theory
- Leader problem-solving theories
- Leader substitutes theory
- Mumford's theory of outstanding leadership
- Path-goal theory
- Path-oriented activities
- Pragmatic leadership
- Relational leadership theories
- Relations-oriented behaviors
- Situational theory of leadership
- Task-oriented behavior
- Trait theory of leadership
- Transformational leadership theory

REVIEW QUESTIONS

1. The early behavioral theories of leadership classified almost all leader actions into two categories: What are they?
2. Which leadership theory suggests that leaders form an in-group and an out-group of followers?
3. Path-goal theory describes four different leadership styles. List and describe each of the four types.
4. Compare and contrast the contingency approach and the situational approach to leadership.
5. Cognitive resources leadership theory discusses how leaders use intelligence and experience; describe how each is used and list one circumstance when intelligence is more important and one in which experience is more important.

DISCUSSION QUESTIONS

1. The implicit theories of leadership suggest that followers' ideas and opinions about their leader and the group have an important effect on how much influence that leader will have over the group. Discuss whether followers' opinions should be taken into account when a leader attempts to influence a group.
2. Contingency theory suggests that a leader should be matched to a situation that matches his or her leadership style. Situational theory suggests that leaders should be flexible and change their style to fit with their situation. Describe the pros and cons of each approach, and present an argument for which one you think is the best strategy.

INDIVIDUAL ACTIVITIES

INDIVIDUAL ACTIVITY 1

List three leaders in high positions of power (such as the head of a company or a world leader), and describe what attributes, actions, or situational factors make them an effective leader.

INDIVIDUAL ACTIVITY 2

Based on what you have read in chapter 2, write a response to three of the following statements:

   a. When a group fails it is due to a failure of leadership.
   b. A good leader can be relied on to turn around a failing group.
   c. A good leader does not need good followers.
   d. A good leader is only as good as his followers.
   e. If you don't have charisma, you will never be an effective leader.
   f. Leadership is an intangible quality—some people have it and some people don't.
   g. A good leader shouldn't worry about what his or her followers think.
   h. If the followers aren't happy, the leader isn't doing a good job.

GROUP ACTIVITIES

GROUP ACTIVITY 1

Leader-member exchange theory suggests that leaders often do not treat all of their followers equally. Some get more responsibilities than others, and some get better task assignments than others. Discuss the following topics with your group: Is this fair for the employees? What problems could this create in a work group? How could someone move from the out-group to the in-group? Is it possible for a leader to have high-quality relationships with all his or her followers, thus resulting in one big in-group and no out-group?

GROUP ACTIVITY 2

The behavioral theories of leadership emphasize the importance of task- and relations-oriented actions. Discuss which of these two types of behavior is more important. Are there certain situations in which focusing on task-oriented actions would be harmful to a group? Are there circumstances when focusing on relations-oriented actions would be harmful to a group? Are the most effective leaders high in both task- and relations-oriented behaviors?

SUGGESTED READINGS

Bass, B. M., & Riggio, R. E. (2005). *Transformational leadership*. Mahwah, NJ: Lawrence Erlbaum Associates, Inc.

Fiedler, F. E. (1967). *A theory of leadership effectiveness*. New York: McGraw-Hill.

Graen, G. B. (2005). *New frontiers of leadership (LMX Leadership: The series)*. Charlotte, NC: Information Age Publishing.

Hersey, P. H., Blanchard, K. H., & Johnson, D. E. (2008). *Management of organizational behavior* (9th ed.). Upper Saddle River, NJ: Prentice Hall.

Mumford, M. D. (2006). *Pathways to outstanding leadership: A comparative analysis of charismatic, ideological, and pragmatic leaders*. Mahwah, NJ: Lawrence Erlbaum Associates.

Methods in Leadership Research

Alison L. Antes

> Men love to wonder, and that is the seed of science.
>
> —*Ralph Waldo Emerson*
>
> Research is formalized curiosity. It is poking and prying with a purpose.
>
> —*Zora Neale Hurston*

lthough you may be tempted to skip this chapter after just a glimpse at its title, you should resist the temptation. In order to fully understand the topic of leadership, you must appreciate how knowledge about leadership is acquired. Because people are commonly exposed to leadership in their daily lives, they may believe that they intuitively understand leadership. Ideas about how leadership works, however, must be evaluated in light of theory and tested through well-designed research studies. Ultimately, knowledge about leadership must be acquired through research. Although this chapter may seem more technical than the others, all of the other topics presented in this book stem from leadership research and the methods researchers use to conduct their studies. Indeed, the topic of methods in leadership research presented in this chapter is fundamental to your understanding of leadership. If you find this chapter challenging, do not be discouraged; good researchers take years to learn about research methods. In fact, there are entire classes and many textbooks just on this topic.

We will begin this chapter by discussing some of the research basics needed to understand the following discussion of the methods used in leadership research. In covering the predominant ways in which leadership research is conducted, we will discuss the advantages and disadvantages of these approaches. The chapter will conclude with some key recommendations for conducting effective leadership research. After reading this chapter, you will have a better understanding and appreciation for the topic of leadership due to your deeper understanding of leadership research. The chapter has several learning objectives, which are outlined here. And then we will address two fundamental questions before we dive into this topic in more detail.

Learning Objectives
- Understand the traditional and emerging methods used in leadership research
- Understand the advantages and disadvantages of different leadership research methods
- Understand recommendations for conducting effective leadership research

WHAT IS RESEARCH?

Research is a formal, systematic process that utilizes observation and/or experimentation to collect information about a phenomenon of interest in order to draw conclusions that contribute to broader knowledge about the topic. In leadership research, the phenomenon of interest is, of course, leadership. Generally speaking, the goals of leadership research include the following: (a) to describe leadership, (b) to determine the causes of leadership, (c) to explain leadership, and (d) to predict leadership.

Which of these goals are addressed by a given leadership study depends on the study and the goals and interests of the researcher.

> **Research**—a formal, systematic process that utilizes observation and/or experimentation to collect information about a phenomenon of interest in order to draw conclusions that contribute to broader knowledge about the topic

Also, as you will learn in this chapter, certain types of studies are better suited to address certain goals than others. In examining leadership, the primary focus may be on the leader, but leadership research also examines the followers, groups, and organizations affected by leaders.

WHAT ARE RESEARCH METHODS?

When researchers develop procedures, or techniques, for addressing their ideas and questions about a phenomenon of interest, they are using research methods. Thus, **research methods** in leadership research are the techniques, or procedures, used to collect information about leadership. Thousands of leadership studies have been conducted in different leadership contexts (i.e., business, military, politics, and education) using a variety of methods. The process of a researcher determining what methods he or she

> **Research methods**—the techniques, or procedures, used to collect information about leadership
>
> **Research design**—the final plan consisting of the research methods and procedures that will be used in a study

will use for a research study is often called designing a study. The final plan, consisting of the research methods and procedures that will be used in a study, is called the **research design.**

THE NUTS AND BOLTS OF LEADERSHIP RESEARCH

This section covers some of the basics of research. Some of this information may be a review for some readers, but it is important to understand the language used by researchers. Therefore, we will cover fundamental research terminology and major distinctions between types of research. We will also discuss the nature of the research process.

THE LANGUAGE OF RESEARCH

Theories are critical concepts in research. A **theory** is a set of concepts (or ideas) that presents a possible explanation for a particular phenomenon. The ideas proposed by theories can be turned into specific hypotheses, which can then be tested in research studies. A **hypothesis** is a statement that arises from a theory that states an expected relationship between variables. For example, a hypothesis based on transformational leadership theory (see chapter 7) might state that emotional messages in leader speeches will influence follower motivation. A **variable** is any factor, trait, or condition that can exist in differing amounts or types.

> **Theory**—a set of concepts (or ideas) that presents a possible explanation for a particular phenomenon
> **Hypothesis**—a statement that arises from a theory that states an expected relationship between variables
> **Variable**—any factor, trait, or condition that can exist in differing amounts or types

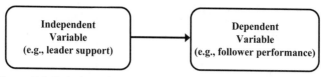

Figure 3.1 Relationship between independent and dependent variables.

For instance, gender, intelligence, and motivation are all variables. Variables are the key objects of interest in research studies.

Two major types of variables are independent and dependent variables. **Independent variables** are variables that account for, or explain, the phenomenon of interest in research studies. **Dependent variables** are variables that depend on, or are affected by, the independent variables. The relationship between independent and dependent variables is demonstrated in Figure 3.1. For example, if a researcher examined the effect of leader support on follower performance, then leader support would be the independent variable and follower performance would be the dependent variable. An independent variable influences, or causes, a dependent variable.

Another important kind of variable is a control variable. **Control variables** are variables a researcher wants to hold constant, or keep from changing. For example, in the leader support example above, it might be important to make sure that follower work experience is controlled. This is because both leader support *and* follower work experience affect follower performance; if follower work experience is not held constant, the researcher cannot be sure whether differences in follower performance are due to leader support

> **Independent variables—**variables that account for, or explain, the phenomenon of interest in research studies
> **Dependent variables—**variables that depend on, or are affected by, independent variables
> **Control variables—**variables that a researcher wants to hold constant

Leader Variables	Follower Variables	Situational Variables
• Personality • Self-confidence • Emotion • Interpersonal skills • Problem-solving • Decision-making • Supportive behavior • Motivation • Power • Influence tactics • Knowledge • Performance	• Experience • Commitment • Satisfaction • Ability • Creativity • Trust • Perceptions of leader • Motivation • Performance	• Organization type • Group Size • Organization Size • Work Structure • Work complexity Interconnectedness of the work • Environmental uncertainty • Group cohesiveness

Figure 3.2 Example variables in leadership studies.

or follower work experience. Many variables may be examined in leadership research. The primary variables of interest in leadership studies include variables pertaining to leaders, followers, and the situation in which leadership takes place (Yukl, 2006). Figure 3.2 provides examples of each of these major categories of variables.

The information collected in leadership studies about variables is called data. **Data** are the pieces of information observed or obtained through research. The people that data are collected about are called **research subjects (or participants)**. Researchers often use the word *measurement*, which means that they are numerically representing the data collected about the variables. Often the questionnaire or test used to

Data—the pieces of information observed or obtained through research
Research subjects (or participants)—the people that data are collected about in a research study
Measurement—a number representing data collected about variables
Measure—the questionnaire or test used to collect numerical data

collect numerical data is called a **measure.** Consider the following example of a measurement that people encounter in their own lives. When you weigh yourself on a scale, you are taking a measurement of your weight (a variable) that is then represented as a number (in pounds).

The tricky thing about leadership research is that many variables are not so simply measured. For example, imagine that you want to measure a leader personality variable, such as conscientiousness (i.e., being self-disciplined, organized, and thorough in one's work). You cannot put the leader on a conscientiousness scale to measure this variable. So researchers commonly measure variables by asking participants to respond to questions or statements about themselves. For instance, "I am always prepared" and "I pay attention to details" (Goldberg, 1999). These questions make up what is commonly referred to as a **survey.** In a survey, participants are given a numerical scale in order to choose their responses. For instance, the above statements would be answered by choosing 1, 2, 3, 4, or 5, where 1 means that the statement is very inaccurate and 5 means the statement is very accurate.

In leadership research, the dependent variable of interest is commonly leader effectiveness, but how can this be measured? This is a difficult question to answer. Researchers have measured leader effectiveness in a number of ways, but generally, leader effectiveness is determined by a leader's effect on his or her followers or organization (Yukl, 2006). There are many effects that a leader might have on his or her followers or organization, so any number of variables might be looked at. For example, organizational growth, productivity, and profit, or follower commitment, satisfaction, and trust, could be examined. As you can see, leader effectiveness is a broad concept that must be broken down into parts in order to be studied. Many times, researchers look at multiple leader effectiveness variables in the same study.

> **Survey**—a set of questions with numerical scales that research participants can use to choose their responses

QUALITATIVE VERSUS QUANTITATIVE RESEARCH

Qualitative research involves collecting data by observing leader behavior or interviewing leaders and/or followers and taking detailed notes. Often qualitative research is exploratory in nature, meaning that the key issues addressed by the study are actually unknown. The study's detailed notes are analyzed by pulling out the themes or patterns and interpreting what they mean about the nature of leadership. **Quantitative research,** on the other hand, focuses on measuring variables when specific hypotheses are tested. Often the major distinction between these types of approaches is the nature of the data arising from them. In qualitative research, the data are in a narrative, nonnumeric form, while the data in quantitative research are measured and expressed in numerical form. Sometimes, the findings from qualitative research provide ideas for hypotheses that are then tested in quantitative research.

> **Qualitative research—** research that collects data by observing leader behavior or interviewing leaders and/or followers and taking detailed notes
>
> **Quantitative research—** research that measures variables when specific hypotheses are to be tested

EXPERIMENTAL VERSUS NONEXPERIMENTAL RESEARCH

In addition to the qualitative-quantitative distinction, research methods can be classified as nonexperimental or experimental. In **nonexperimental research,** relationships between variables of interest are studied by observing or measuring them as they naturally occur. In **experimental research,** the variables of interest are isolated and studied directly by the researcher, who manipulates the independent variable of interest and controls, or holds constant, all other variables.

To **manipulate** an independent variable means that the researcher changes the independent variable for research participants in different groups to see the impact on the dependent variable. For example, if a researcher wanted to examine the effect of a leader giving feedback (i.e., telling followers how they are doing) on follower job commitment (i.e., the follower's attachment and loyalty to the job), the researcher could manipulate the type of feedback given to participants by giving one group positive feedback and another group negative feedback. The positive and negative feedback options are often called

Nonexperimental research— research that involves relationships between variables of interest that are studied by observing or measuring them as they naturally occur

Experimental research— research where variables of interest are isolated and studied directly by the researcher, who manipulates the independent variable of interest and controls all other variables

Manipulate—to change an independent variable as so the researcher can see the impact on different groups

Experimental conditions— the different groupings of participants for whom different treatments of the independent variables are applied

Control group—a group in an experiment that is given no treatment

experimental conditions, because the research participants are exposed to different treatments in these conditions. You may have heard of a control group in experiments. A **control group** is given no treatment (in our example, given no feedback), and the experimental groups are compared to the control group.

By controlling, or holding constant, all other variables that might affect the dependent variable, the researcher can establish how the independent variable affects the dependent variable in experimental research. Control of all other variables is made

Random assignment—the act of putting research participants into different experimental groups at random

possible by randomly assigning participants to the experimental groups, including the control group. **Random assignment** means that the research participants are put into the different experimental groups at random. This procedure controls for other variables because, on average, it ensures that the groups are equal on all other variables prior to exposure to the treatment. Because this amount of control is possible in an experiment, the researcher is able to conclude whether the independent variable *causes* the dependent variable. In nonexperimental research, conclusions about the cause-effect relationship between the independent and dependent variable cannot be made with certainty.

In the previous example, if follower commitment was different in the positive feedback group compared to the negative feedback group, then the researcher would be able to conclude that type of feedback *causes* different amounts of follower commitment. If a nonexperimental study found that feedback was related to follower commitment, three possibilities would exist about the relationship between the individual variable and the dependent variable. These three possibilities are illustrated in Figure 3.3. One possibility is that feedback (variable A) causes follower job commitment (variable B). Another possibility is that job commitment (variable B) causes feedback (variable A). The last possibility is that some other unknown variable (variable C), such as follower conscientiousness, causes both feedback (variable A) and job commitment (variable B).

FIELD VERSUS LABORATORY RESEARCH

Another distinction to keep in mind is that of field versus laboratory research, which pertains to the setting in which the research is conducted. **Field research** is conducted in the natural context—for

Variable A causes Variable B

Variable A
(e.g., feedback) → **Variable B**
(e.g., job commitment)

Variable B causes Variable A

Variable B
(e.g., job commitment) → **Variable A**
(e.g., feedback)

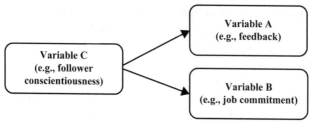

Variable C causes both Variable A and B

Variable C
(e.g., follower conscientiousness) → **Variable A**
(e.g., feedback)

→ **Variable B**
(e.g., job commitment)

Figure 3.3 Possible variable relationships in nonexperimental studies. In nonexperimental research, there are three possibilities that can explain why the independent and dependent variables are related. The researcher cannot be sure that the independent variable (variable A) causes the dependent variable (variable B).

Field research—research conducted in the natural context

example, top executives being studied at their companies. Field research can be valuable because research participants are examined in their natural settings, but the researcher has less control over variables that might influence the key variables being studied.

From a practical perspective, field research can be difficult to conduct because it is time consuming, costly, and often interrupts the normal functions of the groups or organizations studied.

Laboratory research, on the other hand, studies the variables of interest in a laboratory setting. In laboratory studies, it is easier to control other variables that could affect what the researcher is actually interested in studying. The downside to laboratory research, however, is that its context is not realistic. Thus, the degree to which research findings in the laboratory match what happens in the real world is questionable. Another common issue in laboratory studies is the use of undergraduate college students as participants. College students are used in research studies because they are easily accessible in the university setting, whereas real-world leaders are unlikely to take time out of their schedules to participate in a laboratory study. Sometimes researchers debate whether college students are an appropriate sample for studying leadership in the real world.

> **Laboratory research**—research conducted in a laboratory setting

THE RESEARCH PROCESS

To conclude this section on research basics, we will briefly review the phases involved in the research process (Graziano & Raulin, 2004). Figure 3.4 provides an illustration of these research phases. First, a leadership scholar must develop a general idea, theory, or question about how leadership works. Next, it is necessary for the researcher to become well-informed about existing research and theory on the topic of interest by examining what other leadership researchers have theorized and found in their studies. Next, a specific research question or hypothesis needs to be developed by refining the initial idea or theory into a testable hypothesis or research question. After the hypothesis is developed, a research method for addressing this hypothesis must be chosen, and a study must be designed to address it. In this step, a researcher must decide what research method he or she will use. The remainder of this chapter will cover the various options available for research methods and the key advantages and disadvantages of each method.

Although the next stages in the research process are beyond what is covered in this book, it is important to keep in mind what follows the selection of a research method and the design of a research study. After the study is designed, it is conducted by applying the research procedures developed in the previous phase. It is in this phase that data are collected. Following data collection, the next phase is to analyze the data, typically using statistics, although content analysis might be used for qualitative data. **Statistics** are a set of concepts, rules, and procedures that help researchers organize, understand, and draw conclusions from quantitative (i.e., numeric) data. **Content analysis** is a process of reviewing collected qualitative (i.e., nonnumeric) data where the information is examined for certain variables, themes, or patterns, and then conclusions are drawn accordingly. Often, content analysis is called content coding, especially when judges are used to examine the information and categorize, classify, and assign numerical values to it. Judges are usually experts on the topic being studied

> **Statistics**—a set of concepts, rules, and procedures that helps researchers organize, understand, and draw conclusions from quantitative data
> **Content analysis**—a process of reviewing collected qualitative data where the information is examined for certain variables, themes, or patterns; often called content coding when numerical values are assigned to qualitative data

or individuals who have been trained to recognize and code the variables of interest. Finally, conclusions are drawn about whether the hypothesis was correct, or an answer is articulated to address the research question.

After these phases are complete, there are other important phases. For instance, the conclusions from the study must be written and communicated to other researchers. The research findings will be used by the researcher, and others, to develop new ideas about how leadership works or to develop new hypotheses to further test the present theory. This process of using what is learned in the study to inform future research

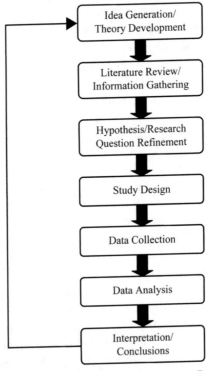

Figure 3.4 Key phases in the research process. Research involves a number of phases, starting with developing an idea and moving to designing a research study, and then collecting and interpreting the data. The conclusions from research studies then inform new ideas about the research topic.

is demonstrated in Figure 3.4 by the arrow that goes from the conclusions phase back to the beginning of the research process.

It is important to keep in mind that this is a simplified explanation of the research process. When research is conducted in the real world it does not necessarily progress exactly in this step-by-step fashion. For instance, the examination of existing research and theory and the development of an idea about leadership often go hand in hand, instead of an idea coming first and then examination of the existing research second. Furthermore, while this gives the reader a basic understanding of the research process, there are countless decisions made by the researcher in each of these phases and numerous details that are not discussed here.

METHODS IN LEADERSHIP RESEARCH

We now turn to the specific research methods used to address research questions and hypotheses about leadership. First, we cover survey methods, which have historically been the most popular methods for studying leadership. Next, we discuss experimental studies, followed by historiometric studies and qualitative studies. Each of these research methods has advantages and disadvantages that will be highlighted.

SURVEY RESEARCH

In **survey research**, the researcher selects a sample of participants, commonly a leader's followers, and asks them to complete surveys in order to obtain data

Survey research—a research method where surveys are administered to a sample of participants in order to collect data about leadership. For example, a particular survey based on leader-member exchange theory (see chapters 2 and 5) asks followers to respond to questions about the quality of their relationship with their leader. One question asks, "Does your leader recognize your potential?" (Graen & Uhl-Bien, 1995). Followers choose an answer between 1 and 5. One means "not at all," 3 means "moderately," and 5 means "fully." In a survey study examining the influence of leader-member exchange (the independent variable) on follower motivation (the dependent variable), the researcher would also collect data from another survey about follower motivation.

Data in survey studies are commonly collected about more than just two variables because, to study something as complex as leadership, more than just the relationship between one independent variable and one dependent variable must be examined. For example, in addition to examining follower motivation, the researcher might also measure follower performance. Sometimes researchers administer surveys to measure control variables that they want to control for in their study. In this case, the relationship between leader-member exchange and follower motivation and performance might also be affected by the length of time a follower has worked with a leader. Therefore, the researcher might collect data about the length of time they have worked together and use this as a control variable.

In addition, there are two special types of variables researchers commonly want to measure and examine in their studies. These variables are shown in Figure 3.5. The first type is called a **mediator variable**, which is a variable that explains the relationship between the independent variable and the dependent variable. For example, the effect of leader-member exchange on follower performance might be mediated, or explained, by follower access to work-

Mediator variable—a variable that explains the relationship between the independent variable and the dependent variable

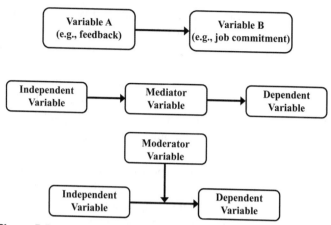

Figure 3.5 Mediator and moderator variables. Recall Figure 3.1 where only independent and dependent variables are shown; here mediator and moderator variables are added. Mediator variables explain the relationship between the independent and dependent variables, while moderator variables influence the strength of the relationship between the independent and dependent variables.

place knowledge, because leader-member exchange is likely to impact access to knowledge. The second special type of variable is called a **moderator variable,** and it influences the strength

> **Moderator variable**—a variable that influences the strength of the relationships between two other variables

of the relationship between two variables. For example, if the relationship between leader-member exchange and follower motivation increases when the work the followers are doing is interesting and decreases when it is uninteresting, then the interest level of the work is a moderator.

A study conducted by Johnson (2008) is a good example of a survey study. Johnson studied the role of emotion in leadership. Schoolteachers were the followers and principals were the leaders. The teachers completed three surveys about emotion. One survey measured the teachers' general emotional state (i.e., whether they generally felt positive or negative), another measured their general emotional state at work (i.e., whether they felt positive or negative *while at work*), and a third survey measured how likely the teachers were to be influenced by the emotions of other people. The teachers also completed the Multifactor Leadership Questionnaire (MLQ), a survey about transformational leadership (see chapter 7). In this survey, the teachers reported whether their principals demonstrated charismatic leadership behaviors, such as expressing confidence that goals would be achieved and talking about values (Bass & Avolio, 1995). Finally, the teachers completed a survey about how likely their principals were to engage in helpful, beneficial behaviors at work, such as cooperating with others.

In this study, the principals also completed surveys. They completed two of the same surveys as the teachers—the surveys about how positive or negative they felt in general and at work. They also completed a survey that measured personality characteristics such as conscientiousness and agreeableness, which were used as control variables.

Based on her data, Johnson (2008) concluded that leader emotion at work influences follower emotion at work, especially for followers who are more likely to be influenced by the emotions of others. In her study, when leaders were positive at work, followers were more positive at work, and when leaders were negative at work, followers were less positive. Her study also showed that follower positive emotion at work was related to viewing one's leader as charismatic and being more likely to engage in helpful, beneficial work behaviors.

Advantages and Disadvantages

One advantage of survey research is that surveys are relatively inexpensive and can be given to research participants fairly easily. The use of the Internet to conduct survey research is becoming popular because people can access the surveys from anywhere, and the data is easily collected through the computer. When research participants are able to complete a research study at their own convenience, without coming to researcher's lab, it is relatively easy to collect data from a large number of participants. Nevertheless, it can be a challenge to conduct a good survey study due to a number of disadvantages of this type of research.

First of all, in order for a survey study to contribute something unique and important to our understanding of leadership, a lot of work must go into developing hypotheses and determining which variables should be examined. It is especially important for a researcher to determine which variables need to be included in the study; some important variables might not be as obvious as the key independent and dependent variables. Specifically, the researcher must determine whether control, mediator, and moderator variables need to be included in the study.

Another challenge to survey research is choosing the surveys to be included in the study. Many surveys already exist that researchers can use in their studies, and this can sometimes be an advantage. It can also be a challenge, however, because a survey must be shown to be effective before it can be used in a research study. When a survey does not already exist to measure a certain variable, then developing a new survey can be a difficult and time-consuming process. In fact, a whole chapter, or even an entire book, could be filled with just explaining how to develop a measure and then ensure that a survey is effective. In the end, it is important to remember that the data coming from survey research are only as good as the surveys used to collect them.

Related to this idea is another major disadvantage of survey research. This is that survey research assumes that research participants can accurately answer the questions in the survey. There are a number of reasons why participants may not be accurate. First of all, participants may remember incorrectly if they are asked about their leaders' behavior, or they just may not be exposed to all their leaders do. Another problem might be that participants may think they are answering accurately, but really they are answering the questions based on something other than reality. For example, simply liking or disliking one's leader may influence how the follower responds (Brown & Keeping, 2005). So a leader might be very effective, but if the follower personally does not like him or her, then the participant might answer questions about the leader's effectiveness inaccurately.

Finally, another significant drawback to survey research is that not all leadership phenomena may be captured through surveys. For instance, how leaders think when they are solving problems is an important issue to research, but it would be difficult to study this issue using a survey study (Mumford, Friedrich, Caughron, & Antes, in press b). Moreover, survey research is limited because it does not capture the complexity of how leadership really takes place. Important variables such as context and social dynamics may be left out. Finally, survey research is nonexperimental; thus, it is not possible to firmly determine cause-effect relationships between variables in this type of research.

EXPERIMENTAL RESEARCH

The use of experimental research to study leadership has grown in popularity, as it addresses some of the limitations of survey research. For example, Jaussi and Dionne (2003) conducted an experiment to examine the effect of unconventional leader behaviors on follower creativity. The sample consisted of college students, and there were two independent variables—transformational leadership (see chapter 7) and leadership behavior. Participants were put in conditions where transformational leadership was either low or high and leader behavior was either conventional or unconventional. These independent variables were manipulated by having a research assistant pretending to be a group leader act out the role of either a low or high transformational leader and engage or not engage in unconventional behaviors. The unconventional behaviors included things like the leader spelling out his name on a table with magnetic letters, telling followers to wear special T-shirts, and standing on chairs. Participants were asked to develop an argument for a controversial topic (i.e., doing away with grades in school) and to give a group presentation. Judges evaluated the group presentations for their quality and creativity. In their study, Jaussi and Dionne concluded that unconventional leader behavior caused followers to see their leader as a role model for creativity and it helped to unify each group. Ultimately, unconventional leader behavior led the followers to be more creative.

In contrast to Jaussi and Dionne's (2003) study, where a person playing the role of a leader was used to manipulate the independent variables, another approach to experimental studies of leadership involves asking research participants to imagine taking on the role of a business leader. Participants are then asked to work through a task that is similar to the real-world tasks that leaders do in their work (Mumford et al., in press b). This type of study is often called a simulation study. Simulation studies are particularly valuable for examining leader cognition (i.e., how leaders think), including leader decision making, problem solving, planning, and creativity.

In a simulation study, the independent variables are manipulated in the task that participants are asked to complete. For example, if the research question was about the influence of past or future thinking on problem solving, then participants in one condition would be asked to think about their past experiences, while participants in another condition would be asked to think about their likely future experiences, before working on the problem (Antes & Mumford, in press). Another example of a potential manipulation would be the complexity of the problem. Problem complexity could be manipulated by presenting the participants in one condition with a problem containing two main issues versus a problem containing five main issues in the other condition. In order for a simulation study to be effective, the research task that participants complete must reflect the actual nature of leadership situations (Mumford et al., in press b).

Advantages and Disadvantages

Perhaps the most notable advantage of experimental studies is the ability to draw conclusions about cause-and-effect relationships.

Additionally, experimental methods allow researchers to examine variables that cannot be examined in survey research, especially phenomena such as leader thinking or decision making. Experimental studies, however, are not without their disadvantages.

The most common criticism of experimental studies is that they are unrealistic given their lack of real-world complexity. Experiments can only examine a limited number of variables in a limited context; thus, understanding how these findings apply to the real world can be limited. However, when the variables to be examined in the study are carefully chosen based on theory, it is much more likely that the results can be interpreted in terms of how they might work in the real world (Mumford et al., in press b). Along these lines, leadership experiments are often criticized for being unable to accurately create the social interactions that take place between actual leaders and followers. Related is the criticism that experiments are short-term, typically taking place within the span of just one day, and usually in several hours or less. Obviously, real-world

NOTE ON FIELD EXPERIMENTS

The studies described in this chapter thus far focus primarily on experiments conducted in the laboratory, which is an artificial environment, instead of the leader's natural environment. Although experiments conducted in the laboratory enable the most control, field experiments can be valuable because they examine behavior in the real world, meaning that real situations and real relationships are examined. Field experiments are commonly called quasiexperiments because they are like real experiments, but they are not true experiments because there is not complete control over the experimental conditions. Field experiments can be even harder to conduct than lab experiments, especially because many variables unknown to the researcher can influence the variables that he or she is trying to study. In addition, it can be difficult to get real leaders to participate in field experiments.

leadership takes place over a much greater span of time, which cannot be captured in experiments. In addition, leaders exert influence at multiple levels, which is often not examined in experiments. Typically, leadership experiments only examine leadership at the individual or group level, but leaders also influence organizations and sometimes even the larger society. Leadership research in general struggles to adequately examine leadership across these levels, but experiments are especially limited in this respect.

HISTORIOMETRIC RESEARCH

In **historiometric research,** historical information is studied to draw conclusions about leadership. Historical documents, including leader speeches, autobiographies, and biographies, represent a large potential source of information about leadership. In fact, historiometric studies are one

> **Historiometic research**—a research method where historical information is studied

major approach to studying outstanding leadership (see chapter 7) because historical information provides access to outstanding leaders who are typically difficult to study (Mumford, 2006). The historical information examined in historiometric studies is typically qualitative (i.e., nonnumeric) to begin with—for instance, recorded speeches or written paragraphs in books. Through content coding, however, historic qualitative data becomes quantitative data by having judges assign numerical values to it.

In a study by Strange and Mumford (2002), biographies of 60 famous historic leaders were coded for specific leader behaviors. The researchers wanted to see whether charismatic and ideological leaders—both types of leaders who base their leadership on visions but who focus on different values (i.e., charismatic leaders focus on social needs and ideological leaders focus on personal values and standards)—would engage in distinct types of behaviors.

The content analysis was done by reading passages about leader behaviors and comparing those behaviors to a checklist of behaviors characteristic of charismatic (e.g., the leader is a role model of his or her values) and ideological (e.g., the leader discredits those who currently have power) leaders. Each time a passage about a particular leader included a behavior characteristic of charismatic or ideological behavior, this was recorded. These checkmarks were then counted and became the scores for each of the behaviors. In addition to coding for charismatic and ideological behaviors, the leader's accomplishments (e.g., contributions to society and people's lives affected by the leaders' actions) were coded. The results from this study provided evidence that charismatic and ideological leadership are distinct types of vision-based leadership because they clearly engaged in different behaviors.

Advantages and Disadvantages

One advantage of historiometric studies of leadership is the great deal of historical information available about leaders. Another key advantage is that the use of historical information often allows multiple variables to be examined in the same study, providing rich information about leadership and the context of leadership. Furthermore, given the nature of historical information, studying historic data allows leadership to be studied over time, which is a key limitation of survey and experimental research.

There are, however, a number of shortcomings of historiometric research. The first concern relates to the material to be studied. In order to obtain good data about leadership, the historic data must be as accurate and complete as possible. When using autobiographies and biographies, a common concern is whether the information reflects reality or the interpretation and opinion of an author, since the information is presented from an author's perspective. Another weakness of historiometric studies is that the historical information available examines only certain aspects of leadership and only select leaders, commonly very influential or notable leaders (Mumford et al., in press b). Finally, the development and implementation of the content coding procedure can be a complex and time-consuming process. The coding scheme must be based on theory and appropriate for the historic information to be coded. Sometimes creativity on the part of the researcher is necessary to determine how to best assess the variables of interest.

QUALITATIVE RESEARCH

The survey and experimental research methods described previously are quantitative in nature, and historiometric research is considered a hybrid that is both qualitative and quantitative, but purely qualitative research can also be a valuable approach to leadership research (Bryman, 2004). In a study by Murphy and Ensher (2008), television directors were interviewed for a study about leadership in creative teams, specifically television production crews. The researchers used qualitative methods in their study because they wanted to collect detailed information that would allow them to elaborate theory about leadership in creative teams. The interviews lasted for about 1 hour, and the researchers took detailed notes and recorded the interviews. The questions in the interview were about career history, developmental experiences, past mentoring relationships, and charismatic leadership. The detailed notes collected in the interviews were examined using content analysis. Specifically, the researchers read the interview responses and coded for whether the leaders discussed any of six charismatic leadership behaviors—for example, vision articulation and sensitivity to followers' needs. The researchers also used a computer program to analyze the interviews. The program searched for the directors' use of leadership words when talking about their leadership style. Based on their data, Murphy and Ensher concluded that charismatic leadership may be an important leadership style for leaders of creative teams.

Interviews are a common technique for collecting data in qualitative leadership studies, but other approaches can also be used. For example, leaders could be observed and detailed notes could be taken about their behavior. In another approach, leaders might be asked to write their thoughts and experiences in a journal. In an approach called critical incidents, people are asked to describe particularly good and bad examples of leadership. Once this information is collected, researchers examine it to find important themes and patterns.

Advantages and Disadvantages

One of the primary advantages of qualitative research is that it is typically conducted in the actual leadership context, allowing for leadership to be examined in the real world. In addition, qualitative research methods allow for rich, detailed data to be collected; for instance, leadership can be examined at multiple levels (e.g., individual, group, and organizational) and over time (Mumford et al., in press). In addition, leadership can be studied from multiple perspectives; followers, peers, and leaders might all provide information about leadership. Often, as in the directors' study described previously, qualitative research is used to study unique cases of leadership, which can provide a great deal of insight into leadership theory. Overall, qualitative research is valuable for developing and expanding leadership theory.

Although qualitative research has several advantages, it also has some disadvantages. One criticism of qualitative research is that the information gathered may be interpreted based on the opinion of the researcher, so it may not be accurate. Quantitative research, on the other hand, is typically considered less likely to be inaccurate due to researcher opinion affecting the study. Ultimately, in order for qualitative research to be effective, it is critical that the data collection be guided by theory as much as possible. Likewise, the coding procedures used to analyze the data must be clearly outlined and based on theory as well. A final disadvantage of qualitative research is that because the data are often collected in a single, unique setting, the findings may not apply to other leadership contexts. For example, the findings about television directors may not apply to creative leadership in technology companies.

RECOMMENDATIONS FOR CONDUCTING LEADERSHIP RESEARCH

Although conducting leadership research is quite challenging, some general recommendations can be made for conducting effective leadership research (Hunter, Bedell-Avers, & Mumford, 2007; Mumford et al., in press b). First, and most important, leadership research must be based on theory. Another critical aspect of conducting effective leadership research is to make sure that important control variables are measured. If control variables are not included, it can be difficult to understand the actual relationship between the main variables of interest.

Another important recommendation is to be certain the variables to be examined in the study are clearly defined. It must be clear what is to be examined in the study, and the way the variables will be measured (in nonexperimental studies) or manipulated (in experimental studies) must be appropriate given the variables. Another recommendation for effective leadership research is to study multiple variables in the same study. This allows for a more realistic picture of leadership. It can be particularly important to study multiple dependent variables in the same study because the independent variables might affect different dependent variables in different ways. For example, the effect of leader problem solving on follower satisfaction may not be as important, or strong, as its effect on organizational performance.

In order to overcome some of the disadvantages of the leadership research methods mentioned in this chapter, the use of multilevel research and longitudinal studies has been suggested (Hunter

Multilevel research—research examining, in the same study, relationships among variables at multiple levels

Longitudinal research—research that examines a phenomenon over time by collecting data at multiple points over time

et al., 2007). **Multilevel research** involves examining, in the same study, relationships among variables at multiple levels—for example, individual, group, organizational, and environmental (Bliese, Halverson, & Schriesheim, 2002). **Longitudinal research** examines a phenomenon over time by collecting data at multiple points over time. This approach to leadership research has been suggested in order to take into account how leadership develops over time, instead of only examining leadership at one point in time.

Given the challenges of conducting effective leadership research, the design of a leadership study often takes a great deal of time. Sometimes, even once a study is designed, the researcher will "pilot test" the study. This means that the researcher will collect some initial data to see if the study is working as he or she intended. This is especially important in experimental research, where the researcher must make sure that the manipulations of the independent variables are working. Because leadership research is so complex, and because different researchers have expertise in different areas of leadership and are better at different parts of the research process, leadership researchers often work together to conduct studies. It is actually unusual for a researcher to work completely alone in designing and conducting a leadership study.

CHAPTER SUMMARY

The traditional approach to leadership research was the survey method, but leadership research methods have recently been extended to experimental, historiometric, and qualitative methods. In this chapter, you learned the key characteristics of these research methods and examples of each. You also learned about the advantages and disadvantages of each research method. It is important for researchers to take these issues into account when designing leadership studies, but it is also important to keep in mind that no research study is perfect. All studies, no matter how well designed and conducted, have limitations. Thus, it is common practice for researchers, in reporting their findings, to explicitly describe the limits of their research study.

The issues and challenges in leadership research covered in this chapter make it clear that researching leadership is no simple task. The complexity of conducting leadership research is second only to the complexity of the leadership phenomenon itself. Thus, perhaps the first step in conducting leadership research is simply to recognize the complexity of leadership and the multiple variables involved. Well-designed and conducted research studies are critical to our understanding of leadership, as research is the source of our knowledge about leadership. Research is a process that builds on the past and present. That is, the basis of future research and our knowledge about leadership rely on the conclusions drawn from the leadership studies of yesterday and today. In this chapter, we only touched on the issues pertaining to research methods; entire books and whole courses exist about research methods. Moreover, the skills needed to be an effective researcher require years to learn and years of practice to perfect. An aspiring leadership researcher should not be discouraged by this fact, but rather excited by the challenge.

KEY TERMS AND PHRASES

- Content analysis
- Control group
- Control variables
- Data

- Dependent variables
- Experimental conditions
- Experimental research
- Field research
- Historiometric research
- Hypothesis
- Independent variables
- Laboratory research
- Longitudinal research
- Manipulate
- Measure
- Measurement
- Mediator variable
- Moderator variable
- Multilevel research
- Nonexperimental research
- Qualitative research
- Quantitative research
- Random assignment
- Research
- Research design
- Research methods
- Research subjects (or participants)
- Statistics
- Survey
- Survey research
- Theory
- Variable

REVIEW QUESTIONS

1. Why is it important to understand the research methods used in leadership research?
2. What is a theory?

3. What is an independent variable and how is it different from a dependent variable?
4. What is the major difference between experimental and non-experimental research?
5. What is the primary nature of survey research?
6. What are the advantages of historiometric research?

DISCUSSION QUESTIONS

1. Other than through research studies, what are other ways that knowledge can be gained about leadership? What do you think are the advantages and disadvantages of these ways of gaining knowledge about leadership?
2. Which type of research method do you think would be the most difficult to use? Which type of research method do you think would be the easiest to use? Explain your answers.
3. If you were a researcher, which phase of the research process do you think you would find the most exciting?

INDIVIDUAL ACTIVITIES

INDIVIDUAL ACTIVITY 1

Imagine that you are a leadership researcher. Think about which variables are the most important to study in leadership research. Determine what three variables you think are important to study in each of the three main categories of leadership research variables: leader, follower, and situational variables.

INDIVIDUAL ACTIVITY 2

You are about to design a leadership research study. What are some of the most important things you need to think about before you design the study?

GROUP ACTIVITIES

Instructions: Get into small groups for these activities. Do the activities in your small groups, and then share your ideas with the other groups.

GROUP ACTIVITY 1

You want to study how leaders influence the self-esteem of their followers. Self-esteem is how someone judges his or her own self-worth. Generate a hypothesis about how leaders influence follower self-esteem.

GROUP ACTIVITY 2

Imagine that you are going to design a study to test the hypothesis generated in group activity 1. Outline the design of a study to test your hypothesis. Specifically, address the following issues:

1. What type of research method will you use?
2. Who will be your participants, or from where will you get your data?
3. What are your independent and dependent variables?
4. How will you measure or manipulate your variables?
5. What are the advantages of your research study for addressing your hypothesis?
6. What are the disadvantages of your research study for addressing your hypothesis?

SUGGESTED READINGS

Antonakis, J., Schriesheim, C. A., Donovan, J. A., Gopalakrishna-Pillai, K., Pellegrini, E. K., & Rossomme, J. L. (2004). Methods for studying leadership. In J. Antonakis, A. T. Cianciolo, & R. J. Stemberg

(Eds.), *The nature of leadership* (pp. 48–70). Thousand Oaks, CA: Sage Publications.

Cozby, P. C. (2006). *Methods in behavioral research* (9th ed.). New York: McGraw-Hill.

Hunter, S. T., Bedell, K. E., & Mumford, M. D. (2007). The typical leadership study: Assumptions, implications, and potential remedies. *The Leadership Quarterly, 18,* 435–446.

Mumford, M. D., Friedrich, T. L., Caughron, J. J., & Antes, A. L. (in press). Leadership research: Traditions, developments, and current directions. In D. A. Buchanan & A. Bryman (Eds.), *Handbook of organizational research methods.*

Simonton, D. K. (2003). Qualitative and quantitative analyses of historical data. *Annual Review of Psychology, 54,* 617–640.

4

Leader Traits, Skills, and Behaviors

Cheryl K. Beeler

> All the adversity I've had in my life, all of my troubles and
> obstacles, have strengthened me. . . . You may not realize
> it when it happens, but a kick in the teeth may be the best
> thing in the world for you.
>
> —*Walt Disney*

W alt Disney is considered by many to be a successful leader. Disney made a name for himself
as a leader in several industries, including media
entertainment and business. He managed to
overcome many obstacles to build an extremely successful company, and he was able to see the future of animation that others
failed to see. How would you describe Walt Disney to someone
who had never heard of him? What is it about Walt Disney that
made him so successful as a leader?

When describing Walt Disney, you would probably use
terms like *creative*, *bold*, *determined*, or *good problem solver*. When
most people think of what makes a good leader, they usually

LEADER SPOTLIGHT: "DISNEY'S FOLLY"— SNOW WHITE AND THE SEVEN DWARFS

When Walt Disney decided to make his first feature-length animated movie, most people, including his wife, thought he was crazy, and they told him so. People in the entertainment industry called Disney's vision for the project "Disney's Folly," and they were convinced it would destroy the Disney studios. Walt Disney decided to continue with his vision, despite what other people said. He put a great deal of effort into planning for the film, including bringing in a famous artist to train the animators and investing money and time developing special effects. Disney wanted to make sure this film was of the highest quality possible. Disney's team had been working on the project for almost 3 years when they ran out of money. In order to get the money to finish, Disney actually showed some rough cuts of portions of the film to loan officers at a bank. Luckily, the bank agreed to finance the completion of the film based on what they had seen.

When the film was released, *Snow White and the Seven Dwarfs* received a standing ovation from the theater audience. This film was the first English, Technicolor, feature-length animated film, and it was a huge success. In fact, it was the most successful film of 1938, and it earned over $8 million. Because of the film's success (which won Walt Disney one full-sized and seven miniature Oscar statuettes), Disney was able to expand his studio, and the film ushered in what came to be known as the Golden Age of Animation for Disney. (Gabler, 2006)

think in terms of what a person is like (traits), what they are good at (skills), or what they do (behaviors). When thinking about leadership, we often consider the aspects of a leader's behavior that are most visible to us as we watch what they do. When you see a successful person, you tend to think of his or her traits and skills as what make that person successful. In fact, many people already have an idea of the traits, skills, and behaviors that make a person a good leader. These ideas make up implicit leadership theories, which will be discussed in chapter 6.

In this chapter, we will cover the personal traits, skills, and behaviors that are associated with effective leadership. We will talk about several different types of traits, including cognitive traits, personality traits, motivational traits, and interpersonal traits. Next, we will talk about various types of skills that are often associated with good leadership, including problem solving and planning. Then, we will talk about some of the behaviors that are important for leadership. Finally, we will discuss the implications for trait, skill, and behavior research.

Learning Objectives

- Understand the history of leadership trait research
- Understand how different traits are related to effective leadership
- Understand how different skills are related to effective leadership
- Understand how different behaviors are related to effective leadership
- Understand the implications of trait, skill, and behavior leadership research

TRAITS

THE NATURE OF TRAITS

Traits are characteristics of a person that describe the person's thinking, personality, motivation, or how they deal

Traits—characteristics of a person that describe the person's thinking, personality, motivation, or how they deal with people

> **Cognitive traits**—the characteristics of a person's ability to think or style of thinking
> **Personality traits**—relatively stable characteristics that influence the way a person acts in certain situations
> **Interpersonal traits**—characteristics that describe the way a person treats and interacts with other people
> **Needs or motives**—the impulses that motivate a person to act in a particular manner

with people. **Cognitive traits,** such as wisdom or intelligence, are characteristics of a person's ability to think or style of thinking. **Personality traits,** such as extroversion, conscientiousness, and emotional stability, are relatively stable characteristics that influence the way a person acts in certain situations. **Interpersonal traits,** like integrity, are characteristics that describe the way a person treats and interacts with other people. Finally, a person's **needs,** or **motives,** such as the need for achievement or power, are what motivate a person to act in a particular manner. Needs and motives influence what types of things people pay attention to and also help guide their behavior.

WHAT IS THE HISTORY OF TRAIT RESEARCH?

Early leadership researchers were looking for a formula of traits common to all leaders. They studied these traits by comparing leaders to nonleaders and effective leaders to ineffective leaders. In doing so, the researchers studied any traits they could think of in order to find the perfect set of traits that would guarantee good leadership. They studied physical characteristics (like height and attractiveness), personality traits, and academic achievements (Bass, 1990).

In two extensive reviews of leadership research from 1904 to 1970, Stogdill concluded that a primary aspect of being a leader is helping a group accomplish its goals. Some traits that early researchers found relevant in leadership included intelligence, dependability, knowing how to get things accomplished, persistence in dealing with problems, confidence, and a willingness to have power and control. Although the studies that Stogdill reviewed looked at a very large number of traits, he concluded that there was no formula of traits that lead to effective leadership. Individual traits tended to be more or less important for leadership depending on the situation, and there was no set of traits that could be associated with effective leadership in *all* situations (Bass, 1990).

More recently, researchers at the Center for Creative Leadership (CCL) compared successful managers to those who had failed (McCall & Lombardo, 1983). Like Stogdill, these researchers did not find traits that guaranteed success or failure, but their findings were interesting. Successful managers and failed managers actually had some traits in common: They were ambitious, technically skilled, and had risen quickly in their companies. On the other hand, the researchers concluded that a number of traits seemed especially relevant for predicting if a manager would succeed or fail. These traits included: (a) emotional stability, (b) not

CENTER FOR CREATIVE LEADERSHIP RESEARCH CONCLUSIONS

- Emotional stability: failed managers were more likely to be easily stressed and feel pressure
- Defensiveness: managers who failed were more likely to be defensive about failure
- Integrity: managers who failed were more likely to compete with others and were more concerned about advancing their own careers at the expense of others
- Interpersonal skills: managers who failed were usually weaker in interpersonal skills than successful managers
- Technical and cognitive skills: managers who failed had high levels of technical skills, which led to overconfidence and arrogance

getting defensive, (c) integrity, (4) interpersonal skills, and (5) technical and cognitive skills. The following table summarizes the researchers' findings on these traits.

WHAT TRAITS ARE IMPORTANT FOR SUCCESSFUL LEADERS?

As mentioned earlier, researchers have looked at many different traits to see how they relate to successful leadership. Several traits seem to be important for leadership across a number of studies. This section will summarize the research findings on some of the traits that appear most relevant to successful leadership.

Cognitive Traits

Intelligence. **Intelligence** is very important for leaders. Leaders must perform extremely complicated tasks and understand the complexities of organizations and the processes and products of those organizations. They must be able to remember large amounts of information, and they must be able to use and retrieve that information quickly and efficiently. You will see that a high level of intelligence is also necessary for many of the other important traits, skills, and behaviors that leaders must have to be successful (Mumford, Marks, Connelly, Zaccaro, & Reiter-Palmon, 2000).

Intelligence—the capacity to acquire, store, and apply knowledge (general mental ability, verbal reasoning, analytical reasoning, etc.)
Wisdom—the successful use of intelligence, creativity, and experience to reach a common good

Wisdom. Sternberg (2007) has studied **wisdom** and leadership extensively. He proposed that wisdom involves the successful use of intelligence, creativity, and experience. There are four components to wisdom: (a) seeking to reach a common good; (b) balancing the goals of oneself, others, and an organization;, (c) considering both the short- and long-term elements of a situation; and (d) adapting to and shaping one's environment. Successful, wise leaders recognize that there are several sets of goals operating in any situation, and they work to balance these goals and interests in their plans and actions. When leaders are unsuccessful, it is often because they ignored the interests of one or more parties who should have been taken into account. Research on wisdom and its relationship to successful leadership is still limited; however, several researchers have found evidence that wisdom is important for successful leadership. One notable finding shows that organizational leaders exhibit more wisdom than people not in leadership positions. Also, people characterized as wise tend to have the same characteristics as those who are successful leaders.

Expertise. **Expertise** is a deep understanding and knowledge of a specific area or situation. Expertise comes from experience; the more experience a person has with a certain area or situation, the more likely that person is to become an expert in that area. Leaders must have expertise in the specific organizational area where they serve as leaders. Researchers have found that expertise (technical expertise, specific to the task at hand) is highly associated with the performance of a leader's team (Mumford, Hunter, Eubanks, Bedell, & Murphy, 2007).

Expertise in the specific work domain is important for several reasons. Leaders must understand the work very well before they can plan work activities and distribute the resources that their employees need to do the work. Also, especially in very specialized fields, if a leader does not have a high level of expertise in the work domain, his or her employees will not trust the leader or see him or her as credible or worthy; thus, they will be less likely to take direction from the leader. Additionally, without the necessary expertise, leaders will not be able to give

> **Expertise**—a deep understanding and knowledge of a specific area or situation

their employees direction and feedback on their progress toward accomplishing tasks and goals (Mumford, Friedrich, et al., 2007).

Personality Traits

Big Five. The **Big Five** model is a popular way of categorizing personality traits into five broad traits that encompass most of what distinguishes one person's personality from another's. The five constructs that the Big Five uses to describe personality are the following: openness, conscientiousness, extroversion, agreeableness, and neuroticism (a good way to remember them is that they spell out *OCEAN*). Openness describes how willing a person is to experience new things. Conscientiousness is how dependable and hard working a person is. Extroversion is how outgoing a person is and how much he or she enjoys being around other people. Agreeableness is being cheerful and optimistic. Neuroticism has to do with how controlled and emotionally stable a person is.

Most leadership research on the Big Five suggests that each of the personality traits is important for successful leadership. However, results have not been entirely consistent. This could be because different researchers use different tests to measure these personality traits, and it could also be because different researchers use different measures of leader success. While these personality traits do appear to be important in leadership, more research is needed to see how they specifically relate to successful leadership.

Big Five—a common set of personality characteristics: openness, conscientiousness, extroversion, agreeableness, neuroticism

Energy level and stress tolerance—the abilities of remaining alert for prolonged periods of time and handling stressful situations

Energy Level and Stress Tolerance. Research has shown that **energy level**, physical stamina, and **stress tolerance** are important for successful leadership. Having a high level of energy and a

94

tolerance for stress allows leaders to cope with the demands often involved in leadership positions, including a fast pace and long hours. Leadership positions often involve stress because of the pressure to make decisions, especially in times of crisis, and the ability to remain calm and think through problems thoroughly will lead to effective leadership (Yukl, 2006).

Self-Confidence. For the most part, leader self-confidence seems related to leadership success. **Self-confidence** influences a leader's behavior primarily by giving him or her the assurance to attempt and accomplish difficult tasks and influence people. Clearly, self-confidence can be good for a leader, but too much

> **Self-confidence**—the a belief in one's ability to accomplish difficult tasks

self-confidence could actually be bad for a leader's performance. Too much confidence can cause leaders to take excessive risks and be arrogant and annoying to people around them, minimizing their success (Yukl, 2006).

Locus of Control. The term **locus of control** describes how a person views the causes of his or her behavior. People with an internal locus of control believe that the events in their lives are determined and controlled by them personally. People with an external locus of control believe that the events in their lives are controlled by chance, or some other ex-

> **Locus of control**—the way a person views the causes of his or her behavior (e.g., internal or external)

ternal factor; they believe they have little control over their lives and, thus, cannot do anything to change (Rotter, 1966). Because people with an internal locus of control believe they can control and influence their lives, they are more future oriented and more likely to actively attempt to solve problems. They are more flexible, and when they experience failure, they are more likely to learn from their mistakes than people with an external locus of control. Research on the relationship between locus of control and leadership is still limited, but it suggests that having an internal locus of control is related to successful leadership.

Emotional Maturity. People who exhibit **emotional maturity** have a realistic view of their own strengths and weaknesses, and they work toward self-improvement instead of denying their weaknesses and focusing only on their strengths. They are less self-centered, they have more self-control, and they are less prone to mood swings. Leaders who are emotionally mature have more cooperative relationships with other people in their work environment (Cantoni, 1955).

> **Emotional maturity**—a realistic awareness of one's emotions and abilities

Interpersonal Traits

Machiavellianism. **Machiavellianism** refers to a person's tendency to deceive and manipulate others for personal gain. People who are high in Machiavellianism resist the influence of other people, and they are more concerned with completing their own personal tasks, rather than with emotional and moral concerns. They are game players. Researchers have studied specific Machiavellian manipulation tactics in organizational leaders. Some tactics they found include lying, acting like other people have a say when they really do not, changing information, exaggerating the importance of a task, and ignoring others. The game playing of Machiavellian leaders does not seem to impact a group's ability to function, but the

> **Machiavellianism**—a person's tendency to deceive and manipulate others for personal gain

group members typically do not get along socially when they work under a Machiavellian leader (Bass, 1990).

Authoritarianism. **Authoritarianism** is a person's tendency to stress authority and power in relationships. People who are high in authoritarianism are said to be conservative, emotionally withdrawn, power seeking, and resistant to change. Authoritarianism is related to several aspects of a leader's behavior. For the most part, authoritarianism is associated with negative leadership behaviors. People high in authoritarianism are more likely to give punishments for bad behavior than rewards for good behavior. Also, authoritarianism is related to fewer successful leadership behaviors, like displaying sensitivity toward other people and contributing to the accomplishment of group goals (Bass, 1990).

> **Authoritarianism**—an individual's tendency to stress authority and power

Integrity. **Integrity** means that a person's behavior is consistent with their personal values, and that the person is honest, ethical, and trustworthy. In fact, integrity is an important part of trust. Several types of behavior are related to personal integrity. First, people with integrity are honest and truthful, rather than deceptive. Leaders lose credibility when people discover they have lied or stretched the truth. Second, people with integrity keep their promises. People do not want to make agreements with leaders who cannot be trusted to keep promises. Third, people with integrity are loyal to their followers. The trust of followers will be lost if a leader does not demonstrate loyalty. Fourth, these people will not tell secrets. People will not tell a leader important, confidential information if he or she cannot be trusted not to

> **Integrity**—the extent to which a person's behavior is consistent with his or her personal values, honesty, and ethicality

tell others. Finally, people with integrity are responsible for their own actions. Taking responsibility for their actions makes leaders look strong and dependable to others (Yukl, 2006).

Motivation. What motivates a leader's behavior can also impact that person's success as a leader. For instance, most people who hold leadership positions are motivated by a need for power. This motivation allows them to work toward higher positions of authority, frequently gaining them leadership positions. McClelland (1985) proposed a group of needs that motivate people, including the need for achievement, the need for affiliation, and the need for power.

McClelland's **need for achievement** describes people who are motivated by the satisfaction they feel when they complete a difficult task. These people prefer to have tasks that depend on their own unique abilities and effort. They like jobs where they can complete their duties in their own way, and they like to receive frequent, concrete feedback about their performance. People with a low need for achievement are content to do things as they are told, and they do not try to push standards of excellence. McClelland's **need for affiliation** describes people who are motivated by feeling liked and accepted by others. These people are especially sensitive to feelings of rejection or hostility from others. They like jobs where they can have social interactions with their friends, and where they can work in friendly and co-operative teams. People with a low need for affiliation tend to be loners who avoid social activities and feel uncomfortable at social gatherings like

> **Need for achievement**—a characteristic of individuals who are motivated by the satisfaction they feel when they complete a difficult task
> **Need for affiliation**—a characteristic of individuals who are motivated by feeling liked and accepted by others
> **Need for power**—a characteristic of individuals who are motivated by their ability to influence and control other people

parties. McClelland's **need for power** describes people who are motivated by their ability to influence and control other people. These people seek out positions of authority in which it is possible to influence and control others. People with a low need for power are timid and dislike telling people what to do.

TWO TYPES OF NEED FOR POWER

People with a high need for power can actually be grouped into two subgroups: socialized power orientation and personalized power orientation. People with a socialized power orientation have strong self-control and seek to satisfy their need for power in socially acceptable ways, including influencing people to take part in a worthy cause or helping others to develop their skills and confidence. In contrast, people with a personalized power orientation satisfy their need for power in selfish ways by dominating others and using their power to accomplish their own desires.

Many studies have looked at how these needs affect a leader's success. Generally, the pattern of needs that seems to be best for successful leadership is a strong socialized power orientation, a moderately high need for achievement, and a relatively low need for affiliation. This general pattern may change, however, depending on the exact business context. For instance, in small businesses, the need for achievement seems to be most important for the success of owner-managers. On the other hand, the need for power may be more important for people seeking higher levels of management in larger businesses (Yukl, 2006).

SKILLS

A **skill** is the ability to do something well. Skills can be talked about in both general

> Skill—the ability to do something well, in both general and specific ways

and specific terms. Examples of general skills include conceptual skills or interpersonal skills. Examples of specific skills include decision making and problem solving. This section will concentrate on the specific skills that have been found to be important for successful leadership.

WHAT SKILLS ARE IMPORTANT FOR LEADER SUCCESS?

Decision Making

Leaders must make high-stakes decisions rapidly, so they must be skilled at **decision making**. They often do not have time to thoroughly think about each and every decision they make, and each decision often has multiple, complicated consequences. Because of this need to make quick decisions with little in-depth thought, leaders have been said to be **intuitive** thinkers, meaning that they do not spend valuable time analyzing complex situations. While intuition is likely to play a large role in the decisions leaders make, there is also a strategic element to leaders' decisions. These decisions involve long time frames and broad organizational elements—for example, product lines and areas of innovation. Because of the complexity and high stakes involved with strategic decisions, leaders cannot simply use intuition for these decisions; they must actively analyze the elements of the situation. When leaders are faced with major strategic decisions, they analyze the following: (a) the goals to be accomplished, (b) the actions or tactics that will be most effective in accomplishing these goals, and (c) the causes involved in the situation (Marcy & Mumford, in press).

Decision making—the process of understanding a complex situation in order to make a high-stakes decision
Intuitive—the characteristic of thinking quickly, without analyzing the situation in-depth

Problem Solving

In their day-to-day work, leaders encounter several different types of social problems. These problems are extremely complex and poorly defined. Not only do leaders have to address complex, ambiguous problems, but they have to address these problems in very short time frames; leaders do not have time to think extensively about

> **Problem solving**—the process of understanding many aspects of a complex problem in order to solve that problem

every aspect of every problem they encounter. Therefore, leaders must be able to solve problems quickly and efficiently, and it is best if their solutions can address multiple problems at one time. In order to come up with these solutions quickly, leaders must focus on the restrictions that apply to potential solutions to determine the best action to take to solve a problem. There are a number of important elements that must be considered when thinking about leader **problem solving** (Mumford, Marks, et al., 2000). We will discuss more about how leaders go about solving problems in chapter 6.

Planning

Planning is an ongoing process that leaders must do every day in organizations. Leaders must think about their future actions and the consequences of these potential actions, and how their actions will help them and their followers achieve their goals. Planning is very important to organizations. Leaders must plan their own day-to-day activities (when and how they are going to work on their own tasks),

> **Planning**—the ability to forecast, and predict, potential actions and their consequences in order to determine the best course of action

leaders must plan how to divide other work tasks among their subordinates (how to delegate effectively), and leaders must help their organizations plan responses to competitors and environmental change. It takes a lot of time and cognitive resources to develop a good, thorough plan (Mumford, Schultz, & Van Doorn, 2001).

Planning is always based on the goal a leader is trying to accomplish. Planning begins with a leader recognizing an opportunity to take an action that will lead to goal achievement. Then, the leader thinks about the situation and the best way to accomplish the goal. Next, the leader comes up with an initial plan, and he or she revises the plan when changes need to be made to avoid potential problems. Finally, a good plan involves ways to mark progress toward goal accomplishment and backup plans in case something goes wrong (Mumford et al., 2001).

Emotional Intelligence

Emotional intelligence is also important for leadership success. Emotional intelligence is the ability to recognize one's own feelings and the feelings of others. It also involves the ability to manage emotions such that they do not interfere with a person's thinking and behavior (Goleman, 1995). Because emotions are strong feelings, they can distract people from their normal thinking and behavior. Even when a person stops immediately experiencing a particular emotion, the feeling often remains as a good or bad mood; moods can also impact leaders' performance. Emotional intelligence is important for leadership success. A leader who has emotional intelligence is better able to solve problems, make decisions, and manage time and crises. Not much research has been done on leadership suc-

Emotional intelligence—the ability to recognize one's own feelings and the feelings of others

cess and emotional intelligence. However, the limited research thus far does suggest that emotional intelligence is relevant to leadership performance, and emotional intelligence in leaders can lead to higher job satisfaction and performance for their followers.

Social Intelligence

Social intelligence is the ability to recognize and choose the best way to address a situation. Social intelligence goes beyond what we commonly think of as social skills. The two elements of social intelligence are social perceptiveness and behavioral flexibility. **Social perceptiveness** is the ability to recognize the needs, the potential problems, and the potential opportunities for an organization. It also involves understanding the characteristics of an organization and the relationships involved in that organization. Finally, a person who is socially perceptive understands how different actions will help or hurt the group. Basically, a leader with high social perceptiveness understands what needs to be done to make a group or organization more effective and how to do it.

Behavioral flexibility is the ability and the willingness to change one's behavior in response to a situation. It involves taking a variety of different actions and judging their effectiveness, changing one's behavior as needed (Zaccaro, Gilbert, Thor, & Mumford, 1991).

Social intelligence—the ability to recognize and choose the best way to address interpersonal situations
Social perceptiveness—the ability to recognize the needs, the potential problems, and the potential opportunities for an organization
Behavioral flexibility—the ability and the willingness to change one's behavior in response to a situation

Ability to Learn

In today's fast-paced, competitive, technology-heavy,

103

industrial environment, adaptability has the highest premium; organizations must be able to not only gain new knowledge, but also use this new knowledge to adapt to this constantly changing environment. The **ability to learn** from experience and adapt to change is very important for leaders in such turbulent environments. The ability to learn involves the ability and the willingness to look at one's own thoughts and behaviors and consider ways to improve. It also involves self-awareness, or the recognition of one's own strengths and weaknesses. Studies of military leaders have shown that the ability to learn was related to leadership success. Furthermore, the CCL researchers found that the ability to learn and adapt is important for executives (Yukl, 2006).

> **Ability to learn**—the ability to recognize a learning experience and use that experience to adapt to changes in the environment

BEHAVIORS

When researchers were unable to find a specific set of traits that would lead to successful leadership, they decided to look at specific leader behaviors that are important for success. Leadership researchers have looked at four broad categories of behaviors: (a) consideration, (b) initiating structure, (c) participation, and (d) change-directed behaviors. Some researchers have also studied several more specific behaviors, like role modeling and feedback behaviors. This section will go over the relevant findings on leadership behaviors.

OHIO STATE LEADERSHIP STUDIES

The Ohio State University leadership studies began in the 1940s. These studies were designed to study leadership behaviors that were related to success. These studies identified two general types of behavior that are important for leadership: consideration and initiating structure (Fleishman, 1953).

Consideration

Consideration involves a leader showing concern for the well-being of his or her employees. Considerate leaders show appreciation of their employees' work, help increase the self-esteem of their employees by treating them well, and work to make their employees feel comfortable in the organization. Considerate leaders are oriented toward relationships and trust. On the other

> **Consideration**—leader behavior that involves a leader showing concern for the well-being of his or her employees

hand, inconsiderate leaders criticize their employees publicly, do not consider their feelings, and make them feel uncomfortable.

Initiating Structure

Initiating structure involves a leader planning and organizing a work group's activity. A leader who initiates structure sets and maintains standards for work, meeting deadlines, and deciding how the work will be done. A leader who initiates structure establishes clear standards and rules for communication and work

> **Initiating structure**—a leader planning and organizing a work group's activity

organization. These leaders are oriented toward the work tasks, as opposed to establishing relationships with other employees.

UNIVERSITY OF MICHIGAN STUDIES

Around the same time as the Ohio State leadership studies, another major program of leadership studies took place at the

University of Michigan. The University of Michigan studies found some of the same categories of leadership behavior, and they also found another category. They identified relations-oriented behavior (similar to consideration), task-oriented behavior (similar to initiating structure), and participative leadership (Foundation for Research on Human Behavior, 1954).

Participative Leadership

With **participative leadership,** a leader involves his or her subordinates in making important decisions and doing supervisor-type tasks. The University of Michigan studies found that successful leaders engaged in participative leadership by having group meetings to encourage individuals to contribute to important decisions and to improve communication. The leader's role in group meetings is to guide the discussion and make sure it is constructive and that the group is solving problems. It is important to remember, however, that the leader is still responsible for what the group decides, even though the group is more involved in decisions (Yukl, 2006).

> **Participative leadership—** leader behavior that involves a leader involving his or her subordinates in making important decisions and doing supervisor-type tasks

Change-Oriented Behavior

Yukl (2006) realized that these types of behavior did not adequately cover the range of behaviors that successful leaders engage in. He and other researchers identified another type of leader behavior: **change-oriented behavior.** Change-oriented behaviors involve behaviors that are directed at encouraging and facilitating change in organizations.

> **Change-oriented behavior—** leader behaviors that are directed at encouraging and facilitating change in organizations

Organizations can no longer be competitive by maintaining their current processes, products, or services. They must continually create new products and processes in order to achieve long-term success. One of the most important factors involved in successful adaptation for organizations is effective leadership (Mumford, Scott, Gaddis, & Strange, 2002).

SPECIFIC BEHAVIORS

There are a number of different specific behaviors that have been researched to see how they relate to successful leadership. Most of these behaviors are important in terms of working with teams of employees and developing and putting different projects into operation in organizations. This section will describe some of the specific behaviors found to be important for successful leadership.

Role Modeling

Role modeling can be a useful tool for leaders. Some people may think the purpose of role modeling is for a leader to show the other employees what types of behaviors are appropriate for a work environment. Actually, role modeling helps leaders because it helps them set the climate of a work group. Work performance is enhanced when employees perceive that the work environment, or climate, is supportive (Amabile, Schatzer, Moneta, & Kramer, 2004). In general, when people work in a climate in which they feel safe and supported, they will be better workers (Mumford, Eubanks, & Murphy, 2007). Leaders may influence these aspects primarily by role modeling behaviors that indicate acceptance of these values (Jaussi & Dionne, 2003). Think about what a leader would do if that leader wanted to make sure his or her employees made the organization of their work materials a priority. Would the leader be organized or disorganized?

> **Role modeling**—behaviors that a leader uses to set a work climate

Support

Organizational tasks and projects can be costly; therefore, these projects will not succeed if **support** and resources are not available (Amabile et al., 2004; Ekvall & Ryhammer, 1999). It is important that leaders make sure the necessary time and resources are available to complete projects. When employees feel pressure to complete their tasks in a short amount of time, their performance will deteriorate. In order to make sure that their employees have enough time and resources to complete their tasks, leaders must often convince upper-level management of the importance of their projects (Jelinek & Schoonhoven, 1990). This can be done by involving these senior executives in the project early on, and then working to keep them interested in the project until it is complete (Mumford, Eubanks, & Murphy, 2007).

> **Support**—leader behaviors that allow employees to have enough time and resources to complete their tasks

Championing

Another part of getting different projects accomplished involves making sure that an organization as a whole is prepared to accept and adopt these new projects. In order for new projects to be adopted, it is important that leaders take part in **championing**, or showing enthusiasm for, a project to gain support from the rest of an organization (Howell & Boies, 2004), in effect serving as representatives for their team within the organization (Ancona & Caldwell, 1992). In order to gain support, leaders must show the other organization members how these new projects

> **Championing**—behaviors that leaders use to create interest and excitement for new projects

promote existing organizational values and processes, and how these projects will have a positive impact on the organization if they are implemented (Howell & Boies).

Feedback

Another important behavior of leaders when working with project teams is directing the work. Leaders help guide the work of their employees in the right direction. One important way leaders direct project work is by evaluating the work of employees and providing **feedback.** Leaders should try to provide constructive

> **Feedback**—behaviors that provide evaluation and direction for a subordinate's work

feedback in evaluating their employees' work. Also, leaders must make sure they are evaluating the work based on appropriate standards; depending on the stage and goals of the project, different evaluation standards will be more or less relevant (Mumford, Eubanks, et al., 2007).

WHAT ARE THE LIMITATIONS OF THIS RESEARCH?

We now know a lot about the traits, skills, and behaviors that are important for leadership success. The research that has been done on these concepts, however, has encountered some problems; the research methods, theories, and definitions we have for studying leadership are not perfect. Many of the traits we study in connection with leadership are relatively abstract, which makes them difficult to study and to understand. These traits are usually studied indirectly in terms of how they influence leaders' behaviors, which is not a perfect way to learn about traits. But it is difficult to study traits directly. Also, many trait studies are not based on theories that can explain *how* these traits may be related to leadership success (Yukl, 2006).

Another limitation of studies looking at leader traits and skills is that most only look at individual traits or skills and how they are related to leadership success. Looking at traits or skills one at a time makes the results less clear than looking at several traits and how they interact. Looking at only one trait or skill at a time ignores the idea that traits may be related to each other and may interact with each other to affect the behavior of leaders. For example, self-confidence and stress tolerance make leaders better able to control their emotions and think clearly during times of stress. Studies that consider many different traits and skills and measure their impact on each other will help identify patterns of traits and skills that may lead to leader success (Yukl, 2006).

CHAPTER SUMMARY

As you can see, researchers have identified many different traits, skills, and behaviors that are important for successful leadership. You may be wondering, however, what this means to you. How do people and organizations use this research? This section will wrap up the chapter by examining one important use for this extensive line of research: leadership training and development.

TRAINING AND DEVELOPING LEADERS

Now that you know what traits, skills, and behaviors are important for leadership, you might be asking, can people learn them? Can people learn to be successful leaders? Luckily, the answer is yes. There are, in fact, many different leadership development programs; in a quick Internet search of leadership development, you would probably get more hits than you would even be able to look at. These leadership development programs vary in several ways. The type of instruction ranges from short, classroom-type training to longer, more real-world training. The content of the programs ranges widely, from those that cover specific leadership models to those that cover broad areas relevant for many different leadership positions. Importantly, these programs also vary in the extent to which they are based on relevant leadership research and theories. The leadership programs that are based on leadership research and theories will most likely be more useful and effective than the ones that are not. Mumford, Friedrich, Caughron, and Antes (in press a) explored how these leadership development programs actually work. They proposed that successful leadership development programs should consist of two main elements: (a) teaching knowledge, and (b) teaching the skills to apply the knowledge.

CONCLUSION

You may have noticed that some of these traits and skills overlap. For instance, intelligence is highly related to planning and problem-solving skills. Intelligence is also necessary for wisdom. This highlights the complexity of the nature of leadership and what is necessary for successful leadership. This chapter has discussed many individual traits, skills, and behaviors that have been shown to be important for leadership in various situations. While some traits, skills, or behaviors may be more important in some situations than others, the traits, skills, and behaviors discussed in this chapter appear to have a wide range of usefulness across many different job situations. Organizations can also use this type of traits and skills research to develop and hire their employees, and you can use this research to develop your own skills as a leader.

KEY TERMS AND PHRASES

- Ability to learn
- Authoritarianism
- Behavioral flexibility
- Big Five
- Championing
- Change-oriented behavior
- Cognitive traits
- Consideration
- Decision making
- Emotional intelligence
- Emotional maturity
- Energy level and stress tolerance
- Expertise
- Feedback
- Initiating structure
- Integrity
- Intelligence
- Interpersonal traits
- Intuitive
- Locus of control
- Machiavellianism
- Need for achievement
- Need for affiliation
- Need for power
- Needs or motives
- Participative leadership
- Personality traits
- Planning
- Problem solving
- Role modeling
- Self-confidence
- Skills
- Social intelligence

- Social perceptiveness
- Support
- Traits
- Wisdom

REVIEW QUESTIONS

1. What are the three different types of traits that are important for successful leadership? Give an example of each.
2. Name and describe the three different types of motivation that McClelland discusses.
3. How does locus of control relate to successful leadership?
4. What are the three elements of a situation that leaders consider when they make decisions?
5. Name and describe the four general categories of leader behavior proposed by the Ohio State and University of Michigan studies and Yukl.
6. What are the two key elements that are taught in successful leadership development programs?
7. What are some of the limitations of leader trait and skill research?

DISCUSSION QUESTIONS

1. If you had to choose one trait, which would you say is the most important trait for successful leadership and why?
2. Have you encountered any leaders who you consider good or successful but who are lacking in any of the traits, skills, or behaviors discussed in this chapter? If so, which one(s) were lacking, and how do you think the leader made up for his or her weaknesses?

CHAPTER 4

3. Have you ever held a leadership position? Did you feel you expressed the traits, skills, and behaviors discussed in this chapter? How did you use your traits and abilities to do the best you could?
4. What is the difference between wisdom and expertise?
5. Think of your supervisor(s) at a job you held in the past. Of the four leadership behavior categories proposed by Ohio State, University of Michigan, and Yukl, which was most influential when used by your leader(s)?

INDIVIDUAL ACTIVITIES

INDIVIDUAL ACTIVITY 1

Think about three different leaders you have had. Do the leaders have many of the important traits and skills? Did you ever see them engaging in the important behaviors? Think about how good and bad leaders you have had compare to each other.

INDIVIDUAL ACTIVITY 2

Search the Internet for leadership training programs. Search terms you might want to try include *leader/leadership development*, *leader/leadership training, management training*, and other related terms. Find a program for leader development that is described (for free) on a Web site—if you have to pay for the description, don't do it! Answer the following questions below about the program you found:

1. Provide the URL of the program you found.
2. Describe the program. Elaborate as much as possible, and be specific.
3. Do you believe this program would be effective or ineffective? Using evidence from the chapter, explain your answer.

GROUP ACTIVITIES

GROUP ACTIVITY 1

If you have ever watched a professional sporting event on television, you may have noticed the way the commentators talk about the game. Often, they notice specific elements of the game that you did not notice. This is because they are experts in that game. Think about something you are an expert in. It could be a sport or a school subject (like math), or anything that you are really good at. In your groups, talk about the things you notice when doing that activity that other people may not notice. This activity demonstrates how having expertise in an area allows a person to view the activity differently and see things other people cannot see.

GROUP ACTIVITY 2

Have you ever held a leadership position? How would you go about training someone to take over that position for you? In your groups, discuss your leadership positions and how you would train someone to do those jobs. Discuss the differences among your positions.

SUGGESTED READINGS

Bass, B. M. (1990). *Bass and Stogdill's handbook of leadership: Theory, research, and managerial applications.* New York: Free Press.

McCall, M., & Lombardo, M. (1983). *Off the track: Why and how successful executives get derailed* (Tech. Rep. No. 21). Greensboro, NC: Center for Creative Leadership.

Mumford, M. D., Friedrich, T. L., Caughron, J. J., & Antes, A. L. (in press). Leadership development and assessment. In K. A. Ericsson (Ed.),

The Development of Professional Performance. Cambridge, UK: Cambridge University Press.

Mumford, M. D., Friedrich, T. L., Caughron, J. J., & Byrne, C. L. (2007). Leader cognition in real-world settings: How do leaders think about crises? *The Leadership Quarterly, 18*, 515–543.

Mumford, M. D., Hunter, S. T., Eubanks, D. L., Bedell, K. T., & Murphy, S. T. (2007). Developing leaders for creative efforts: A domain-based approach to leadership development. *Human Resource Management Review, 17*, 402–417.

Mumford, M. D., Schultz, R. A., & Osburn, H. K. (2002). Planning in organizations: Performance as a multi-level phenomenon. In F. J. Yammarino & F. Dansereau (Eds.), *Research in multi-level issues: The many faces of multi-level issues* (pp. 3–35). Oxford, England: Elsevier Science.

Yukl, G. (2006). *Leadership in organizations* (6th ed.). Upper Saddle River, NJ: Prentice Hall.

Followers and Situational Factors

Jamie D. Barrett

> The ear of the leader must ring with the voices of the people.
>
> —*Woodrow Wilson*

lancing at the title of this chapter, you may be thinking, "Shouldn't leaders just lead and let everyone else fall in line?" or "If a leader is good, then why does the situation matter?" Perhaps you took this perspective: "I know that followers and situations affect leadership. Why do I need to read more?" Sit back for a moment and think about who leaders lead. Do they always lead the same people? Is the situation always the same? Obviously, the answer to both of these questions is no. It follows, then, that the type of people and the situational factors are important for leaders to consider.

Leaders do not function alone; they must have a person or a group to lead. These people are their followers. Followers may be employees, students, players on a sports team, volunteer workers, or even family members. Anyone who works with a leader toward a common goal is considered a follower. There are so many kinds of followers that it can be difficult for leaders to decide how to act toward all of them. One may become confused about how best to lead a wide variety of followers. This chapter will discuss the most prominent theories of leader-follower interactions. Within each discussion, you will not only learn about the theory and relevant research, but you will also be given practical advice about how to implement the ideas presented in each theory. This advice will help you understand how followers impact leadership, and what you, as a leader, can do about it.

Now that you can see how important followers are, what about situational factors? Are the situations that leaders encounter really that different? Think, for a moment, about some common situations leaders face. If your high school was having a budget crisis, your principal would likely lead very differently than if the school had plenty of money. The CEO of a major company will change his or her behavior toward the company's employees when he or she is trying to implement an organization-wide change, such as a merger with another company. These situations require different kinds of leadership behaviors and actions. In order to understand how different situations affect leaders, and what actions a leader should take, leadership theories involving situational factors must be closely examined.

As you can see, followers and situational factors both have unique roles in leadership. To begin this discussion, we will first look at how power and influence are involved in leadership, specifically regarding leader-follower interactions. Next, topics involving followers will be discussed. After understanding how followers have an impact on leadership, we will take an in-depth look at various situational factors. Theories, research, and practical implications will be presented for both followers and situational factors. The goals of this chapter are listed in the following.

Learning Objectives
- Understand the importance of power and influence in leadership

- Understand how followers and situational factors influence leadership
- Understand the strengths and weaknesses of the theories related to followers and situational factors
- Gain a practical understanding of how to deal with followers and situational factors

POWER AND INFLUENCE

Power is an important force behind any leader's effectiveness. Without power, it would be impossible for leaders to exert their influence to get things done. Think about how the leaders around you are able to get others to listen and act. Would the American people listen to the president if he had no power? Would your teachers or professors be able to command their classrooms without influence over their students? Before diving into a discussion of followers and situational factors, the concepts of leader power and influence must first be mentioned. This section will cover the interpretations and implications of power and influence, and then the discussion will move on to followers and situations, which will be explored in depth.

POWER

In leadership, **power** is generally understood as the capacity of one person to influence the behavior or attitudes of others. Power can be exercised over groups as well as individuals. Power is derived from **authority**, which includes a right or claim of legitimacy that serves as a justification to exercise the

> **Power**—the capacity of one person to influence the behavior or attitudes of others
> **Authority**—a right, or claim of legitimacy, that serves as a justification to exercise power

power. Sometimes power is viewed in relative terms, such as the amount of power a leader has compared to that of a follower. Usually, a leader has more sway over his or her follower; thus, the leader has more power. In the same way, your teacher has a greater influence on you than you have on your teacher, so your teacher has more power than you.

Attempts to understand power have identified many different types, and further efforts distinguished among those types. Some of the most influential work in this field was done by French and Raven (1959), who developed a classification system describing five kinds of power. Although their work had a great affect on power research, it did not include all sources of power involved in leadership. The five types of power in this taxonomy include the following:

> **Legitimate power**—power that involves a follower's internalization of values or norms that grant rights to the person in power
>
> **Expert power**—power that involves a follower's beliefs that the person in power is knowledgeable and competent
>
> **Referent power**—power that involves a follower liking or admiring the person in power
>
> **Reward power**—power that involves a follower seeking rewards provided by the person in power
>
> **Coercive power**—power that involves a follower avoiding punishment from the person in power

1. **Legitimate Power** involves a follower's internalization of values or norms, and the belief that the person in power has a right to his or her power, often as a result of his or her position.

2. **Expert Power** involves a follower's beliefs that the person in power is knowledgeable and competent.

3. **Referent Power** involves a follower liking or admiring the person in power.

4. **Reward Power** involves a follower seeking rewards provided by the person in power.

5. **Coercive Power** involves a follower avoiding punishment from the person in power.

Another approach to power sources is Bass's (1960) theory of position versus personal power. This model describes the two major sources of power. Position power occurs when one is given a certain position that involves influence over one's subordinates, such as a manager of a restaurant. On the other hand, personal power is that which is attributed to an individual in power, usually involving expertise or one's friendship with the person in power. For example, if your favorite political science teacher from high school ran for mayor, you might attribute personal power to him or her because you think your teacher has expertise in that area and the two of you were friends. Research has found support for Bass's view and has revealed types of power subsumed within each factor. The types of power within position power include legitimate, reward, coercive, information (control over access to information), and ecological (control over the situation) power. The different types of personal power include referent and expert power (Yukl & Falbe, 1991). Due to the complexity of position and personal power, it can be difficult at times to distinguish between the two; however, Bass's approach is still widely accepted among researchers.

Now that you have learned what power is and some of the different types of power, you may be asking yourself, "So how does a person gain or lose power?" Because a leader's amount of power can change over time and in different situations, two theories have been proposed to explain how power is acquired and lost. First, **social exchange theory** defines changes in power in terms of the relationship between leaders and followers over time. In this way, social interactions between members of a small group determine how power is gained or lost. These social

Social exchange theory—a theory that defines changes in power in terms of the relationship between leaders and followers over time

Idiosyncrasy credits—credits that a leader builds up with successful ideas over time

interactions tend to involve the exchange of material or psychological benefits (e.g., approval, respect, affection). As leaders show involvement in a group and propose successful goals and actions, they will accumulate what are called **idiosyncrasy credits** and gain power. Idiosyncrasy credits are credits that a leader builds up with successful ideas over time. These will be discussed in more detail later in the chapter. However, if a leader appears selfish or uninvolved and his or her actions fail, then he or she loses power. In evaluating this theory, problems arise with the theory's application of the different types of power. Social exchange theory focuses only on expert power and authority and fails to consider how reward and referent power are involved in interpersonal exchanges. Furthermore, the discussed findings were based on laboratory research of small groups; the long-term effects have not been investigated. Overall, more research is needed in this area.

The second theory proposed to explain how power is gained or lost is called **strategic contingencies theory.** This theory attempts to describe how power is distributed among various subunits, or departments, in an organization. Strategic contingencies theory contends that, in each group, power depends on (a) expertise in handling major problems, (b) the importance of the subunit to the overall work of the organization, and (c) how easily the subunit's expertise can be replaced. In short, as a subunit exhibits unique expertise at solving problems critical to the organization, it gains power. Gained power will first come in the form of expert power and, over time, can evolve into legitimate power. This theory has generally been supported by research; however, it fails to consider the organizational politics that might be involved with a particularly dominant subunit, such as how a subunit might intimidate others in order to maintain power.

> **Strategic contingencies theory**—a theory that attempts to describe how power is distributed among various subunits, or departments, in an organization

INFLUENCE

Related to power, influence also plays an important role in successful leadership. In fact, influence lies at the core of leadership, and without influence it would be impossible to rally follower support, implement decisions, or get anything done. As mentioned in chapter 1, **influence** involves altering the motives or perceptions of another to accomplish a given goal. As such, **influence attempts** are actions geared toward bringing about a desired outcome. A **proactive influence attempt** refers to a single request from one person to another. While influence attempts are actions, the psychological view considers influence to be a process. This view of **influence processes** maintains that one person's influence on another depends upon the follower's perceptions of the leader regarding the actions within the context of the situation. Key points to take from these explanations of influence are that it involves a goal, it affects interactions between leaders and subordinates, and it must be considered in context.

> **Influence**—altering the motives or perceptions of another to accomplish a given goal
> **Influence attempts**—actions geared toward a desired outcome
> **Proactive influence attempt**—a single request from one person to another
> **Influence processes**—the processes involved in a leader influencing others, such as perceptions of the leader and the situation

Another way of understanding influence is the behavioral approach. This approach views influence in terms of behavioral tactics. **Influence tactics** are behaviors intended to sway the attitudes and behaviors of others. Three types of influence tactics have been identified by Yukl and Chavez

> **Influence tactics**—behaviors intended to sway the attitudes and behaviors of others

Impression management tactics—behaviors that influence how leaders and followers are perceived

Political tactics—behaviors intended to affect broad organizational decisions, or how such decisions can benefit the individual or his or her group

Proactive influence tactics—behaviors geared toward achieving a particular outcome

(2002). **Impression management tactics** are behaviors used by a leader to make followers like him or her. **Political tactics** are behaviors intended to affect broad organizational decisions, or how such decisions are made, to benefit an individual or his or her group. **Proactive influence tactics** involve behaviors geared toward achieving a particular outcome. These differ from proactive influence attempts in that they do not necessarily have to be a single request from one person to another. These influence tactics can generalize across situations, but also must be considered in the context of specific situations, where one tactic may be more appropriate than another. For example, impression management tactics may be useful at work meetings or social events; however, when working on a specific project with followers, proactive influence tactics would be more beneficial.

POWER AND INFLUENCE BEHAVIOR

Although distinct concepts, power and influence in the leadership context maintain a complex relationship that causes leaders to behave in different ways in attempts to enhance their effectiveness. One important factor in understanding how power and influence are exhibited is the direction of the interaction. To understand the directions of influence tactics, Yukl and Tracey (1992) developed a model to help identify which influence tactics would be most useful. This model consists of the following interrelated factors: (a) adherence to existing social norms and role expectations about using the tactic in a given situation, (b) the appropriateness of a leader's power being used as a base for the tactic in a given situation, (c) the extent to which the tactic will lead to a goal of an influence attempt, (d) the amount of follower resistance expected, and (e) the expected cost compared to the benefits of using the tactic. For a given situation, a leader will assess the relevance of these five concerns and decide which influence tactics will be most useful. The main idea from this model is that leaders should use influence tactics that are accepted socially and by their followers, appropriate for the goal and situation, and not overly costly to accomplish their goals. Support for this model has been somewhat inconsistent due to the complex relationships between the factors in the model, the behaviors of those involved, and potential influence tactics utilized in different contexts. In general, however, the model has been supported (Yukl, 2006).

In addition to identifying which tactics should be used in various situations, the same researchers addressed the question, How can a person know which influence tactics will be successful? Thus, the researchers proposed a second model in response to this question, which contained the following five factors intended to predict influence tactic effectiveness: (a) the extent to which followers resist because they disagree with a request, (b) the likelihood that the tactic will affect follower attitudes regarding the attractiveness of a request, (c) the appropriateness of a leader's power being used as a base for the tactic in a given situation, (d) a leader's proficiency in using the tactic, and (e) existing social norms and role expectations about using the tactic in a given situation. Application of this model reveals that an effective influence tactic will be one that is socially acceptable, appealing and supported by followers, and appropriate for use by the leader in that context. As one can see, these models are very similar.

FOLLOWERS

Leaders cannot act alone. In order for a person to become a leader, he or she must have someone to lead. If you wanted to paint your bedroom, you could work alone or ask friends to help. When you involve others in completing a task, you become the leader and they become your followers. When painting your bedroom, you could choose to enlist the help of one friend, or maybe you would want many friends to help. In this way, leadership can involve one follower or multiple followers. Additionally, some people are easy to lead, while others are more difficult. These issues, and many more, make followers a very important factor in understanding leadership. This section of the chapter will discuss the role that followers play in leadership endeavors.

INDIVIDUALS VERSUS GROUPS

It has already been stated that leadership can be geared toward a single person or many people. Also, the leader may be leading multiple independent individuals, but more often than not, the leader is leading a *group* of individuals. Dealing with an individual is much different than dealing with a group. When a single follower is involved, a leader has only one person's concerns, preferences, and activities to consider. If a leader must oversee an entire group, then he or she must consider not only the group as a whole but also each member individually.

When leading groups, it is important that the group members get along with each other and that they work together effectively. In doing so, each member creates an identity within the group, causing him or her to feel associated with the other members of the group as a whole. When group members stick together, they become **cohesive**. However, sometimes members become too close and fall into a process called **deindividuation**. Deindividuation happens

> **Cohesive**—the status of a group when members are highly attracted and connected to the other members of the group
>
> **Deindividuation**—a situation where members become too entrenched in a group and lose their own identities

when members become too entrenched in the group and lose their own identities. This is a bad thing because individual members might act differently than they normally would and might participate in uncharacteristic behaviors. Group members do this because they feel they are exempt from the consequences of their actions as individuals, and that the group will likely take the blame for negative consequences. This tends to happen when leaders motivate their followers with punishment for bad behavior. When leaders offer rewards for good behavior, group members tend to maintain their own identities yet are still cohesive. Because of this, it is essential that leaders avoid punishments and instead offer rewards to groups for their accomplishments.

ATTRIBUTIONS

The way leaders and followers interact can depend on a number of things. One very strong influence on these interactions is perceptions. If a follower is perceived as capable and trustworthy, then a leader may act differently toward him or her than if the follower is perceived as incapable and untrustworthy. The same holds true for follower perceptions of a leader. These perceptions about others' behavior are called **attributions.** It is important to note the impact that these attributions have on leader-follower relations.

Leader Attributions

As previously mentioned, the way a leader perceives a subordinate can affect the way the leader treats that person. Research by Green and Mitchell (1979) suggests a two-stage model that describes the actions of leaders when a follower is performing poorly. In this model, the leader first attempts to locate the cause of the unacceptable performance. It may be due to either causes internal to the person, such as the follower

Attributions—perceptions about others' behavior

127

being lazy or incapable of performing, or external causes, such as a lack of resources or the difficulty of the task. Mitchell and Kalb (1982) found that leaders who had experience with tasks similar to those encountered by an underperforming follower were more likely to attribute performance problems to external causes (those out of the follower's control). The second part of the model states that a leader will then select an appropriate response to the situation. Later studies have consistently supported this model, lending support for its usefulness for understanding how leaders react to their followers' poor performance. Another study looking at leader attributions found that when leaders do not often interact with their followers, they tend to attribute poor performance to internal causes and good performance to external causes. On the other hand, in highly interactive relationships, poor performance is attributed to external causes and good performance to internal causes. Further, if a follower has succeeded in the past and has proven to be a dependable employee, then he or she will not be docked for poor performance—it will be attributed externally. This reveals a serious downside for followers who are not highly active in the leader-follower relationship.

Follower Attributions

Follower attributions can have a strong impact on the success of leaders. Leaders seen as competent are more likely to gain power and prestige and will be more likely to advance to a higher position. Follower attributions are generally made regarding a leader's loyalty, competence, and, most importantly, success. When leaders implement successful ideas, they gain idiosyncrasy credits. Again, these are credits that a leader builds up with successful ideas over time. Leaders with many idiosyncrasy credits are more likely to have their ideas initially accepted and later tolerated even if they fail. Leaders are allotted a number of failures based on the number of credits they have earned. Followers will be more critical of leaders with fewer idiosyncrasy credits and more lenient on those with several credits (Hollander, 1958, 1978). The concept of idiosyncrasy credits offers an explanation of how followers attribute the performance of leaders as good or bad.

In addition to idiosyncrasy credits, leaders can be evaluated by followers with implicit leadership theories. Discussed in chapters 2 and 6, this type of evaluation involves beliefs and assumptions, typically involving stereotypes, about how effective leaders are supposed to behave. These can be influenced by the beliefs, values, and personality of both individual followers and groups of followers. Implicit leadership theories tend to affect ratings of leadership because follower expectations of successful leadership may not be accurate.

IMPRESSION MANAGEMENT

Just as the perceptions of others influence leader-follower interactions, both leaders and followers engage in behaviors to influence how others perceive them. These are called impression management tactics. The process of accomplishing this is called **impression management.** Leaders engage in impression management by drawing attention to their accomplishments and pointing out events that they control. Leaders

> **Impression management—** the process by which leaders and followers engage in behaviors to influence how others perceive them

also highlight their successes and downplay their failures. Think about the way candidates behave right before elections. They will usually air television advertisements where they celebrate all the good things they have done. These ads rarely mention the failures they have had, or if they do, the failures are made to seem insignificant or perhaps are presented to highlight a successful response to the failure.

Followers differ from leaders in their impression management behaviors. Instead of promoting their accomplishments at

129

work, which is often looked upon negatively by superiors, followers will try to look like good people. Followers use upward impression management tactics to influence their bosses by looking like a person who is nice, caring, considerate, and so forth. This tactic is typically more successful for followers than self-promotion.

LEADERSHIP THEORIES: FOLLOWERS

Leader-Member Exchange (LMX) Theory

Because the theories mentioned in this chapter were already discussed in chapter 2, the basics of each theory will only be summarized before our in-depth discussion in terms of research and application. To begin, **Leader-Member Exchange (LMX) theory** is a theory that suggests leaders establish an in-group of followers and an out-group of followers and that they influence these two different groups of followers in different ways. High-exchange relationships are developed with followers a leader perceives as competent, and low-exchange relationships are formed with followers that a leader perceives as incompetent. This theory is sometimes viewed as the high school theory of leadership because it suggests that leaders develop high-exchange or high-quality relationships with their closest followers and low-exchange or low-quality relationships with everyone else, much like the formation of cliques. Furthermore, a leader's inner circle of followers (in-group members) will be more liked, given better tasks, and allowed leniency when they fail. Members of the out-group will not be liked as much and, thus, will be perceived as less capable. These members will be given less interesting tasks and will be personally blamed for their failures.

Measuring LMX has been far from consistent. Several aspects of the leader-follower relationship vary significantly from study to study. However, one measure that defined seven specific items is a measure called LMX-7. For example, one item from the measure is, "How well does your leader understand your job problems and needs?" (Graen & Uhl-Bien, 1995). These items are used to evaluate the relationship between leaders and followers. Other researchers suggest that there are more dimensions that must be considered. However, more research is needed before additional items can be added to the existing seven (Liden & Maslyn, 1998; Schriesheim, Neider, Scandura, & Tepper, 1992). In addition, studies have not yet been able to present clear evidence of this relationship from both leader and follower viewpoints.

Although research on LMX has somewhat ebbed over the years since its conception, some great strides have been made in studies of this relationship. Research looking at outcomes for subordinates found that positive exchanges with leaders lead to higher satisfaction, commitment, and performance. Specific studies of these outcomes found that increases in follower performance and satisfaction were observed when leaders were told to form high-exchange relationships with their subordinates (Graen, Novak, & Sommerkamp, 1982; Scandura & Graen, 1984). Graen and Uhl-Bien (1995) updated their theory to include these findings by suggesting that leaders should try to develop high-quality relationships with all of their followers, not just a few of them.

Since its emergence, the weaknesses of LMX have been frequently discussed. Most importantly, the relationships suggested in this theory take a long time to develop; thus, this theory cannot be researched in-depth in a lab. Because of this, the causal linkages between the various factors in the theory cannot easily be determined and tested. But even when accounting for these issues, the implications of LMX are useful for leaders in a practical setting. In general, it is important for leaders to attempt to get to know their followers. This will help leaders understand their subordinates' capabilities and character from specific interactions with them, and not from assumptions based on in-group or out-group membership. Think about the high school view. If a high school leader got to know people outside his or her inner circle, then that leader would have more realistic views of the outsiders. If this occurred, there would be more understanding of the outsiders' points of view, thus making the leader better able to make decisions that benefited everyone.

Participative Leadership

The foundation of participative leadership is that followers have some say in the decisions being made by the leader. Four specific decision procedures, ordered from least to most participative, have been agreed upon by researchers in this area: (a) autocratic decision, (b) consultation, (c) joint decision, and (d) delegation. Autocratic decisions involve no follower involvement whatsoever. In consultation, a leader seeks the opinions of others and makes a decision with those opinions in mind. With joint decision, a leader works with his or her followers to come to a decision together. Lastly, delegation involves a leader choosing an individual or a group to make a decision within bounds set by the leader.

Research in this area has caused a few changes to the original premise. To begin, Tannenbaum and Schmidt (1958) narrowed autocratic decision into two types: "tell" style, in which a leader only lets his or her followers know what decision was made; and "sell" style, in which a leader uses influence tactics to convince others of the decision. Later research by Vroom and Yetton (1973) broke consultation down into consulting with individuals and consulting with groups. Further, Strauss (1977) contended that it is necessary to distinguish between overt procedures and actual influence when dealing with participation in decisions. In other words, sometimes leaders might ask for other's opinions and then ignore them, or leaders might intimidate their followers while asking for opinions so that the followers are scared to reveal their true thoughts.

Some of the first research studies looking at the consequences of participative leadership were conducted by Lewin, Lippitt, and White (1939) and Coch and French (1948). Most of these first studies looked at follower satisfaction and performance; however, later research could not find consensus on the true effects of participation due to a lack of strong results and similar methodology (e.g., Leana, Locke, & Schweiger, 1990; Sagie & Koslowsky, 2000; Spector, 1986). Experiments looking at goal setting and participative leadership found that goals assigned by a leader were just as effective as goals set by a leader and a follower together (participative goals), as long as the tasks were equally difficult and the leaders involved equally helpful and persuasive (Latham, Erez, & Locke, 1988). Although these findings were not very strong, they still suggest that participation can be useful in some contexts. Other studies contended that managers who engage in a lot of consultation and delegation tend to be more effective because they help employees feel they have a legitimate influence on the decisions being made (Kanter, 1983; Kouzes & Posner, 1987; Peters & Waterman, 1982).

Given this research history, participative leadership has several weaknesses. As mentioned earlier, many of the findings of past studies are not strong or consistent, leaving it very difficult to draw accurate conclusions. As for the methodologies employed in the research, few studies have used the same methodology, and the various methods have their own problems. For example, causation is difficult to determine from field, qualitative, and quasiexperiments (see chapter 3 for more detail). Also, many studies conducted within organizations did not involve a single leader, but the organization as a whole. Due to these weaknesses, one must be careful when interpreting the implications of this research. The major practical application one can extract from this research, however, is that participation tends to be a good thing. Overall, studies seem to lean toward the idea that leaders are better off when their followers are allowed a stronger say in the decision-making process.

SITUATIONAL FACTORS

As one can see, followers play a large role in how leaders behave. However, there is another factor that has an influence on leadership—the situation. It is easy to overlook the idea that different situations require different types of leadership. However, think about how football coaches lead. During a team meeting in the middle of the week, a football coach will lead his or her team one way, but Friday night in the fourth quarter, with the game on the line, the coach will act very differently toward his or her players, utilizing a very different style of leadership. Keep this concept in mind as we move on to the next section of the chapter, which first discusses the most common types of situations and then takes a detailed look at several theories of leadership that take the situation into account.

TYPES OF SITUATIONS

In modern research studies, situational aspects are nearly always considered as either determining leadership behavior or strongly influencing it (Vroom & Jago, 2007). There are several different kinds of situations that can impact leadership; the most frequently discussed are the following: (a) environment, (b) organization, (c) culture, (d) crisis, and (e) change. First, several aspects of an environment can determine how leadership occurs. Some examples of this are the stability of the environment; whether the environment centers on politics, society, or legal issues; or the types of relationships and social networks that exist in the environment. For example, when an environment is unstable, perhaps during an organizational change or merger, leaders must behave differently than when the organization is stable. They must take into account the instability of the environment in order to lead successfully.

Next, the nature of leadership may change depending on the character of an organization. For instance, organizations may have different philosophies, outlooks, types, or structures. Organizational culture can also affect leadership through its values, the views of those who founded the culture, and any emergent countercultures. Crisis is another important example of a situation impacting leadership. Crisis situations are delicate because they require a different kind of leader than noncrisis situations. Crisis situations are situations that involve high levels of stress—usually involving an unclear problem or unclear outcomes—and require a leader to create a new solution. Hunt, Boal, & Dodge (1999) conducted a study that focused on varying types of leadership exhibited in crisis situations; they found that visionary leaders, or leaders who develop visions similar to their followers' values and goals, are most accepted by their followers in a crisis.

The last type of situation is change. Change is a broad concept that refers to any new efforts to alter an organization. Change can be carried out through mergers, divisions, or a revision of the way things are done within the organization. An organization can change for a number of reasons, including survival and competition. A continuing question within the study of change is what type of leader is best at accomplishing change. In addition, resistance to change is also a significant issue for leaders attempting organizational change. Interestingly, Levay (in press) found that charismatic leaders—leaders who develop visions and unique ways of carrying out those visions—are not only the best at making change, but also the most influential in combating resistance to change. Charismatic leadership, along with other types of outstanding leadership, will be discussed in further detail in chapter 7. Now we will move on to a discussion of the leadership theories associated with situational factors.

LEADERSHIP THEORIES: SITUATIONS

Least Preferred Co-Worker (LPC) Contingency Model

Because these theories were previously discussed in chapter 2, they will only be summarized before being discussed in terms

Least preferred co-worker model (LPC contingency model)—the most accepted and applied contingency theory of leadership, which explains two types of leaders, task oriented and relationship oriented

of research and practical applications. Fiedler's (1967) **least preferred co-worker model (LPC contingency model)** is the most accepted and applied contingency theory of leadership. This theory explains two types of leaders: task oriented and relationship oriented. These two types of leaders may act within three situations: highly favorable, moderately favorable, and highly unfavorable for the leader.

Research applying the LPC contingency model has shown some, although not complete, support for the model. For instance, results from field studies have not been as strong as for laboratory studies (Peters, Hartke, & Pohlmann, 1985; Strube and Garcia, 1981). These studies suffer from several weaknesses. First, the methods used to test the theory have undergone much scrutiny. The most serious complaint is that the results from studies looking at this theory do not support it strongly enough (Graen, Alvares, Orris, & Martella, 1970; McMahon, 1972; Vecchio, 1983). Also, the methods used in these studies combine different aspects of the situation in arbitrary ways that do not naturally fit the model (Shiflett, 1973). Therefore, it is difficult to conclude that the theory is supported.

Criticisms over the concepts in the model are also quite frequent. Yukl (1970) critiques the model by arguing that its interpretation has changed over time. He goes further to suggest that not only have interpretations changed, but also individual LPC scores may change over time and might be more complex than researchers in this area assume. A more practical critique by Ashour (1973) contends that because LPC does not actually explain *how* leadership affects performance, it is not a theory. Fiedler (1973, 1977) has replied to some of these criticisms; however, issues concerning the accuracy of the model have yet to be resolved.

Some practical implications of the LPC contingency model can be applied to types of leaders and situations. Task-oriented leaders tend to do better in situations that are highly favorable and highly unfavorable. This means that leaders who focus on tasks, planning, and organizing to achieve goals will be more successful in situations with cooperative followers, high-performing groups, and high leader control or in situations with difficult followers, low-performing groups, and low leader control. On the other hand, in situations that are only moderately favorable, relationship-oriented leaders will be more successful. This means that in situations with moderate levels of follower cooperation, group performance, and leader control, leaders who focus on building relationships and supporting followers will perform best. The key idea to take from this, before directly applying the components of this theory to practice, is that leaders should first evaluate what type of leader they are and what type of situation they are in. By identifying these things, leaders can then apply the theory in the most appropriate way.

Path-Goal Theory of Leadership

The **path-goal theory** of leadership states that leadership involves reinforcing change in a subordinate (House, 1971). First, a leader must make rewards visible to a follower. Next, the leader will show the path that the follower needs to take in order to receive those rewards. In doing so, the leader must clarify the goals of the subordinate as well as the path he or she must take in order to reach the goals and be rewarded. The two major factors in determining how leaders decide to lead in path-goal theory are the followers and the task. Besides the follow-

> **Path-goal theory**—a theory that emphasizes the role of a leader as setting, defining, and clarifying goals; motivating followers to achieve those goals; and helping followers see a clear path toward goal attainment

ers and the task, this theory identifies four different overarching leadership styles: supportive leadership, directive leadership, participative leadership, and achievement-oriented leadership. Participative leadership was discussed previously in this chapter.

Research on this theory has yielded inconclusive results. Studies have found it difficult to test relationships in the theory and other variables associated with leadership (Podsakoff, MacKenzie, Ahearne, & Bommer, 1995; Wofford & Liska, 1993; Yukl, 2006). Because of these mixed results, this theory has had little support and has been viewed as somewhat weak. Applying this theory is risky because of its weaknesses, so it is recommended that one only use it to explain existing leadership efforts, not as a guide for appropriate leadership behaviors. For example, one might approach a leader in a particular situation by first addressing the pertinent goals and the expected path to reach those goals. Next, one can determine the followers involved and the task performed to help explain why the leader behaved in that particular way. As mentioned before, this theory has little support, so one must not follow it too closely in practice.

Situational Leadership Theory

Hersey and Blanchard (1993) developed a theory called the **situational theory of leadership,** which predicts how leaders should act depending on the relative maturity of their followers regarding their work. Followers with high maturity have the ability to complete the task at hand and feel self-confidence in their performance. Alternatively, low-maturity followers lack the ability necessary for the task, and they do not have self-confidence with regard to their work. This theory supposes that the maturity level of a leader's followers

Situational theory of leadership—a theory of leadership suggesting that leaders should be able to recognize the circumstances they are facing and adjust their leadership style to match that situation

is the characteristic of the situation that will affect the leader's behavior. In response to their followers' maturity levels, leaders should act in ways that are appropriate for the situation.

Although this theory has been applied quite a bit in management, very few studies have addressed whether or not the situational theory of leadership actually works (e.g., Blank, Weitzel, & Green, 1990; Fernandez & Vecchio, 1997; Norris & Vecchio, 1992). Some researchers have focused on the conceptual weaknesses of this theory. First, Graeff (1983) pointed out that leadership behaviors, along with task- and relations-specific behaviors, are vaguely and inconsistently described throughout this theory. As for leader behavior and follower performance, this theory does not clearly explain how the two are related (Barrow, 1977).

Given the overwhelming lack of research, and the apparent weaknesses in the theory's basic concepts, one must again be careful when applying the tenets of the situational theory of leadership to real-life leadership endeavors. However, taking this theory as it is, a leader could pay close attention to the maturity of his or her subordinates with regard to their work, determining whether they have high or low maturity levels. Doing so will help a leader act appropriately for a specific situation. For example, if you are working with friends on a project, using the situational theory of leadership could help you discern which friends have the abilities necessary to complete the task, and which friends have self-confidence in their abilities. This analysis should give you insight into how to interact with each follower so that the task is completed successfully.

Leadership Substitutes Theory

Another theory that looks at how a situation influences leadership is **leadership substitutes theory**, developed by Kerr and

> **Leader substitutes theory**—a theory that suggests that in some circumstances, groups do not need a leader to function effectively

> **Neutralizers**—the aspects of a situation that make a leader ineffective, such as a leader's lack of authority or a follower's lack of interest
>
> **Substitutes**—the aspects of a task, a group of followers, or an organization that replace leadership, making it unnecessary

Jermier (1978). This theory differentiates between two situational variables, **substitutes** and **neutralizers.** Substitutes affect leadership by making a leader's role unnecessary. Substitutes live up to their title in that they essentially substitute for leadership. Substitutes include aspects of the task, followers, or organization that show followers how to do their work, understand their place in the organization, and feel motivated and generally satisfied. Thus, when these substitutes are present, leadership becomes unnecessary. On the other hand, neutralizers, such as a leader's lack of authority or a follower's lack of interest, basically make a leader's actions pointless. Neutralizers take away a leader's effectiveness, while substitutes take the place of a leader.

The research on leader substitutes theory suggests that the wrong parts of the theory are being tested and evaluated. Specifically, most studies have found little support for the idea that elements of a situation (substitutes and neutralizers) affect the relationship between leaders and followers, but other studies show that the direct impact of a situation on followers has a strong effect (Podsakoff, Niehoff, MacKenzie, & Williams, 1993). McIntosh (1988) agreed with this view and suggested that studies should focus more energy on looking at the direct effects of a situation on followers and leaders instead of looking at substitutes and neutralizers as middlemen in the relationship.

The lack of research on leader substitutes theory may be, in part, due to the weaknesses of the theory. The biggest weakness is that it does not address how to determine what is a substitute or a neutralizer. There are no specific directions on how to pick out components of a situation and categorize them as either substitutes or neutralizers. Further, even if one were to attempt to define what makes something a substitute or a neutralizer, actually labeling an element of a situation as one or the other is extremely difficult. Because of this ambiguity, applying this theory is not easy, although it is still possible. Similar to the recommendations for the situational theory of leadership, appropriate application could involve attempts to identify which parts of a situation fit into each category of variable—substitutes or neutralizers. Then, leaders could try to avoid or counter these variables so that their efforts are not wasted.

Multiple Linkage Model

Yukl (2006) built upon previous theories of leadership and group effectiveness and proposed a model to explain the causal relationships in leadership. The **Multiple Linkage Model** is an integrated theory that evaluates the relationships between managerial variables (leader behaviors), intervening variables (variables that affect how a leader's behaviors influence group performance), criterion variables (group performance or other outcomes), and situational variables (substitutes, neutralizers, or other components of a situation). This model links these four variables in complex ways to explain how leadership, affected by a situation and other constraints, predicts group effectiveness.

Previous research on individual and group performance was applied to this model in the form of specific intervening variables. These specific intervening variables are the following: (a) commitment to the task, (b) the ability and clarity of members' roles, (c) work organization, (d) cooperation and mutual trust between group members, (e) the resources and support available, and (f) coordination with other parts of the organization (Hackman, Brousseau, & Weiss, 1976; Likert, 1967; McGrath, 1984; Porter & Lawler, 1968). The model also outlines differences in the short- and long-term behaviors of leaders, suggesting that leaders must work quickly in the short-term to correct their followers' deficiencies and gain long-term control to identify and appropriately address the sources of deeper problems.

Research is lacking in evaluating the accuracy of the multiple linkages model. Without studies investigating how appropriate the model is for leadership, one cannot determine how well it explains the relationship between leaders and followers. Nonetheless, several conceptual weaknesses of this theory have been identified. First, the theory does not explain how the complex linkages work within the model, especially involving different leader behaviors and situational variables. Also, specific hypotheses or predictions about how the long-term actions of leaders impact a group simply have not been developed and tested. Due to the lack of research on the model and explanations of how the model works, practical application of the Yukl model is currently a difficult task.

CHAPTER SUMMARY

In order for a person to be a leader, he or she must have followers. To effectively lead these followers, a leader must take the followers' characteristics into careful consideration before acting. Along with considering his or her followers, a leader must also understand the situation and identify factors that can make leadership successful. This chapter discussed how followers and situational factors can have an impact on leadership. Leaders are affected by power and influence. Theories related to the effects of followers are leader-member exchange theory and participative leadership. Theories about situational factors include the LPC contingency model, path-goal theory, the situational theory of leadership, leadership substitutes theory, and the multiple-linkage model. After reading this chapter, you should understand how important it is for leaders to take followers and situational factors into account.

KEY TERMS AND PHRASES

- Attributions
- Authority

- Coercive power
- Cohesive
- Deindividuation
- Expert power
- Idiosyncrasy credits
- Impression management
- Impression management tactics
- Influence
- Influence attempts
- Influence processes
- Influence tactics
- Leader-member exchange (LMX) theory
- Leader substitutes theory
- Least preferred co-worker model (LPC contingency model)
- Legitimate power
- Multiple-linkage model
- Neutralizers
- Path-goal theory
- Political tactics
- Power
- Proactive influence attempt
- Proactive influence tactics
- Referent power
- Reward power
- Situational theories of leadership
- Social exchange theory
- Strategic contingencies theory
- Substitutes

REVIEW QUESTIONS

1. In what situations should a leader use each influence tactic?
2. What happens when group members become too close? What are the consequences for leaders?

3. What are idiosyncrasy credits? How do they impact leaders and followers?

4. What are impression management tactics? What are some examples that you've seen or experienced?

5. Describe leader-member exchange theory. What are its strengths and weaknesses?

6. Describe participative leadership theory. Is it a good theory? Why or why not?

7. Describe LPC contingency theory. Is it a good theory? Why or why not?

8. Describe path-goal theory. Is it a good theory? Why or why not?

9. Describe the situational theory of leadership. What are the major problems with this theory?

10. What are the two types of situations in leadership substitutes theory?

11. What are the four types of variables in the multiple linkage model?

DISCUSSION QUESTIONS

1. Why are followers and situational factors important for leaders to understand?

2. What are some ways that leaders exert their power?

3. Have you ever experienced difficult followers? What did you do to complete the task or achieve your goal?

4. What are some examples of situations that affect leadership behaviors?

INDIVIDUAL ACTIVITIES

INDIVIDUAL ACTIVITY 1

Think about a time when you, as a leader, experienced a difficult situation. How did you react to the situation? Apply two of the situational factors theories to your experience. What could you have done differently to be a more effective leader? Now, think of a time when you encountered difficult followers. Do the same exercise that you did with situational factors and think about how these theories can help you be a better leader in the future.

INDIVIDUAL ACTIVITY 2

Think of a leader who you admire. Look up the details of his or her life and career. What issues did he or she encounter regarding followers and situational factors? How did that leader react to these issues? How did his or her leadership develop over time? What theories best fit the actions of the leader you chose?

GROUP ACTIVITIES

GROUP ACTIVITY 1

Pretend that you are the principal of a school for gifted children. This school has been very successful in the past; lately, some serious issues arose that have affected the school's success. The following three problems regarding students at the school have been identified as the source of the schools troubles: lack of motivation, low attendance, and low test scores. How would you go about solving these problems? What are the key factors you should consider?

GROUP ACTIVITY 2

Imagine that you are the project leader for a marketing team at a large organization that specializes in new technology. Your team must come up with 10 new ideas to market the company's new cell phone. Your job is to make sure the team produces 10 great new ideas by the end of the week. With this large assignment and fast-approaching deadline, how would you go about leading your team to reach the goal? What factors do you need to consider? Now take on the role of a team member. How would you want to be led?

SUGGESTED READINGS

Bass, B. M. (1990). *Bass and Stogdill's handbook of leadership: Theory, research, and managerial applications.* New York: Free Press.

Conger, J. A., & Riggio, R. E. (2007). *The practice of leadership: Developing the next generation of leaders.* San Francisco, CA: Jossey-Bass.

Yukl, G. (2006). *Leadership in organizations* (6th ed.). Upper Saddle River, NJ: Prentice Hall.

How Leaders Think

Cristina L. Byrne

THINK.

—Thomas J. Watson, President of IBM

homas Watson was the president of International Business Machines (IBM) from the 1920s to the 1950s. During his time as president, the country faced the one of its most difficult economic hardships—the Great Depression. Watson and IBM faced difficult financial times and had to make tough decisions about how to keep the company going during the depression. Watson was often heard saying to his followers, "Think." This simple phrase became the motto for the company. The word could be found on the wall of every room in the building. Every employee carried around a THINK notebook so that they could write down any ideas during the day. This motto is carried on today in the naming of products, including the IBM ThinkPad notebook computer (Maney, 2003).

Watson found it very important to take some time to really *think* about the problems the company was facing during the depression. He not only set an example by mentioning how he was giving the problem careful consideration but also made it clear that it was a big problem that all of them would have to spend time really thinking about, together (Maney, 2003). Clearly, *thinking*, as well as being able to guide the thinking of others, is one of the most important jobs of a leader, especially when faced with a problem or crisis.

In this chapter, we will learn about *how* leaders think. To do this, we will cover research aimed at understanding leadership from a cognitive perspective. In other words, this research examines the thinking, or **cognition,** of leaders. The first theory to be presented is the **cognitive resources leadership theory** (Fiedler & Garcia, 1987). This theory argues that effective leadership depends on both the **intelligence** and the **experience** of the leader. However, an important concept in this theory is that a leader's experience will be more useful than his or her intelligence when a situation is stressful. Next, we will cover another model of how leaders think. This model holds that *how* leaders go about solving problems and making decisions helps their followers understand and make sense of complex situations (Connelly et al., 2000; Mumford, Friedrich, et al., 2007). We will also discuss how a leader's ability to solve problems *creatively* can help his or her followers (Mumford et al., 2003). Next, we will cover **implicit theories of leadership.** Implicit theories of

Cognition—mental events where perceptions, memories, and thoughts are processed
Cognitive resources leadership theory—a theory that emphasizes the type of intelligence a leader uses when dealing with problems or making decisions
Intelligence—the capacity to acquire, store, and apply knowledge (general mental ability, verbal reasoning, analytical reasoning, etc.)
Experience—active participation that leads to the accumulation of knowledge or skill
Implicit theories of leadership—theories that examine how peoples' beliefs and assumptions about leadership influence their perceptions of and behavior toward leadership

leadership are beliefs and assumptions people make regarding what makes an effective leader (Yukl, 2006). This theory is more about how people think about a leader than how that leader

> **Cognitive frameworks**—the categories and their connections into which individuals place events, behaviors, objects, attributes, and concepts

thinks. Both leaders and followers have implicit leadership theories, and these theories, or **cognitive frameworks**, impact both how leaders are perceived by their followers as well as what leaders believe are the appropriate leader behaviors for a given situation. Finally, we will cover a theory of how leaders are developed, or made, using a cognitive perspective (Lord & Hall, 2005). This theory argues that as leadership skills are developed, there are changes in how a leader processes information. This theory attempts to understand changes in how information is processed as a person moves from being a novice to being an expert leader.

Learning Objectives

- Understand the importance of learning and researching how leaders think
- Understand cognitive resources leadership theory and its implications for leaders
- Understand how leaders solve problems, make decisions, and employ creativity
- Understand implicit theories of leadership and their implications for leaders
- Understand that how leaders think is related to their development and acquisition of new leadership skills

COGNITIVE RESOURCES LEADERSHIP THEORY

Cognitive resources leadership theory was developed by Fiedler and colleagues (Fiedler, 1986; Fiedler & Garcia, 1987). In this theory, it is argued that a leader's performance (and, thus, his or her followers' performance) is influenced by cognitive resources like intelligence and experience. It is thought that performance is determined by a combination of a leader's cognitive resources, his or her behavior, and the aspects of a situation. One type of situation Fielder and colleagues were interested in was a high-stress situation. This theory argues that stress moderates the relationship between a leader's intelligence and his or her followers' performance. When something is said to be a moderator, it means that it influences the relationship between two other things. High-stress situations could include, for example, frequent work crises, interpersonal conflicts, or unrealistic demands placed on a leader. This relationship is shown in Figure 6.1.

When the situation is not stressful, the intelligence of leaders has a positive impact on their followers' performance. In other words, the more intelligent leaders are, the better their followers perform. However, when a situation is highly stressful, this relationship becomes very weak or disappears completely (Bass, 1990). Why is this the case? Why wouldn't intelligence help in a stressful situation? One explanation for this change is that stress interferes with the way a leader processes information and makes decisions (Yukl, 2006). Stress causes a leader to be distracted and lose focus on the task at hand. Thus, a leader's intelligence will not provide an advantage in a high-stress situation.

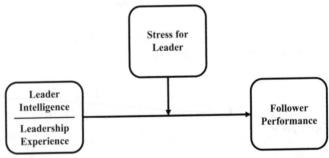

Figure 6.1 Causal model of cognitive resources leadership theory.

Figure 6.2 Mediated relationship between leader intelligence, experience, behavior, and follower performance.

When a situation is stressful, leaders' experience becomes a greater influence on their followers' performance than does their intelligence. In this case, followers who are led by more experienced leaders tend to perform better. In this theory, experience is usually thought of in terms of time on the job. With greater experience, leaders tend to learn successful behaviors, especially behaviors that have previously led to the successful resolution of problems. These behaviors become habits for successful leaders. It is thought that when people become stressed, they revert back to previously learned behaviors and habits instead of relying on their intelligence to solve the problem.

Additionally, cognitive resources leadership theory argues that a leader's behavior will mediate the relationship between that leader's cognitive resources and his or her followers' performance. Mediation refers to something that has an indirect influence. In other words, a leader's cognitive resources can only have an impact *through* his or her behavior. It is unlikely that a leader will have any impact at all unless they actually *do* something. Cognitive resources will only influence follower performance through a leader's behavior. This relationship is shown in Figure 6.2.

In this case, this theory suggests that cognitive resources impact performance through a behavior style we call **directive leadership.**

> **Directive leadership**—letting subordinates know what they are expected to do, giving specific guidance, asking subordinates to follow rules and procedures, and scheduling and coordinating work

Directive leadership is discussed in greater detail in chapters 2 and 5 in the explanation of the contingency theory of leadership. House and Mitchell (1974) defined directive leadership as "letting subordinates know what they are expected to do, giving specific guidance, asking subordinates to follow rules and procedures, and scheduling and coordinating the work." Directive leadership involves the leader *doing* something to help the group.

In contrast, **participative leadership** involves coordinating *with* followers and considering their opinions and suggestions. Participative leadership often involves a leader letting the group members do their work with minimal interference. With participative leadership, neither the leader's intelligence nor experience will have much of an impact. But when a leader is being directive—structuring work, developing plans, and making decisions—his or her intelligence and experience will have an impact. This theory assumes that leaders who are intelligent will make better plans for guiding work. Intelligent leaders will also better communicate these plans to their followers. This applies only when a task is complex. If a task is simple or routine, the followers already know how to perform it and will require little in terms of guidance (Yukl, 2006). For more information about moderation and mediation, see chapter 3.

> **Participative leadership**— leader behavior that involves a leader involving his or her subordinates in making important decisions and doing supervisor-type tasks

Much of the research done on cognitive resources leadership theory was conducted by Fiedler and his colleagues. Additionally, much of this work was done using samples of military leaders. In an early study, Fiedler and colleagues (1979) found that the experience, but not the intelligence, of infantry squad leaders who were under a high degree of stress was related to their performance. When the squad leaders were not under a high degree of stress, their experience was not related to their performance.

They found, instead, that in low-stress situations, intelligence was related to performance. In general, under conditions of low stress, the intelligence of leaders will have a greater impact on follower performance than will their experience. Several other studies have found similar evidence and have suggested similar conclusions (Borden, 1980; Fiedler & Leister, 1977; Frost, 1983; Knowlton, 1979; Potter, 1978; Zais, 1979).

Much of this work has demonstrated that these proposed relationships do exist. However, very few studies have been able to examine the reasons *why* they do. Gibson, Fiedler, and Barrett (1993) conducted a study using a sample of ROTC cadets. In the experiment, the cadets, in groups, were asked to come up with a creative solution to a problem, and the leaders of these small groups were examined. The study showed that under high-stress conditions, intelligent leaders tended to talk more, but they rambled and actually contributed few good ideas. Because they dominated the group conversation but did not really help, the other group members were not able to contribute as much, thus reducing overall group performance on the task.

All in all, the evidence suggests that these relationships do, in fact, exist. However, there is far too little research to be certain why these relationships exist. More studies must be conducted on cognitive resources leadership theory. In particular, it would be informative to know if specific cognitive skills, like problem solving, are driving these findings.

COMPLEX AND CREATIVE PROBLEM SOLVING

COMPLEX PROBLEM SOLVING

Try to think of a time when you were at work and a crisis or situation had to be handled by your manager or supervisor. What did you supervisor do? Were they able to resolve the problem effectively? Now, try to imagine all the things that were going through your manager's head when he or she was thinking about how to solve the problem. **Problem solving** is something that leaders at every level are required to do. From the manager of a small convenience store to the CEO of a large corporation, problem solving is a major part of being a leader. Leadership, as generally defined, usually involves influencing others to understand what needs to be done and how to do it in order to achieve a common objective (Yukl, 2006). However, as Mumford, Zaccaro, Connelly, and Marks (2000) noted, "Unless leaders can identify significant organizational problems and formulate solutions to those problems, all the planning and all the persuasion in the world are to no avail." While problem solving is a skill that leaders typically use on a regular basis, it is a relatively new area of research for leadership scholars.

> **Problem solving**—the process of understanding many aspects of a complex problem in order to solve that problem

While we know that leadership involves substantial problem solving, we also need to understand what kind of problems leaders are required to solve. Mumford, Zaccaro, Harding, Jacobs, and Fleishman (2000) described the problems that leaders typically face as highly complex, novel, and ambiguous. On first reading, this might seem like a vague description of these problems; however, it is intentionally broad so it can accurately describe the types of problems all leaders might face regardless of their position or situation. In other words, the complex problems that executives face do not look like the complex problems that politicians or military leaders face.

The following is a problem that was used in a research study to examine the problem-solving skills of military leaders. This scenario was presented to real military leaders in order to simulate a problem they might encounter in their work. This is a good illustration of what is meant by a complex, novel, and ambiguous problem. As you read, notice that there are several variables operating in the situation that must be attended to by the leader (i.e., it contains high complexity). Additionally, this particular situation had never been faced before by the United States military. Thus, it was novel to the participants in this study. Finally, it is important to recognize that this problem does not have a single right answer. There are a variety of responses and courses of action that the leader could pursue—all of which could potentially lead to positive outcomes.

Burma has invaded Indonesia. Indonesia has requested assistance from the U.S. government. You have 24 hours to develop a plan for a military response. The information you have is that one enemy force of 75,000 soldiers is located in the western part of Indonesia, while another 25,000 soldiers are located in the eastern part of the country. These armies are well armed in terms of tanks and artillery, but weak in terms of tactical air support. In your planning, you can utilize any and all aspects of the U.S. Armed Forces personnel and material. (Zaccaro, Mumford, Connelly, Marks, & Gilbert, 2000, p. 44)

In 2000, Mumford, Zaccaro, Harding and colleagues suggested a model describing the factors that influence effective leadership. This model focuses on the characteristics and capabilities of leaders, specifically leaders' abilities to solve complex problems, their **social judgment skills,** and their knowledge, which are all thought to influence leader performance. This model is shown in Figure 6.3.

While this figure is complex, it offers some rather

Social judgment skills—the ability to understand and monitor social dynamics within the problem domain and integrate potential solutions with the practical demands of an organization

155

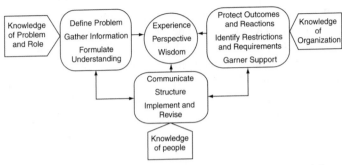

Figure 6.3 Model of effective leadership and problem solving.

straightforward suggestions. Basically, this model describes the factors that influence leaders' abilities to solve problems and their performance in general. In the first box on the left, you can see that part of being able to solve a problem involves defining the problem, gathering information about that problem, formulating an understanding of the problem, and, ultimately, generating initial solutions to that problem. While these are probably the most critical elements of a leader's ability to solve problems, it is also recognized that a leader must be able to consider factors associated with his or her followers. For example, leaders must be able to communicate potential solutions to their followers and structure how their followers go about implementing, or putting into action, the solution. Additionally, leaders must know their organization, or company, well enough to deal with any obstacles that might arise when implementing a solution. For example, a leader who wants to implement a new safety program to reduce accidents in the workplace must be able to sell that idea to top management to get funding and other support for the program to be effective.

Studies designed to examine pieces of this model (Connelly et al., 2000; Zaccaro et al., 2000) have demonstrated that leadership is not simply a matter of intelligence; it requires skills that go beyond intelligence, including problem-solving skills. In their study, Connelly and colleagues (2000) examined the problem-solving skills of army leaders. The leaders were asked to solve several military scenarios where multiple solutions were acceptable.

The researchers measured each leader's problem-solving skill and showed that those skills were related to the quality of the solutions proposed. The evidence provided by this, as well as other studies, suggests that leaders do, in fact, need more than just intelligence. They also need to be able to effectively solve problems.

CREATIVE PROBLEM SOLVING

A related area of research involves the need for leaders to be creative when they solve problems. When we think of creativity, we often call to mind an artist or a musician; you might be asking yourself, "What does creativity have to do with leadership?" The definition of creativity has been expanded to include not just art, music, and literature, but, more generally, any production of a *new*, socially valued product. When you think of creativity in this way, it becomes easier to see its connection to leadership. Imagine the director of a marketing firm. Marketing directors are constantly tasked with developing new ways to capture the attention of customers through advertisements and promotions. When leaders are tasked with such problems, they must help their followers generate something *novel*. By doing so, they engage in **creative problem solving**.

You might be wondering how creative problem solving differs from the problem solving described in the previous section. In the last section, we said the types of problems leaders typically face are complex, novel, and ambiguous. For creative problems, the definition basically remains the same, with a few changes. First, the solutions called for in problem solving do not require that the solution be *novel*. However, in creative problem solving, the solution *must* be novel and unique. In other words, in traditional problem solving, a leader could rely on solutions that worked in the past for similar situations, making only minor ad-

> **Creative problem solving**— cognitive processes that produce a novel, useful solution

157

Recombination of existing knowledge—the process of restructuring or reorganizing existing concepts to provide new understandings that can serve as the basis for generating alternative solutions

justments for the particular situation. In creative problem solving, a leader would have to generate a solution that was novel or unique in some way. Another way these problems and solutions differ is that, in creative problem solving, the solutions generated typically come from the reorganization or **recombination of existing knowledge.** For example, a marketing director could take the techniques used in Campaign A (e.g., mailer promotions) and combine them with techniques used in Campaign B (e.g., Internet advertising) to generate something that had not been used before by the group (e.g., e-mail promotional ads).

Usually, however, it is not a leader who must generate a novel solution to a problem calling for creative thought. This is more often the role of the followers. However, leaders must still use their creative problem-solving skills to help their followers develop a final product. Often, in this type of situation, the leader will serve as an evaluator of initial ideas. Mumford and colleagues (2003) suggested a process that leaders would go through to help their followers in such a situation. First, the followers would present their ideas to their leaders. The leaders would then evaluate those ideas and engage in their own idea generation and combination, which would, in turn, produce refinements to improve the ideas (or discard unusable ideas). The leaders would then give feedback to their followers, and the followers would take those refinements and incorporate them into the final product. This model suggests that leaders must, depending on the situation, serve in two capacities. In one role, they must use creative problem-solving skills in order to generate a novel, useful solution to a problem that the group is facing. In the second role, they serve as sounding boards for the novel and useful solutions generated by their followers. In this role, however, they are still required to use creative problem-solving skills, but these skills may focus on different areas of the creative process (i.e., the evaluation of ideas).

In a review of the creative problem solving of leaders, Mumford and Connelly (1991) discussed a variety of studies that indicate that creative problem solving is an important skill for leaders. Many of these studies examined real-world leaders and provided evidence for the connection between leader performance and effective creative problem-solving skills. For example, studies examining the relationship between creative ability and leadership performance have suggested there is, in fact, a relationship where the more the creative leaders are, the better they perform. Additional studies suggest that when leaders are given **creativity interventions,** or training designed to enhance their creative problem-solving skills, their performance increases. Overall, there is a substantial body of evidence suggesting good leaders have good creative problem-solving skills.

> **Creativity interventions—** training designed to enhance creative problem-solving skills

Cognitive resources leadership theory suggests that intelligence and experience play a large role in leader performance. The models of leader complex problem solving and creative problem solving described above add to that suggestion by arguing that not only do leaders need to be intelligent, knowledgeable, and experienced, but they also need to have good problem-solving skills in order to be effective leaders. Additionally, there are many situations and problems that leaders face that require them to generate creative solutions to problems and evaluate the creative ideas of others. In these cases, leadership also calls for creative problem-solving skills.

IMPLICIT THEORIES OF LEADERSHIP

A third area of research that examines how leaders think involves a concept called implicit theories of leadership. These theories involve how both leaders and followers think about good leadership. It is best to think about implicit leadership theories as beliefs people have about what good leaders do, how they behave, and what characteristics they have. Both leaders and followers have implicit leadership theories, and these theories affect both how leaders are perceived by their followers and what leaders believe is the appropriate leader behavior for a given situation. Bass (1990, p. 375) said, "Both the leader and the led are affected in their exchange relationship by the implicit theories of leadership they carry around in their heads." To help you understand these theories, answer the following questions: What is leadership? What makes a good leader? What does a good leader do? Your answer . . . well, that is *your* implicit theory of leadership.

People's implicit theories of leadership, however, can change over time as they are exposed to different types of effective leaders, as they read more about effective leadership (like you are doing right now), or as they are exposed to other sociocultural influences (Lord, Brown, Harvey, & Hall, 2001). Additionally, people's implicit theories of leadership are different in different situations. For example, what makes the president of the United States an effective leader? Are those the same characteristics and behaviors that are required to be a good manager of a small team? Implicit theories of leadership change given the type of position held (e.g., president vs. manager), the context (e.g., crisis vs. noncrisis situations, different cultures), and individual differences (e.g., male vs. female leaders) (Yukl, 2006). It is also important to remember that implicit theories of leadership are affected by a person's beliefs, values, and personality traits. This means that every person's implicit theories can be different. However, people existing in the same culture, whether it is a national culture or a corporate culture, will likely have relatively similar perceptions of how a leader should behave and what makes a good leader.

Implicit theories of leadership are important because they affect how people evaluate their leaders, as well as their expectations of leadership. This will ultimately have an impact on leadership research and evaluation, and it should be taken into account when the research involves followers' evaluations of the behavior of their leaders, managers, or supervisors. Expectations of how a leader *should* behave in a given situation could ultimately affect and potentially bias how people rate that leader's performance (Yukl, 2006). For example, when followers are unable to observe their supervisor's behavior, but are then asked about it in a survey, they will use their implicit theory of leadership to fill in the blanks or missing information. If they believe their leader is generally a good leader, and if they believe good leadership involves intelligence, honesty, and strong character, then they are likely to describe their leader as intelligent, honest, and of good character, even though they may not have had many opportunities to see the leader demonstrate these qualities. Thus, it is absolutely critical that we consider implicit theories of leadership when conducting leadership research.

LEADERSHIP DEVELOPMENT

In this section, we will review a recent theory regarding the development of leadership skills (Lord & Hall, 2005). This theory argues that as leadership skills are developed, changes occur in how a leader processes information. This theory attempts to understand changes in how information is processed as a person moves from a novice to an expert leader.

Lord and Hall (2005) suggested that the development of leadership skills occurs over an extended period of time. First, **novice**, or inexperienced, leaders will attempt to use skills that are loosely connected and not integrated. This will likely be an effortful process. When novice leaders attempt to use newly learned skills, they will likely be

> **Novice**—a person who is new to a field or activity (i.e., a beginner)

guided by their desires to do what they think leaders should do (remember that leaders have implicit theories of effective leadership, too). They will attempt to display the behaviors they associate with good leaders. Novice leaders might believe (and rightfully so) that good leaders organize and structure the work of their followers. They may attempt to perform these behaviors to the best of their abilities. Because they are novice leaders, this may take a lot of effort, and other behaviors associated with good leadership may be put aside for the time being.

However, once leaders become comfortable structuring the tasks of others, these behaviors will become habitual. When leaders are comfortable in their roles and have gained some experience, they will gradually progress to an intermediate level of leadership skill. Lord & Hall (2005) argued that as leaders move into this intermediate phase, they will begin to integrate their leadership skills into their leader identity (i.e., how they view themselves as leaders). In other words, leaders will begin to see themselves as leaders who are capable of a variety of skills (structuring work activities, etc.). Leaders' views of themselves will have an impact not only on how they perform their role, but also on how motivated they are to become better, more experienced leaders. At this level, leaders will likely seek out learning experiences to help them further develop their own leadership skills.

Once leaders have acquired a great deal of experience, they begin to have a deeper understanding of themselves as leaders (i.e., their leader identity) and their core values. This understanding becomes an important source of flexibility in leadership skills. When they understand themselves and their skills and have experienced a variety of situations, leaders are better able to handle a variety of situations and can apply the appropriate leadership skills for a given situation (i.e., they are flexible). In other words, they no longer rely on a small set of skills, but, rather, they have a large library of skills they can turn to under different circumstances. Once leaders have developed sufficiently, the integration of their leadership skills with their identity is more complete. As Lord and Hall (2005) noted, this integration "can result in an expert and unique manner of leading that can include the development of internal qualities and abilities located not only within the leader but also within the followers." In other words, expert leaders have developed a unique way of leading that integrates a variety of skills and abilities and allows them to develop themselves further but also allows them to develop their followers.

CHAPTER SUMMARY

In this chapter, we have discussed the importance of understanding how leaders think. Leaders' intelligence, experience, problem-solving skills, and perceptions of what leadership is will all affect how they behave in a leadership role. This ultimately has an impact on how effective they will be in that role. Additionally, how leaders think, and how they integrate their experiences into their identities as leaders, will affect their further development.

Much of the leadership research to date has focused on what leaders do, what their personal characteristics are, and what skills they can bring to their followers. Recently, however, researchers have begun to focus on how leaders think, what they think about, and how these modes of thinking help them be better leaders. This trend is likely to continue in the field of leadership research. In a relatively short period of time, the study of leader cognition (thinking), leader problem-solving skills, and how leaders think in general has provided valuable information that can help us better understand how leaders go about developing skills and learning to be good leaders. Additionally, we have learned how leaders effectively perform their roles, how they solve problems, and how they help their followers solve problems. Hopefully, this information can be used to help leaders develop the critical skills they need in order to perform their roles effectively.

KEY TERMS AND PHRASES

- Cognition
- Cognitive frameworks
- Creativity interventions
- Creative problem solving
- Directive leadership
- Experience
- Implicit theories of leadership
- Intelligence
- Novice
- Participative leadership
- Problem solving
- Recombination of existing knowledge
- Social judgment skills

REVIEW QUESTIONS

1. Briefly describe how a leader's intelligence and experience work to influence follower performance according to the cognitive resources leadership theory. What is the moderator in this relationship? What is the mediator in this relationship?
2. Why is it important for leaders to be effective problem solvers?
3. Explain the difference between complex problem solving and creative problem solving.
4. Why is it important for leadership researchers to consider implicit theories of leadership?
5. Explain the flexibility that leaders acquire as they develop from novice to expert leaders.

DISCUSSION QUESTIONS

1. In the cognitive resources leadership theory, it is suggested that leaders' intelligence and experience will only have an impact

if the leaders are being directive. Do you agree or disagree? Why? Can you think situations where this statement might not be true?

2. According to Mumford and colleagues, problem solving is a key component of leadership. Think of experiences you have had where your supervisor has had to solve a problem. Did they do so effectively? What did they do well? What could they have done differently?

3. Creative problem solving has been shown to have a considerable impact on a leader's ability to help his or her followers in their work. Why is it important for leaders to be able to help their followers be creative? Why is creativity so important for our economy today?

4. How has this book changed *your* implicit theory of leadership?

5. Based on what you have learned about leadership so far, why is leadership development so important? Can you think of some ways that leaders can improve themselves?

INDIVIDUAL ACTIVITIES

INDIVIDUAL ACTIVITY 1

Generate a list of occupations or jobs where you think creativity would be important. Describe the ways in which a manager might help his or her followers improve their creativity in these jobs.

INDIVIDUAL ACTIVITY 2

Compare and contrast the implicit theories of leadership that you associate with the president of the United States verses the CEO of a large corporation (e.g., Microsoft). What makes them good leaders? How are they different?

GROUP ACTIVITIES

GROUP ACTIVITY 1

Read the scenario below. As a group, discuss the steps Dr. Whitfield would have to think through in order to solve the problem. Describe what she might need to do or think in regards to each of the elements involved in problem solving (defining the problem, gathering information, formulating an understanding, and generating initial solutions). Generate recommendations, based on what you know about problem solving, that could help Dr. Whitfield come to a workable solution.

> Dr. Whitfield is in charge of a large pharmaceutical laboratory. One of the drugs that the laboratory has been researching could potentially be used to treat patients with heart disease. After a decade of progress, the new drug has been through several rounds of testing and is now ready for clinical trials on a human sample. As the clinical trials begin, one of Dr. Whitfield's employees calls to her attention a patient who has suffered a mild psychotic episode. Dr. Whitfield believes the episode is likely a coincidence and has nothing to do with the drug. Two weeks later, there is another report of a second patient suffering from a mild psychotic episode. What should Dr. Whitfield do in this situation? (Zaccaro et al., 2000)

GROUP ACTIVITY 2

In cognitive resources leadership theory, a high-stress situation has an impact on how leaders perform. As a group, consider other situations that might impact the relationship between a leader's intelligence and experience and his or her followers' performance. Describe how these situations will ultimately impact the followers' performance. What might moderate the relationship? What might mediate the relationship?

SUGGESTED READINGS

Fiedler, F. E., & Garcia, J. E. (1987). *New approaches to effective leadership: Cognitive resources and organizational performance.* New York: Wiley.

Lord, R. G., & Hall, R. J. (2005). Identity, deep structure, and the development of leadership skill. *The Leadership Quarterly, 16,* 591–615.

Mumford, M. D., Connelly, M. S., & Gaddis, B. (2003). How creative leaders think: Experimental findings and cases. *The Leadership Quarterly, 14,* 411–432.

Mumford, M. D., Zaccaro, S. J., Harding, F. D., Jacobs, T. O., & Fleishman, E. A. (2000). Leadership skills for a changing world: Solving complex social problems. *The Leadership Quarterly, 11,* 11–35.

Outstanding Leadership

William B. Vessey

> When the effective leader is finished with his work, the people say it happened naturally.
>
> —*Lao Tse*

> Great necessities call forth great leaders.
>
> —*Abigail Adams*

When you think of a leader, whom do you think of? You probably think of someone like Abraham Lincoln or Gandhi rather than Barry, the manager at your local supermarket. Though they all may lead, there is a clear difference between the leaders that immediately come to mind and a leader you may have never heard of. Leaders like Lincoln and Gandhi have an influence on the world around them that often affects entire countries, if not the world. These people represent a special case of outstanding leadership beyond what we have discussed so far in much of this book. The goal of this chapter is to give you some insight into what outstanding leadership is and how outstanding leaders lead.

In the following sections we will discuss some different types of outstanding leadership. We will describe how these leaders get people to follow them and how they lead. In addition, you will learn about the followers of outstanding leaders.

Learning Objectives
- Understand the different ways of thinking about outstanding leadership
- Learn how and why outstanding leaders are outstanding
- Find out who follows these leaders and why they follow

CHARISMATIC LEADERSHIP

The first theory of outstanding leadership we will discuss is charismatic leadership. **Charismatic leadership** suggests that a leader's authority comes from a follower's perceptions of him or her, along with the leader's ability to inspire others to take action. Just like the name implies, charismatic leaders have charisma—they are seen by their followers as extraordinary, and this perception of the leader motivates people to follow them (Weber, 1947). The key to understanding this definition of charismatic leadership is the word *perception*. The followers of charismatic leaders think these leaders have certain qualities, whether or not they actually possess those qualities. These perceptions can be based on, or magnified by, the behaviors of the leader and the leader's vision (Conger & Kanungo, 1998). Two commonly referenced examples of charismatic leadership are John F. Kennedy and Martin Luther King, Jr. Both were seen as

Charismatic leadership—a leadership style in which the leader tends to express a positive vision of the future, is highly self-confident, appears honest and generous, and attracts a wide variety of followers who are loyal to the leader rather than the leader's agenda or organization

heroes by their followers, and much of their influence came from their ability to outline a vision of the future through inspiring speeches. Kennedy's speech on the future of the space program is a good example. He was able to provide a goal—landing on the moon—that people could work toward, and he inspired his followers to try to achieve this goal. This example brings us to our discussion of how charismatic leaders lead their followers.

VISION

A critical component of charismatic leadership is a leader's vision. For the charismatic leader to inspire his or her followers, that leader must present an appealing vision for the future. So what is a vision? Strange and Mumford (2002) defined **vision** as a set of beliefs about how people should act, and interact, to achieve some ideal future. In other words, leaders develop their idea of what the future should hold and then determine what they and their followers should do to create this ideal future. We can see an example of this in Martin Luther King, Jr. He laid out a vision for a future in which all people would be treated equally, and then he expressed ideas about what actions would be necessary to achieve this equal future.

Now that you know what a vision is, you might be wondering where a leader's vision comes from. Charismatic leaders form a vision by looking at what is wrong with the world around them and noticing the opportunities they have to change it (Conger, 1999). These leaders base their goals on solving the problems they perceive. Charismatic leaders base their vision on **forecasting,** or predicting, what the world would be like if these problems were solved. Through forecasting, a leader can refine his or her ideas in order to develop a better understanding of what things could be like

> **Vision**—a set of beliefs about how people should act, and interact, to achieve some ideal future
>
> **Forecasting**—predicting what the world would be like if certain problems were solved

in the future. A charismatic leader must also be keenly aware of opportunities for change. If there are no such opportunities, a leader may be seen as ineffective for failing to make any significant changes. In addition, followers may think of that leader's vision as unrealistic (Conger & Kanungo, 1998).

Furthermore, simply having a vision is not enough to motivate others; the leader must effectively communicate that vision to his or her followers. How the vision is communicated is critical. A vision for the future that people do not understand has no value. To effectively communicate their vision, a charismatic leader must first set goals either different from the norm or directly opposing it. When communicating these goals, a charismatic leader needs to make his or her followers aware of (a) problems with the norm, (b) how his or her vision is different, (c) why the vision should matter to the followers, and (d) how to achieve the vision (Conger & Kanungo, 1998). By communicating his or her goals in this way, a leader can offer a real alternative to the current way things are done. Simply having a real option may be enough to inspire some people to follow a leader.

When communicating his or her vision, a charismatic leader must also make sure to offer a perspective that can be identified with. Followers can identify with a vision if they understand why a leader thinks certain things about the world (Bass & Avolio, 1993). If a leader can explain why he or she thinks a problem is worth solving, that leader makes others aware of both the problem and the need to do something about it. If people are unable to identify with a leader and the need for change, the leader will have trouble attracting followers. Thus, a leader must not only communicate a perspective that can be identified with, but he or she must also be able to communicate in a way that inspires and motivates others. Leaders can do this by expressing their own motivation and commitment to the vision (House & Podsakoff, 1994). By showing confidence, high levels of energy, persistence, and assertiveness, a leader clearly shows motivation and commitment to his or her followers. Leaders can also inspire others by displaying unconventional behavior to make it clear to their followers that it is acceptable to resist the way things are normally done. By displaying motivation and commitment, a leader can spread these same feelings to his or her followers.

Next, if a charismatic leader has successfully communicated a vision to his or her followers, what effect does this have? By communicating his or her vision, one thing a leader can change is people's attitudes about whether there is a problem (Petty & Cacioppo, 1981). Some people may not perceive a problem or may see it as less important before hearing about it from a leader's perspective. A leader's vision can also give followers a sense of group identity (Shamir, House, & Arthur, 1993). This vision is something for everyone to rally around, regardless of individual differences. If the followers can work toward a common vision for the future, they will tend to act in the interest of the group rather than in their own self-interest. Any given action taken for the group, no matter how big or small, is more meaningful to the followers because of this vision (Bennis & Nanus, 1985). A task may seem meaningless on its own, but in the context of achieving a leader's vision it will be perceived as part of a greater movement. This will give the followers a reason to be motivated regardless of what they are doing at any given moment. In fact, the motivation that comes from a great vision can be long lasting (Berson, Shamir, Avolio, & Popper, 2001). The vision gives the followers something to look forward to in the future, something that can only be achieved through their hard work. We can revisit our example of Kennedy's speech on the space program to see how this works. Putting a man on the moon was a goal that required a long-term commitment from Kennedy's followers. His inspiring vision for the future provided the motivation for his followers to continue their work toward achieving this goal over a long period of time.

Once the followers believe in a charismatic leader's vision, the leader needs to put them to work on achieving goals related to the vision. There are two things a charismatic leader must do to get his or her followers to successfully act toward achieving a vision: build follower trust and demonstrate how to achieve the goals (Conger & Kanungo, 1998). Charismatic leaders can gain the trust of their followers in a variety of ways. First, a leader can communicate the vision's goals as being for the benefit of the followers, not for themselves (Walster, Aronson, & Abrahams, 1966). Secondly, a leader can demonstrate expertise in the area, showing that there is a legitimate reason to believe he or she is competent (Conger, 1989). Also, a leader can show that he or she is taking a personal risk by trying to achieve the vision (Friedlander & Walton, 1964). If a leader has a personal stake in the project, the followers are more likely to trust the leader's commitment to achieving the vision, thereby increasing their own commitment. Once a leader has his or her followers' trust, that leader must demonstrate how to achieve the goals at hand. By acting to achieve goals in a certain way, a leader shows his or her followers appropriate methods to achieve those goals (Conger & Kanungo). Again, we return to the example of Martin Luther King, Jr. He demonstrated to his followers that resistance against authority could be peaceful. By participating in a peaceful protest, Martin Luther King, Jr. showed his followers two things: first, that this method was acceptable; and second, how to correctly engage in the activity.

EMPOWERING FOLLOWERS

Forming and communicating a vision are not the only important activities charismatic leaders need to engage in to be successful. They must also empower their followers (Bass & Avolio, 1993). **Empowering** is a process by which leaders make their followers feel more confident in their own abilities and their importance to the group. Charismatic leaders empower their followers primarily by increasing follower **self-efficacy,** or the extent to which followers feel they are qualified to perform given

Empowering—a process by which leaders make followers feel more confident in their own abilities and their importance to the group

Self-efficacy—the extent to which an individual feels they are qualified to perform a given activity

activities. Increasing follower self-efficacy increases follower commitment to a leader and the extent to which the followers successfully contribute to achieving goals (House & Shamir, 1993).

Charismatic leaders can boost follower self-efficacy in a number of ways. One option is that leaders can give their followers more control of a situation with less supervision or direction. By letting their followers control how to behave when solving a given problem, leaders demonstrate that they trust their followers' abilities to handle a problem on their own. This demonstration of trust makes the followers more confident that they can achieve the goals on their own (Burke, 1986). Another way leaders can increase self-efficacy is through expressing confidence in the abilities of their followers to achieve the goals set for them. A leader telling his or her followers that they are capable is enough to increase their self-efficacy if they believe in the leader (Conger & Kanungo, 1988). Finally, just as expressing commitment to a vision increases follower acceptance of that vision, leaders can also demonstrate their own commitment to a goal in order to empower their followers to achieve that goal. If a leader demonstrates commitment, it makes his or her followers believe that the goal can be accomplished and that the leader has confidence in them to achieve the goal (Thomas & Velthouse, 1990).

FOLLOWERS

Although we've discussed how charismatic leaders treat their followers, we have yet to discuss this topic from the followers' perspective. To begin, why do people follow a leader? What motivates them to follow a charismatic leader over someone else? To answer these questions, we need to look at why charismatic leaders emerge in the first place. The most common situational factor cited for the emergence of charismatic leadership is a crisis or an opportunity for change (Beyer & Browning, 1999; Conger, 1993). Think about Martin Luther King, Jr. and JFK again. Both emerged during a time of social upheaval, a time when major changes could and were being made. Crises and times of change motivate people to seek out leaders to give them direction and stability. They want someone who can increase their confidence that the proposed changes will occur and that the results will be positive for them. Looking back at the discussion on empowering followers, we can see that charismatic leaders tend to instill confidence. In addition to motivating followers to seek out a leader, crises are times when charismatic leaders are more likely to be accepted. The vision proposed by a charismatic leader often involves radical change, and this change may be more acceptable to the public during a crisis (Roberts & Bradley, 1988). Likewise, charismatic leaders also may be more motivated to propose their visions for radical change during times of crisis, when they are more likely to be accepted.

Now that you understand why charismatic leaders emerge, why do people follow them? There are three primary reasons that followers are attracted to a charismatic leader. The first is the vision presented by the leader (Bass, 1985a). We explained earlier how a vision draws in followers, giving them motivation and commitment to work toward a leader's goals. The second reason followers are drawn to a charismatic leader is the leader's personality (Conger, 1989). You have probably heard someone described as charismatic before. This is almost always in the context of their interpersonal interactions. Followers are drawn to this charisma the leader displays in interacting with others. It is no surprise that people want to be around likeable, interesting people such as charismatic leaders. Finally, followers seek approval from charismatic leaders, and this drive for approval motivates them to follow (Shamir et al., 1993). In our discussion of empowering followers, we found that charismatic leaders increase their followers' self-efficacy. As the followers' self-efficacy is influenced by a leader, the followers become dependent on the leader's feedback to keep their self-efficacy high. This results in increased feelings of loyalty and motivation to please the leader.

So what do followers do as a result of their attraction to a charismatic leader, other than follow his or her directions? A few behaviors exhibited by followers of charismatic leaders have been studied. First, followers of charismatic leaders often view their leader as a hero (Conger & Kanungo, 1998). We can see this with Martin Luther King, Jr. and JFK. Followers view a charismatic leader as a special individual with special abilities that most other people cannot or do not possess. This hero worship leads to the second behavior commonly seen in followers of charismatic leaders— imitation (Shea & Howell, 1999). Because the followers view their leader as a special person to be admired, they will try to behave like that leader. Finally, followers of charismatic leaders try to please their leader (Shamir et al., 1993). This relates to the discussion of self-efficacy and seeking approval from a leader. Followers feel that if they please their leader, they will receive positive feedback, which improves their feelings about themselves. As followers base more of their self-worth on a leader's feedback, they have more of a need to please the leader so they will get positive feedback in return.

TRANSFORMATIONAL LEADERSHIP

Transformational leadership is another way to think about out-standing leaders, and it is closely related to charismatic leader-ship theory. **Transformational leaders** are leaders who are able to motivate their followers to achieve above and beyond their followers' own expectations (Conger, 1999). Followers of trans-formational leaders are motivated to attempt tasks they did not believe they could complete without assurance from the leader. Individuals are motivated by a leader to attempt these tasks and often succeed, despite their own initial belief that they would not be able to. Transformational leadership is defined by four basic actions performed by the leader: (a) charisma, (b) inspiration, (c) intellectual stimulation, and (d) indi-vidual consideration (Bass, 1985a). To discuss each of

Transformational leaders— leaders who are able to moti-vate their followers to achieve above and beyond their fol-lowers' own expectations

these components and the effects of each of these behaviors on the followers of transformational leaders, we will again use Martin Luther King, Jr. and JFK as our examples. Here, we should note that many leaders who are categorized as charismatic would also be categorized as transformational. This helps illustrate the connection between the theories of charismatic leadership and transformational leadership, and how multiple theories of leadership can be used to explain outstanding leadership.

CHARISMA

Charisma is considered to be the most important of the four characteristics of transformational leadership (Bass, 1985a). Charisma is often cited as the most immediately noticeable trait of transformational leaders. When people describe both Martin Luther King, Jr. and JFK, they often first talk about their personal charisma. **Charisma** in terms of transformational leadership is defined both by a leader's actions and by the reactions of followers to that leader (Bass & Avolio, 1993). An example of charismatic behavior is presenting a vision for the future. The charismatic behaviors exhibited by transformational leaders are very similar to the behaviors exhibited by charismatic leaders. Reactions from followers are also similar in many respects.

So how are the two leadership styles different? The difference in charisma between charismatic leaders and transformational leaders is how influence attempts are focused. A transformational leader primarily uses his or her individual charisma to inspire loyalty and strong feelings in his or her followers toward the goal or mission set forth by that leader (Bass & Riggio, 2006). Because of their loyalty to their leader, these followers are more likely to accept the leader's ideas for change, while their strong feelings tied to the mission keep them

Charisma—a quality of individuals that makes others perceive them as extraordinary; this perception motivates people to follow them

excited about the tasks they must complete. In addition to inspiring loyalty to a leader and excitement about a mission, charisma also increases feelings of trust in a leader. A charismatic leader is more likely than a noncharismatic leader to be viewed as trustworthy. These feelings of trust enable a leader to set goals that may seem unrealistic to his or her followers. Though the goals may seem unrealistic, the followers trust the leader enough to attempt the tasks anyway. JFK set the seemingly unrealistic goal of putting a man on the moon in 10 years, but his followers trusted him enough to believe it was possible. Charisma also increases follower admiration for a leader (Bass & Riggio). This is similar to our discussion of leaders as heroes in the section on charismatic leadership. Because of the transformational leader's charisma, the leader is viewed as the type of person one should try to emulate. Because of this, people admire and try to imitate transformational leaders.

INSPIRATIONAL COMMUNICATION

Inspirational communication is a method by which a transformational leader motivates his or her followers. There is no one best way to inspire followers, but each method for inspiration basically revolves around emotions (Bass & Riggio, 2006). A transformational leader arouses the emotions of his or her followers through the use of inspirational communication. This is often in the form of emotionally powerful statements and appeals directed toward increasing follower motivation (Rafferty & Griffin, 2004). By appealing to emotions, transformational leaders are able to motivate their followers to work toward a common goal instead of focusing on themselves (Bass, 1985 a).

We previously discussed how charismatic leaders use their vision to inspire their followers. Transformational leaders may also use a vision for the future as part of their

> **Inspirational communication**—emotionally powerful statements and appeals directed towards toward increasing follower motivation

inspirational communication with their followers (Bass, 1999). However, this is not the only method that a transformational leader can use to inspire his or her followers. Any kind of communication that arouses the emotions of one's followers for the purposes of increasing motivation counts as inspirational communication. One common example of inspirational communication is a football coach giving his or her team a pep talk before a game. The purpose of the talk is to inspire the football players to play to their full potential and work hard for the good of the team. You can imagine how a coach may try to illicit emotions, such as excitement, drive, and pride, to get the team motivated.

The transformational leader may emphasize how each follower's role or task fits in with the broader goals (Bass & Riggio, 2006). By expressing confidence in their followers and their followers' abilities to meet the goals that have been set for them, leaders can increase their followers' motivation and confidence in completing their tasks. By focusing on the importance of their followers' tasks, transformational leaders provide meaning to their work (Bass, 1985a). This meaning gives the followers motivation to complete given assignments. When a leader expresses confidence in his or her followers' abilities to get a job done, this motivates the followers to rise up to meet the challenge. Even if a transformational leader puts forth challenging goals, the followers will believe they can accomplish it because of their trust in the leader (Bass).

INTELLECTUAL STIMULATION

While we have seen how a transformational leader may inspire his or her followers to solve a problem, how are those followers first made aware of the problem? This is where intellectual stimulation comes in. Transformational leaders use **intellectual stimulation** to make their followers aware of problems and possible solutions (Bass,

Intellectual stimulation—the process of making followers aware of problems and possible solutions; getting followers to change how they think about problems

1985a). Part of this involves getting the followers to change how they think about problems. When the followers start thinking about problems differently, they may find solutions that were not clear at first. This can make seemingly unsolvable problems much easier.

There are three primary methods used by transformational leaders to intellectually stimulate their followers: (a) reframing, (b) questioning assumptions, and (c) unconventional methods (Bass & Avolio, 1994).

Reframing is putting a problem in a different context, or viewing it in a different way. Essentially, the leader is changing the questions they are asking about a problem. Asking "Why is this business doing poorly?" is very different than asking "What does this business do well?" Even though they are different questions, both are useful if the ultimate goal is to improve the performance of a business. Focusing on just one of the possible questions one could ask about a problem may limit the possible solutions. By reframing a question, the leader is encouraging his or her followers to arrive at a solution by a different path (Bass & Avolio).

> **Reframing**—the act of putting a problem in a different context, or viewing it in a different way

Questioning assumptions is another method for intellectually stimulating one's followers. When a leader asks followers to question their assumptions, the leader is asking them to challenge their own beliefs about a problem (Bass & Riggio, 2006). For example, the Wright brothers had to challenge the assumption that humans could not fly in order to go forward with the idea of the airplane. Similarly, transformational leaders encourage their followers to question what they think are the facts. A follower may think a problem is unsolvable because of some fact they know about the problem. If

> **Questioning assumptions**—the process of challenging beliefs about a problem

the leader questions that fact, the follower may find another way to work through the problem, showing that their assumptions about the problem were incorrect. A transformational leader encourages his or her followers to come up with new ways of looking at a problem by challenging their way of thinking.

Using unconventional methods is similar to reframing and questioning assumptions. It stimulates new ways of thinking about a problem with the intention of encouraging followers to come up with new solutions. When a transformational leader uses **unconventional methods**, he or she promotes the use of methods for solving a problem that are not

> **Unconventional methods—**
> the use of methods for solving a problem that are not normally associated with the type of problem

normally associated with that type of problem (Bass & Riggio, 2006). The use of unconventional methods may lead to solutions that were not originally considered, or solutions that may be more efficient than those previously used. A transformational leader may, at one point, have told his or her employees to find a way to put a nail into a piece of wood without a hammer. By being forced to use unconventional methods to find a solution, they may have come up with a more efficient way of solving the problem, like the nail gun.

All three of these methods do two basic things to help followers solve problems. First, they increase problem identification (Bass, 1985a; Bass & Avolio, 1994). By forcing them to think about a problem in a different way, followers will have to look more deeply at the problem and what is causing it. This makes it more likely that the followers will take into account all aspects of a problem and not just the most obvious. These methods for intellectually stimulating followers also increase follower awareness of alternate problem-solving methods (Bass; Bass & Avolio). Each method encourages followers to come up with solutions in ways they may not have thought about without a leader's encouragement. These methods also make it clear to followers that their leader wants them to think through problems and not just stick to the normal ways of doing things. Without this assurance, followers may be afraid of consequences from a leader and may not engage in the type of thinking encouraged by intellectual stimulation.

INDIVIDUAL CONSIDERATION

The final aspect of transformational leadership is consideration of the individual. **Individual consideration** is where a transformational leader thinks about his or her followers as unique and responds to their individual needs (Bass, 1985a). The specific way this consideration is shown may vary. Bass initially focused on the efforts of a leader to develop followers, but later Avolio and Bass (1995) focused on a leader's general support of

> **Individual consideration—** the process of thinking about followers as unique people and responding to their individual needs

his or her followers. For the purposes of this section, we will focus on Bass's initial definition of individual consideration and the transformational leader's efforts to develop his or her followers.

The process used by a transformational leader to develop his or her followers is a multistep process. First, a leader has to assess each follower's skills and potential to develop new skills. By focusing on the skills a person has, as well as the ones they may be able to learn in the future, a leader can then assign tasks based on what each individual is capable of doing (Bass, 1985a). A transformational leader will assign tasks that individuals can perform with their current skills, that will help develop their skills for the future, and that fill a need toward the leader's overall goal.

By taking into account the individual abilities of their followers, transformational leaders increase the trust they receive from their followers and develop those followers to more effectively

183

perform their assigned duties. When followers believe their leader is thinking about them as individuals and considers them important, they will then associate a strong sense of trust and attachment to the leader (Bass, 1985). Because of their admiration for the leader, this increases their self-confidence and motivation to work toward the leader's goals. The leader's individual consideration of his or her followers increases their skill development (Bass). As the followers develop more skills, they are more able to successfully complete the tasks set for them. This makes it more likely that the leader will be able to accomplish his or her overall goal.

AUTHENTIC LEADERSHIP

A more recently developed way of thinking about outstanding leadership is the theory of authentic leadership. **Authentic leadership** is leadership that is aligned with a leader's personal beliefs and values (Avolio, Gardner, Walumbwa, Luthans, & May, 2004). These leaders act upon their personal beliefs and gain trust from their followers because their actions match their stated values. Authentic leaders believe in what they are doing, which, in turn, leads followers to believe in their leaders' actions. Shamir and Eilam (2005) describe the followers of an authentic leader as **authentic followers**. These people follow their leader because their own deeply held beliefs and values match with their leader's beliefs and values in some way. Authentic leaders are often thought to lead for the perceived good of others rather than for their own personal gain (George, 2003). Authentic leaders believe their actions are for the good of everyone, and their goal in leading is to improve

> **Authentic leadership**—leadership based on personal beliefs and values
> **Authentic followers**—individuals who follow a leader because of personal beliefs and values

people's lives based on their personal perceptions of what is right. We can again use the example of Martin Luther King, Jr. when talking about an authentic leader. Mahatma Gandhi is also frequently cited as an example of an authentic leader. Both King and Gandhi based the work they did as leaders on their personal beliefs of right and wrong. In this section we will discuss the five aspects that make up authentic leadership: (a) a positive outlook, (b) ethics, (c) self-awareness, (d) self-regulation, and (e) setting an example (Avolio & Gardner, 2005). Later, we will move on to discuss the characteristics of the followers of authentic leaders.

The first aspect of authentic leadership is a leader's positive outlook. This is made up of a leader's confidence, hope, resilience, and optimism (Luthans & Avolio, 2003). By showing confidence, or a faith in one's own abilities to accomplish something, a leader can increase the level of trust from his or her followers. Also, showing confidence in one's followers' abilities leads to increased motivation and self-confidence from those followers. Authentic leaders also display hope and keep their followers hopeful. **Hope** is a positive feeling of motivation that a task or goal can realistically be accomplished. Hope in the successful completion of a task increases the effort that is put into that task by followers. The authentic leader's **resilience** is their ability to deal with setbacks or negative outcomes (Luthans & Avolio). Because authentic leaders are highly resilient and able to effectively deal with setbacks, they inspire trust from their followers. The final component of an authentic leader's positive outlook is optimism. **Optimism** is an expectation that events or actions will work out in a positive way (Seligman, 1998). A high level of optimism leads to increased motivation, performance,

> **Hope**—a positive feeling of motivation that a task or goal can realistically be accomplished
> **Resilience**—the ability to deal with setbacks or negative outcomes
> **Optimism**—an expectation that events or actions will work out in a positive way

and morale in one's followers, all of which are important to successful leadership (Seligman).

The next aspect of authentic leadership is a leader's morality or **ethics**. Ethics are an individual's personal beliefs about right and wrong. An authentic leader bases his or her decisions on these beliefs. The authentic leader's personal ethical code becomes clear to his or her followers over time. The extent to which the leader's decisions fit this ethical code increases the respect and trust received from his or her followers. If the leader's behaviors are inconsistent based on their ethics, followers will lose trust in that leader.

> **Ethics**—an individual's personal beliefs about right and wrong

Critical to authentic leadership is the concept of self-awareness (Luthans & Avolio, 2003; Ilies, Morgeson, & Nahrgang, 2005; Shamir & Eilam, 2005). **Self-awareness,** in this case, is the extent to which an authentic leader is aware of his or her values, identity, emotions, and motives. The authentic leader has high levels of self-awareness, allowing decisions to be made with the confidence that they fit with his or her personal values and goals. A leader's awareness of his or her **values,** or personal opinions about what is desirable (Schwartz, 1999), is probably most important to self-awareness. If an authentic leader does not know what they value, then they will not be sure what to try to achieve.

> **Self-awareness**—an awareness of one's own values, identity, emotions, and motives
> **Values**—personal opinions about what is desirable in a given situation

SELF-REGULATION

Self-regulation is a process inherent in being an authentic leader because it is the way an individual matches values with goals and actions (Avolio & Gardner, 2005). Self-regulation is a three-step process made up of the following: (a) setting internal standards, (b) looking for inconsistencies, and (c) addressing inconsistencies (Stajkovic & Luthans, 1998). First, the authentic leader must set **internal standards**, or personal lim-

> **Self-regulation**—a process through which an individual matches values with goals and actions
> **Internal standards**—personal limits on how closely goals and actions must match values

its on how closely goals and actions must match values. If a leader's internal standards do not match with what he or she is doing then the inconsistencies must be addressed (Gardner, Avolio, Luthans, May, & Walumbwa, 2005). Usually one of two methods is used to address an inconsistency. Either leaders (a) change their actions and behaviors or (b) change their internal standards.

SETTING AN EXAMPLE

The primary method used by authentic leaders to influence their followers is setting an example, or acting as a model (Gardner et al., 2005; Ilies et al., 2005). When discussing the different components of an authentic leader's positive outlook, you may have noticed that many of these aspects are passed on to followers by their observation of the leader. For example, followers that spend time around a leader displaying hope will oftentimes become more hopeful themselves. This is an example of vicarious learning, or learning by example. Authentic leaders are particularly successful at acting as models for their followers, since the likelihood of a person being accepted as a good example is based on their trustworthiness, credibility, and prestige (Bandura, 1997). Because authentic leaders possess all of these traits in the eyes of their followers, they are admired as examples of what a person should try to be.

FOLLOWERS

We have already discussed the effects of the different aspects of authentic leadership on followers, so here we will focus on why followers are attracted to authentic leaders. Authentic leaders are attractive to their followers for a number of reasons. First, authentic leaders help develop their followers. The authentic leader develops his or her followers both in terms of their skills and their authenticity (Gardner et al., 2005). Followers of authentic leaders view their leaders as worthwhile examples, so it is desirable for the followers to try to be authentic as well. An authentic leader often develops his or her followers simply by being present as an example of what to be and how to act (Gardner et al.). Authentic leaders also inspire hope and positive emotions in their followers, as we discussed in the section on positive outlook. Finally, authentic leaders are highly trusted by their followers. Because of the clear link between authentic leaders' values and actions, followers see their leaders as extremely trustworthy (Avolio et al., 2004). This, in turn, leads to an authentic leader seeming like a more attractive choice than an inauthentic leader.

CHARISMATIC, IDEOLOGICAL, AND PRAGMATIC LEADERSHIP

The final theory of outstanding leadership we will discuss is another recently developed by Mumford and colleagues. This theory is made up of three types of leadership: charismatic, ideological, and pragmatic. This theory presents the idea that there is not just one type of outstanding leadership; rather, there are multiple ways to be an outstanding leader. However, the different types, while all having the potential to be effective, differ in a number of ways, including the type of followers they attract. These differences between the three types of leaders are discussed in this section. Though all three types of outstanding leaders can accomplish great things, each needs the right situation to be in place beforehand. As with charismatic leadership, this model suggests that outstanding leadership is likely to appear during a period of crisis.

CHARISMATIC LEADERSHIP

The first type of leadership in this theory may sound familiar at this point—it is called charismatic leadership. Much of the following information is similar to the leaders we talked about earlier in the chapter. As a reminder, charismatic leaders influence their followers through the vision for the future they present (Conger & Kanungo, 1998). Charismatic leaders, like the other types of outstanding leaders, appear during crises. Charismatic leaders commonly emerge when people have a strong emotional connection to the crisis at hand and when the crisis affects most people in the same way (Mumford, Scott, & Hunter, 2006). Charismatic leaders appeal to their follower's emotions, meaning they are most effective during crises that have strong emotional components.

Charismatic leaders, according to this theory, have a strong focus on the future. A charismatic leader's primary method of influence is his or her vision for the future. Along with simply having a general vision for the future, charismatic leaders also set specific goals that focus on changing their world in a positive way (Keane, 1996). The charismatic leader strongly believes he or she can change and control events, even if her or she may not be able to. The goals they set for themselves and others are based on trying to institute these changes. In a crisis, a charismatic leader is able to motivate multiple groups to work together based on his or her vision (Shamir et al., 1993). Because the charismatic leader's vision for the future usually involves many complex changes, different parts of the vision can appeal to different groups. This can result in groups that do not normally work together coming together for a common goal. A leader's vision also provides a sense of identity for new members of a group (Mumford, Scott, et al., 2006). The group bases their identity on the leader's vision, and because of this, new members are able to join in relatively easily. This allows the group to increase in size quickly while still functioning as a unit with a single identity.

The followers of a charismatic leader are attracted primarily to the leader's vision for the future (Conger & Kanungo, 1998). Again, using our examples of Martin Luther King, Jr. and JFK, we see that these leaders consistently used a positive vision for the future to motivate and inspire their followers. A leader's personal charisma also appeals to his or her followers. The followers will try to act as much like the charismatic leader as possible because of their admiration for him or her. In addition to acting like their leader, followers will try to earn the approval of their leader. Because these followers look up to their leader, any sign of approval increases their self-worth.

IDEOLOGICAL LEADERSHIP

Ideological leadership, like charismatic leadership, involves a leader who presents a vision to his or her followers. This vision, however, is not based on the future, but the past (Strange & Mumford, 2002). Ideological leaders are also most likely to emerge during crises that affect their followers in an emotional way. However, in the case of the ideological leader, the crisis is usually a conflict—for example, a war. The crisis that causes the emergence of an ideological leader often results in a long-lasting negative feeling among those affected by it. An example would be a war that caused a long-term food shortage in a region. The war may end quickly, but the results are negative and long

> Ideological leadership—a leadership style in which a leader tends to express the desire to return to an idealized past state and attracts a small group of highly devoted followers with a value system similar to that of the leader

lasting. Ideological leaders also commonly come from cultures that are considered strongly defined. This means that the culture has clear rules and regulations for behavior, traditions that are still very active, and little cultural diversity (Mumford, Scott, et al., 2006). Two commonly cited examples of ideological leaders are Vladimir Lenin and George W. Bush. Both emerged as leaders during times of conflict that created strong negative feelings for their respective cultures. In the case of Lenin, the culture surrounding him was clearly defined. In the case of George W. Bush, the culture became much more defined following the 9/11 attacks, with an increased patriotic sentiment in the United States that coincided with his rise to power.

Ideological leaders present a vision that focuses on the past by appealing to people's positive feelings toward the past. Ideological leaders present their vision in terms of the values and traditions from the past that need to be maintained or reintroduced in order to fix problems with the world (Strange & Mumford, 2002). They focus primarily on current problems, and their goals center around fixing these problems using traditional methods (Mumford, Scott, et al., 2006). Their focus on the past makes the ideological leader's argument for solutions to a crisis more interesting to individuals familiar with the past being referenced. Therefore, if an individual saw one food shortage fixed with a certain method, the idea of using it again is more appealing than focusing on a new method that is unfamiliar. Ideological leaders also believe that events are primarily caused by external forces, not by individuals. This means that ideological leaders focus on large changes, such as changing a government, rather than on changing individuals (Mumford, Scott, et al.).

Finally, ideological leaders strongly promote traditions and traditional values. This appeals to those who have the same values (Barreto, Spears, Ellemers, & Shahinper, 2003) but can alienate individuals who do not share those values. This means that ideological leaders are often polarizing figures. They can be extremely popular among their followers and yet hated by others. The followers of ideological leaders form their identity and group identity around the traditional values promoted by their leader. These followers have a strong motivation toward maintaining and promoting the values and traditions they identify with (Post, Ruby, & Shaw, 2002). In general, the longer a crisis has been going on, the more appeal the leader's focus on tradition will have to those within a culture (Mumford, Scott et al., 2006).

PRAGMATIC LEADERSHIP

The last type of leadership we will discuss is **pragmatic leadership**. Pragmatic leaders are outstanding leaders because they are outstanding problem solvers (Mumford & Van Doorn, 2001). A pragmatic leader is an expert at identifying, analyzing, and solving problems, even in a crisis. Unlike a charismatic or ideological leader, a pragmatic leader does not have a vision. Instead, he or she focuses on the present problem and how to solve it. Because of this, pragmatic leaders are most likely to emerge when there is a specific problem with an objective solution. They are also more likely to appear if people have less of an emotional reaction to the problem at hand (Mumford et al., 2005). The classic example of a pragmatic leader is Benjamin Franklin (Mumford & Van Doorn). He was known more for his ability to solve problems than his ability to give a rousing speech and motivate followers. He was considered a great leader because he was able to think through and solve complex problems.

A pragmatic leader focuses on the present, rather than the future or past. This is because focusing on the future and past do not help a pragmatic leader solve the problem at hand. Rather, the pragmatic leader focuses on

> **Pragmatic leadership**—a leadership style in which the leader emphasizes knowledge management, expertise, problem solving, and consensus building rather than a loyal following or adherence to an ideological stance

the present and the specific aspects of a crisis that can be solved in the present (Mumford & Van Doorn, 2001). A pragmatic leader is also much less focused on goals and making changes, unless they are necessary to solve the problem. Changes, unless they definitely help solve a problem, are seen as unnecessary by the pragmatic leader. Because pragmatic leaders look at the objective aspects of a problem when trying to solve it, they believe different problems can be controlled to different degrees. This makes them more flexible than charismatic and ideological leaders when it comes to looking for solutions to problems (Mumford, Scott, et al., 2006).

Pragmatic leaders also try to balance the possible positive and negative consequences when they come up with solutions to a crisis (Mumford & Van Doorn, 2001). Again, this allows them to be more flexible than ideological and charismatic leaders, because the pragmatic leader does not just look for a perfect solution to a problem. Pragmatic leaders will accept solutions that may not make everyone perfectly happy, but that will mostly solve a given situation. This means pragmatic leaders can get support from more people than just those who agree with their value system, as occurs with charismatic or ideological leaders. They can also work more easily with multiple groups and try to come to a compromise if it is necessary to find a solution. Finally, they are more able to identify which actions will cause the greatest changes and whom those changes will benefit (Thomas & McDaniel, 1990). This allows them to set realistic expectations for their followers, which helps build trust in them as leaders.

The followers of a pragmatic leader are most attracted to the leader's past performance when solving problems (Mumford & Van Doorn, 2001). If pragmatic leaders are consistently able to solve problems, they will build up a feeling of trust from their followers. Each problem they are unable to solve undermines their relationship with their followers. The willingness of people to follow a pragmatic leader is nearly entirely based on objective results. The other aspect of pragmatic leadership that attracts followers is a pragmatic leader's willingness to listen to multiple points of view. This allows multiple groups to feel like they matter and that their concerns will be addressed in whatever solution the leader proposes. The followers of pragmatic leaders have two important functions. First, they are likely to produce and voice their own ideas for a solution to the problem (Mumford & Licuanan, 2004). Second, they are more likely to generate creative solutions to the problem that may not have been obvious to others (Mumford & Licuanan). This means the followers of pragmatic leaders may have a more direct impact on the final solution for a problem than the followers of charismatic or ideological leaders.

CHAPTER SUMMARY

In this chapter we have seen there are a number of ways to think about outstanding leadership. Charismatic leaders are leaders who inspire followers using a vision for the future. Their goals often revolve around this vision, and it gives their followers something to work toward. Transformational leaders are similar to charismatic leaders with regard to having a vision for the future. Where transformational leaders differ is their need to inspire, intellectually stimulate, and individually consider their followers. This focus on followers, rather than a vision, is what differentiates transformational leaders. Authentic leaders, on the other hand, are focused on being true to themselves and their values while leading others. Their followers come to trust them because of this authenticity. We see with the charismatic, ideological, and pragmatic framework that there may be multiple ways to be an outstanding leader. Charismatic leaders focus on the future, ideological leaders focus on the past, and pragmatic leaders focus on the present. After reading this chapter, you should realize there are a number of ways to become an outstanding leader and have an understanding of the possible impact outstanding leaders can have on the world around them.

KEY TERMS AND PHRASES

- Authentic followers
- Authentic leadership
- Charisma
- Charismatic leadership
- Confidence
- Empowering
- Ethics
- Forecasting
- Hope
- Ideological leadership
- Individual consideration
- Inspirational communication
- Intellectual stimulation
- Internal standards
- Optimism
- Pragmatic leadership
- Questioning assumptions
- Reframing
- Resilience
- Self-awareness
- Self-efficacy
- Self-regulation
- Transformational leaders
- Unconventional methods
- Values
- Vision

REVIEW QUESTIONS

1. What are the four theories of outstanding leadership discussed in this chapter?
2. Which leaders use a vision to motivate followers?

3. Why are followers drawn to charismatic leaders?
4. What is the benefit of asking followers to question their assumptions about a problem?
5. What are the five aspects of authentic leadership?
6. Why is self-regulation important for authentic leadership?
7. What makes the vision of ideological leaders different than the vision of charismatic leaders?
8. Which type of leader is likely to be the most controversial?
9. In what type of situation is an outstanding leader most likely to emerge?

DISCUSSION QUESTIONS

1. Which type of outstanding leadership do you think is best?
2. What are the main differences between charismatic, ideological, and pragmatic leaders?
3. Is there anyone you have known or worked for whom you would consider an outstanding leader? Why do you think they are outstanding, rather than just a regular leader?
4. Who are some examples of each of the types of outstanding leadership? Which type of outstanding leader would each example be?
5. Do you think a crisis is really necessary for the emergence of outstanding leaders? Explain your position.

INDIVIDUAL ACTIVITIES

INDIVIDUAL ACTIVITY 1

Given the following scenario, write out a possible solution using the approach a transformational leader might use:

The company is in a crisis. The organization is in massive debt, employees are quitting faster than they can be hired, and the organization's services are not in demand anymore in the current marketplace. You are the CEO of the organization and have essentially complete control over the company. What do you do to try to bring the company back from the brink of closing?

INDIVIDUAL ACTIVITY 2

Think of a leader from your own life. Explain which leader type they most closely matched. Then, explain what they would need to do to fit that style and be considered an outstanding leader based on the theories you read about in this chapter.

GROUP ACTIVITIES

GROUP ACTIVITY 1

As a group, pick a well-known leader. Explain why this leader may be an ideological, pragmatic, or charismatic leader. Then decide which type of leader your choice most resembles and justify your answer.

GROUP ACTIVITY 2

Read the following excerpt from John F. Kennedy's New Frontier speech. After reading, explain how the speech can be used as evidence that he was a charismatic leader. Make sure to cite specific examples when discussing which parts act as evidence of charismatic leadership.

> *The New Frontier is here whether we seek it or not. Beyond that frontier are uncharted areas of science and space, unsolved problems of peace*

and war, unconquered problems of ignorance and prejudice, unanswered questions of poverty and surplus. It would be easier to shrink from that new frontier, to look to the safe mediocrity of the past, to be lulled by good intentions and high rhetoric—and those who prefer that course should not vote for me or the Democratic Party. But I believe that the times require imagination and courage and perseverance. I'm asking each of you to be pioneers towards that New Frontier. My call is to the young in heart, regardless of age—to the stout in spirit, regardless of Party, to all who respond to the scriptural call: "Be strong and of a good courage; be not afraid, neither be [thou] dismayed." For courage, not complacency, is our need today; leadership, not salesmanship. And the only valid test of leadership is the ability to lead, and lead vigorously. A tired nation—A tired nation, said David Lloyd George, is a Tory nation. And the United States today cannot afford to be either tired or Tory. There may be those who wish to hear more—more promises to this group or that, more harsh rhetoric about the men in the Kremlin as a substitute for policy, more assurances of a golden future, where taxes are always low and the subsidies are always high. But my promises are in the platform that you have adopted. Our ends will not be won by rhetoric, and we can have faith in the future only if we have faith in ourselves.

SUGGESTED READINGS

Avolio, B. J., & Gardner, W. (2005). Authentic leadership development: Getting to the root of positive forms of leadership. *The Leadership Quarterly, 16*, 315–338.

Bass, B. M., & Riggio, R. (2006). *Transformational leadership* (2nd ed.). Mahwah, NJ: Lawrence Erlbaum Associates.

Conger, J., & Kanungo, R. (1998). *Charismatic leadership in organizations.* Thousand Oaks, CA: Sage Publications.

Mumford, M. D. (2006). *Pathways to outstanding leadership: A comparative analysis of charismatic, ideological, and pragmatic leaders.* Mahwah, NJ: Lawrence Erlbaum Associates.

Strange, J. M., & Mumford, M. D. (2002). The origins of vision: Charismatic versus ideological leadership. *The Leadership Quarterly, 13,* 343–377.

Yukl, G. (1999). An evaluation of conceptual weaknesses in transformational and charismatic leadership theories. *The Leadership Quarterly, 10,* 285–305.

Future Directions

Amanda S. Shipman

> The future belongs to those who see possibilities before
> they become obvious.
>
> —*John Scully*
>
> All progress is initiated by challenging current conceptions,
> and executed by supplanting existing institutions.
>
> —*George Bernard Shaw*

Throughout this book, you have learned about the history of leadership and many theories explaining a leader's influence. So, you may be asking yourself, is that all there is to leadership? The answer to this question is no. Actually, there are many questions researchers have recently been trying to answer, such as why some leaders go bad, how leaders operate in teams, and how diversity influences leadership. These areas and others will be discussed in this chapter.

Since the beginning of time, there have been leaders who used their influence and power to be destructive. In your history classes, you probably learned about leaders who acted in ways that resulted in negative consequences, even for their own followers. We

201

will talk about this destructive leadership, when it is more likely to occur, and when it might actually work. On the other hand, being a leader is not as simple as being good or bad. In reality, leaders face complicated situations that are far from black and white. They have to make decisions that will affect many people. Ultimately, making ethical decisions involves carefully thinking things through to make sense of a situation. The study of ethical leadership is another area of future research discussed in this chapter.

Another emerging area of research is leader relationships. In chapter 5, you learned about leader-member exchange theory and how leaders form different relationships with their followers. Recent research has started to look at how leaders form relationships with other people in their social network. Part of a leader's social network is the team they oversee. Leaders do not just have relationships with each follower individually. Instead, leaders may work within or oversee a team. We will talk about leadership in teams and how leaders can behave in ways that will make these teams more effective. One thing team leaders may do is give power and responsibilities to their team members. In this chapter, we will also talk about how team members may influence the team through shared or distributed leadership, even though they are not formal leaders.

We have already discussed how leadership effectiveness can depend on a situation. You might have also asked yourself if leadership effectiveness depends on where you are. In other words, a leader in China might act differently than a leader in the United States, and they might get different results even if they act the same way. In this chapter, we will discuss whether cultural differences call for different styles of leadership. Leaders may act differently depending on their culture, but do they act differently depending on their gender? Other chapters in this book do not separate findings between male and female leaders. You probably have seen similar numbers of women and men in leadership positions in projects or clubs, but you might have noticed there are fewer women in top leadership positions such as company CEOs. Researchers have explored why this might be the case. This chapter will discuss if there are, actually, any differences between male and female leaders.

Learning Objectives

- Develop an understanding of emerging areas of leadership research
- Become familiar with the dark side of leadership
- Recognize how the social context influences leadership
- Become familiar with the influence of diversity on leadership

DESTRUCTIVE LEADERSHIP

Leadership research has traditionally focused on studying the positive side of leaders. Many have tried to explain what good leaders are like, what they do, and what situations will help them accomplish their goals for the good of others. Yet, we have all seen leaders do bad things. In fact, you have probably experienced firsthand a leader who acted selfishly or bullied others. Acting in ways that are harmful to others may come more easily when people are put in positions of power (Mumford, Gessner, Connelly, O'Connor, & Clifton, 1993). This dark side of leadership has started to receive attention in the field in hopes that a better understanding will help us predict when it may occur and what might be done to prevent it. **Destructive leadership** involves a leader acting in ways that go against the best interests of the organization or his or her followers. The following section describes the components of destructive leadership.

DESTRUCTIVE LEADER

There are a number of ways to explain destructive leadership, and researchers have

Destructive leadership— leader behavior that is harmful to the organization and/or the leader's followers

used a variety of methods for studying destructive leadership. The first approach involves describing the characteristics of a destructive leader. Destructive leaders *act* in certain ways that are harmful to their followers, the broader organization, or both their followers and the organization. One model describes destructive leadership in terms of leader behaviors (Einarsen, Aasland, & Skogstad, 2007). It says leaders may or may not act in the best interest of their followers and/or the organization. So, a leader can engage in behaviors that are good for the organization and good for their subordinates (e.g., constructive leadership), bad for the organization and bad for their subordinates, or bad for one and good for the other. This results in four types of leadership, as seen in Figure 8.1—one that is constructive and three that are destructive.

The three destructive types are supportive-disloyal leadership (good for subordinates, bad for the organization), tyrannical leadership (good for the organization, bad for subordinates), and derailed leadership (bad for the organization and bad for subordinates). **Supportive-disloyal leaders** are overly concerned with having good relationships with their subordinates, and they neglect the organization. They may harm the organization by stealing materials or lying about time worked. The second kind of destructive leader is a **tyrannical leader,** where the organization's best

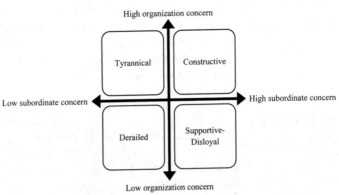

Figure 8.1 Behavioral classification of destructive leaders.

interests are pursued yet the subordinates' best interests are not. Tyrannical leaders may focus on achieving organizational goals and strategies, but they treat their subordinates badly. This abusive supervisor may behave in a number of ways that are harmful to his or her subordinates, like making fun of them, not giving them the information they need, using harsh language, or threatening and intimidating them (Zellars, Tepper, & Duffy, 2002). Have you experienced a leader like this? Someone who acted as if they did not care for you and the other subordinates at all, yet still worked toward the goals of the wider organization? You probably felt stressed out, wanted to quit, and felt the leader was unfair. If so, you are not alone; researchers have found these feelings to be true of followers of destructive leaders (Tepper, 2000). The last kind of destructive leader is the **derailed leader,** who does not pursue the legitimate interest of the organization or his or her subordinates. This may include acting in ways that undermine the organization's goals and objectives as well as manipulating and abusing subordinates. This type of leader may be impatient or short with others when trying to accomplish goals. Additional behaviors of the derailed leader could be ignoring errors or problems due to an unstoppable commitment to his or her own vision.

DESTRUCTIVE LEADER TRAITS

Narcissism

How do we know who might become one of these destructive leaders? Taking a trait-based approach helps us predict what types

Supportive-disloyal leader—a leader who acts in the best interest of his or her followers, while ignoring or acting against the organization's best interest

Tyrannical leader—a leader who acts in the best interest of the organization, while ignoring or acting against his or her followers' best interest

Derailed leader—a leader who ignores or acts against the best interest of both his or her followers and the organization

of personalities may be more likely to act in destructive ways. One such trait is narcissism. Narcissistic people love themselves, think they are more important than others, and think they deserve great things. The confidence and dominance that come from being narcissistic may actually help someone get into a leadership position (Hogan, Curphy, & Hogan, 1994). However, once narcissistic leaders are in leadership positions, they may become destructive because they are often more concerned with their own needs and interests than the interests of their followers or the organization (Rosenthal & Pittinsky, 2006).

Charisma

Another trait that is commonly discussed when describing destructive leaders is charisma. This may seem strange to you at first, because you might consider charisma a positive trait that would help leaders accomplish their goals (see chapter 7). This is true; being charismatic can help leaders sell a vision of the future that inspires and motivates their followers to work toward that vision (Conger, 1989). On the other hand, charisma serves the destructive leader in several ways. First, a destructive leader with charisma can sell a vision that describes the world as scary and unstable in order to encourage his or her followers to think everyone else is a rival threatening their personal safety (O'Connor, Mumford, Clifton, Gessner, & Connelly, 1995). Charismatic leaders are also skilled at communicating with others, and they could use this skill to manipulate other people to accomplish negative goals.

Power Orientation

As mentioned earlier in this chapter, giving power to someone may make them more likely to harm others (Mumford et al., 1993). You have probably heard Spiderman's credo: "With great power comes great responsibility." Even though we may not relate to the power of Spiderman, we can understand that the power associated with leadership positions also has this kind of responsibility.

Leaders who are destructive may use their power for their own selfish needs and desires while ignoring or even acting against the needs and desires of others. McClelland (1970, 1975) described this selfish use of power as **personalized power**, while **socialized power** entails acting for the good of others and not solely

> **Personalized power**—power that is used to serve selfish needs and desires while ignoring or even acting against the needs and desires of others
>
> **Socialized power**—power that acts for the good of others and not solely for oneself

for oneself. Individuals with personalized power motives may be more likely to become destructive than leaders with socialized power motives, because personalized power motives tend to make people ignore the impact of their actions on others.

Radical Belief System

A fourth, and final, trait associated with destructive leaders is an extreme worldview characterized by radical ideals and hate. Evidence for the relationship between ideological beliefs and violence was found in a study of historical leaders by Mumford, Espejo, and colleagues (2007). They concluded that certain characteristics associated with strong ideological beliefs might predispose leaders to engage in violent, destructive behavior. Consider the famous Al Qaeda leader, Osama bin Laden. He relies heavily on his followers' belief systems to commit themselves to his violent goals. Strange and Mumford (2002) suggested that destructive leaders have a worldview that is filled with hate for those who do not support their beliefs. This hate helps them justify using violence or whatever means necessary.

AT-RISK FOLLOWERS

In earlier chapters of the book, the importance of followers was discussed (see chapters 2 and 5). In studying the dark side of

Conformer—a follower who supports a destructive leader because of unmet safety needs and/or low levels of maturity
Colluder—a follower who supports a destructive leader because of shared goals and for personal gain

leadership, the role of followers has not been overlooked. A destructive leader is not going to have an effect without the right followers. Padilla, Hogan, and Kaiser (2007) suggested a number of characteristics that describe two types of followers—conformers and colluders—both of whom are likely to go along and serve the needs of a destructive leader. **Conformers** go along with a destructive leader because they feel unsafe or have low levels of maturity. On the other hand, **colluders** serve a destructive leader because they support his or her goals, usually because these goals will help the follower in some way.

The group of followers who as a whole support the acts of a destructive, violent leader may have certain characteristics as well. Insular groups are those that are tight knit and somewhat removed from others or broader society (Mumford, Espejo, et al., 2007). Groups that are tight knit and separated from others may begin to view outsiders as threatening rivals. These types of groups may be more likely to accept leaders who promote violent, destructive behavior because they no longer have those outside the group as a referent point for good behavior.

CONDUCIVE ENVIRONMENT

In order for a destructive leader to rise to power and obtain significant influence, the right environmental conditions need to be in place. When there are times of instability and crisis in an area (e.g. depression, war), a leader may be able to step in and assume control (Bass, 1985a; Conger & Kanungo, 1987). Because this disruption may require quick action, a leader may be given more power and leeway than normal. Followers will be anxious for someone to save the day and turn things around. So, when circumstances like this arise, a destructive leader is likely to turn the situation to their advantage. Consider the example of Adolf Hitler. One of the reasons Hitler was able to gain power was the dire economy the Germans were facing at the time.

Corrupt environments are also conducive to destructive leaders (Mumford, Espejo, et al., 2007). A corrupt environment exists when organizations are set up so that checks and balances are not in place. Another feature of corrupt environments is how a leader's power is assigned. When a leader is given too much power and has no accountability, he or she may be more prone to becoming destructive. An organization that structures a leader's power so that the leader is allowed to use violence for punishment may encourage destructive leadership.

CONSEQUENCES OF DESTRUCTIVE LEADERSHIP

In addition to describing destructive leaders in terms of traits and behaviors, we can also think about the outcomes they produce. Padilla and colleagues (2007) argued that in order to better identify what is actually destructive, one needs to look at the long-term consequences of a leader's behavior. Using this framework, it is possible for someone who is good (i.e., does not have the personality traits discussed above) to become a destructive leader and do bad things, and the same is also true in reverse. So, for example, someone can be a charismatic leader, but they may or may not become a destructive leader. The effects of destructive leadership on followers can be poor performance, deviant behavior, distress, and a number of other negative outcomes (Zellers et al., 2002). Organizations that employ destructive leaders are likely to have poor performance if the leader is not acting in the organization's best interest. Padilla and colleagues discussed the outcomes of a destructive leader—the former president of Cuba, Fidel Castro. After Castro's regime, the economy was seriously damaged, and one in four Cubans tried to flee the country.

Although negative outcomes are typical when a leader is destructive, a recent study provides an alternative perspective. Several positive outcomes can occur when leaders bully others (Ferris, Zinko, Brouer, Buckley, & Harvey, 2007). More specifically, bullying results in a leader being thought of as powerful, which may actually increase productivity. This productivity increase, however, will be short-lived, rather than long-term. It is likely that these followers increase their productivity in order to avoid abusive behavior. So, positive outcomes might occur for the organization in the short-term, but you can probably imagine things will not be quite so positive from the perspective of the followers, and they will ultimately become resentful, unproductive, or even leave the organization.

In summary, leadership is not always a positive thing; in fact, leaders may not act in the best interests of their organizations or followers. This leadership behavior may be more commonly found in individuals with certain types of personalities or beliefs, but a leader's personality alone does not completely describe destructive leadership. In fact, both the situation and the followers play a large role in whether or not a leader becomes destructive. When all three of these elements are in place (the leader, the followers, and the environment), destructive leadership is more likely to occur.

ETHICAL LEADERSHIP

A related line of research is the topic of ethical leadership. If destructive leadership is doing things to harm one's organization and/or followers, does ethical leadership represent the reverse side of the coin? The answer to this question is *probably* no. Brown and Trevino (2006) suggested that a person who is low in ethical behavior is not the same as a person who is actively behaving unethically (i.e., being destructive). Also, being destructive may include being unethical, but it does not necessarily involve an ethical component. That being said, more research is needed to explore the relationship between ethical leadership and unethical leadership, as well as destructive leadership.

Recently, a definition of **ethical leadership** has been proposed—acting in ways consistent with appropriate norms and promoting this behavior to one's followers (Brown, Trevino, & Harrison, 2005). One thing you should notice is that the behavior should be appropriate based on norms, or the commonly accepted behavior, rules, or procedures of a situation. This is not to say that moral principles are irrelevant. As a matter of fact, moral principles will often influence norms. However, what is ethically appropriate varies depending on the situation, and there are often multiple options that are ethical, unethical, or a mix of both. In the second half of the definition, you see it is not enough for a leader to act ethically in private; rather, ethical leadership involves promoting ethical behavior to one's followers. Leaders can communicate ethical values to their employees or followers. If a leader tells his or her subordinates that a certain rule is not important or goes against a rule in their own work, then that leader's followers will likely do the same. In this way, a leader can set the tone for ethical behavior. So, it is important how the followers perceive the leader's ethical behavior. For these reasons, we can see why ethical leadership is important.

> **Ethical leadership**—leadership characterized by behavior that is consistent with appropriate norms and promoting this behavior to followers

Now that you have a better understanding of ethical leadership, we will turn to a model that has been proposed to describe it. This model, developed by Brown and Trevino (2006). is likely to serve as the basis for future research in this area. Within this model, an underlying assumption is that ethical leadership is most important in terms of follower perceptions. Followers perceive how ethically a leader behaves, which will in turn influence their own ethical behavior. This model suggests that ethical behavior is influenced by both situational influences and leader characteristics.

SITUATIONAL INFLUENCES

Situational influences, like the presence of ethical role models and the ethical context, affect how ethical a leader will be. You probably have had a role model, somebody that you looked up to and tried to imitate. Researchers have found that followers who claim to have an **ethical role model**—someone who not only behaves in an ethical manner, but who also learns from his or her mistakes and shows humility—were shaped in their own ethical leadership (Trevino, Hartman, & Brown, 2000). The next situational influence is the ethical context in the organization. The **ethical context** is strongly related to the ethical climate of the organization, which deals with the normal practices and processes related to ethics (Victor & Cullen, 1988). When an organization has an ethical climate, its employees tend to be more committed to the organization and have better attitudes about ethics (Trevino, Weaver, Gibson, & Toffler, 1999).

Ethical role model—an individual others can look up to who behaves in an ethical manner, learns from mistakes, and shows humility

Ethical context—the normal practices and processes within an organization that dictate and guide ethical behavior

LEADER CHARACTERISTICS

An ethical leader may have certain attributes that come into play. These personality characteristics were probably the first thing that came to mind when you thought about what determines if a leader is ethical. You may have thought, "Well, if the leader is a *good* person, then they will be ethical." Remember, though, that situational influences have a strong impact on whether a leader will be ethical or not, so putting too much emphasis on this particular factor would be a mistake. Brown and Trevino (2006) believe

> **Moral reasoning**—the ability to understand and work through complex ethical situations

moral reasoning, or the ability to understand and work through complex ethical situations, influences ethical leadership. However, just having the ability to reason through moral situations does not mean that someone will use this ability. For this reason, those who actually use this moral reasoning ability will be more ethical than those who simply have the ability.

It is not uncommon for leaders to have a desire for power, and this may actually help them be more effective. How a leader *uses* this power helps us predict whether they will behave ethically. Followers are likely to think of leaders who use their power for the good of others as more worthy role models than leaders who use their power only to meet their personal needs (Brown & Trevino, 2006). Another leader characteristic related to ethical leadership is Machiavellianism (see chapter 4). Remember that this trait has to do with a leader manipulating others in order to get what he or she wants. Since this trait involves being comfortable with manipulating others, these people are more open to engaging in unethical behavior.

OUTCOMES OF ETHICAL LEADERSHIP

There are a number of outcomes that may occur if a leader is ethical (Brown & Trevino, 2006). These outcomes reflect an influence on follower behavior and, in particular, their ethical behavior. First, followers will learn how to make ethical decisions without the immediate supervision of a leader if they have been able to see that leader behaving ethically. Beyond making ethical decisions, followers will develop trust in their leader and will feel personally obligated to him or her. When followers feel personal obligation toward their leader, they may be more willing to go outside of their formal job requirements to help the leader and the organization. For the same reasons, followers will probably be less inclined to engage in behavior that is harmful to the organization if their leader is a strong ethical role model. In addition to follower behavior, ethical leadership has an influence on follower attitudes such as satisfaction and dedication (Brown et al., 2005). It is clear that ethical leadership is beneficial for a number of reasons.

MAKING ETHICAL DECISIONS

The model described above is useful in understanding the influences and outcomes of ethical leadership. While the focus on follower perception is useful because of the impact leaders may have on their followers' ethical behavior, it is also critical to think about *how* leaders work through ethical dilemmas or problems. Recent research has attempted to explore what processes scientists go through to make ethical decisions (Mumford, Connelly, et al., 2008). Though this model focuses on the ethical decision making of scientists, the thought processes may be similar for leaders because they both face complex, ambiguous situations. This process starts with identifying the ethical problem, experiencing and managing emotional responses, predicting the likely outcomes of potential actions, and reflecting on past experiences to evaluate these potential outcomes. When a scientist works through these thought processes, he or she is able to make sense of the situation and is then better equipped to make an ethical decision. Whether this or a similar process is relevant for leaders will be an avenue of future research.

After a leader has made a decision, determining if it was ethical can be based on several factors—the decision's purpose, its consistency with moral standards, and, lastly, the outcomes associated with the decision (Yukl, 2006). It is possible that these three things are at odds; for example, where the purpose may justify adopting less than virtuous moral standards. Typically, the moral component is a gray area, because multiple factors can influence whether something is considered moral or not. For leader behavior, moral standards are often determined by things like inconsistency with laws, blocking others' rights, putting individuals in harm's way, or the deception and exploitation of others (Yukl). Remember, the norms of a situation count in evaluating whether a decision was ethical or not.

In conclusion, ethical leadership is affected by a number of factors, including situational influences and leader characteristics. Being an ethical leader means not just behaving ethically, but also promoting ethical behavior to others. When organizations have ethical leaders in place, desirable outcomes may be more likely to occur.

LEADER SOCIAL NETWORKS

Recent research has started to emphasize the fact that leadership occurs in a social context. Balkundi and Kilduff (2006) described how the **social network**, or the set of social relationships a leader has, will influence a leader's effectiveness. These authors also suggest that the way a leader *thinks* about his or her network plays a critical role in the leader's effectiveness. Studying leader social networks is related to leader-member exchange (LMX) theory (see chapter 5). Remember that LMX describes how leaders form relationships with their followers. The social network perspective takes a broader approach and is not just limited to the relationships the leader has with his or her followers, but extends to all other relationships.

There are three critical concepts for social network researchers (Kilduff, Tsai, & Hanke, 2006). First, social

> **Social network**—a set of relationships that a leader has with other individuals, groups, and organizations

Social capital—the idea that relationships are a valuable resource, and that knowing the right people can help leaders in a number of ways (e.g., providing information, getting permission, obtaining funding)

network researchers study the relationships between different individuals, groups, and organizations, as opposed to just the individual. Second, human behavior does not occur in a vacuum; it occurs within the context of social relationships. Thus, it is inappropriate to study the behavior of an individual without considering their social network. The third, and final, idea critical to studying social networks is that relationships are a valuable resource called **social capital.** Knowing the right people—having social capital—can help leaders in a number of ways, such as by providing information, permission, funding, and many other things.

TYPES OF LEADER NETWORKS

Figure 8.2 presents a model of leadership networks as proposed by Balkundi and Kilduff (2005). Within this model, three types of leadership networks are suggested: the ego network, the organizational network, and the interorganizational network. All three networks are influenced by how a leader thinks about and understands these networks. The **ego network** represents the immediate ties a leader has to others. In order to be effective, a leader should maintain relationships with a variety of different people. Having relationships with different kinds of people will allow a leader to get different kinds of information and resources. However, having rela-

Ego network—relationships that a leader has with other individuals

tionships with different kinds of people is typically easier said than done. Most people tend to develop relationships with those who are similar to them (McPherson, Smith-

Figure 8.2 Types of leader social networks.

Lovin, & Cook, 2001). This preference to surround ourselves with those like us stands in the way of developing a diverse network.

The next kind of network is the **organizational network** (Balkundi & Kilduff, 2005). A leader's effectiveness will depend not only on his or her relationships, but also on how well he or she understands the relationships between others in the organization (Sparrowe & Liden, 2005; Sparrowe, Liden, Wayne, & Kramer, 2001). It is beneficial for the leader to not only understand the relationships of others in the group, but also in the broader organization. The leader needs to know to whom others in the organization go for help with particular kinds of problems or how certain individuals get along. The leader can encourage relationships to form, which can then help the leader perform better and can also serve the organization. So, the leader may want the subordinates in his or her workgroup to develop relationships with others with specific knowledge or authority. The last type of network involves relationships outside of a leader's organization,

> **Organizational network—** relationships that exist within an individual's organization

Interorganizational network—relationships that the leader and individuals within the leader's organization have with others outside of the organization

which may be crucial to his or her performance and the organization's performance. This type of network is labeled an **interorganizational network**. Developing connections with other organizations or external leaders may help a leader share information or form alliances. The leader should also be aware of other people's ties to important figures outside the organization. This understanding can be used to the leader's advantage.

In sum, the literature on leader social networks is rapidly growing. This research helps us better understand the nature of leader relationships and how these relationships ultimately influence leader performance. Leaders should develop relationships in three types of networks, including the ego network, the organizational network, and the interorganizational network. Having relationships with others important people is not enough, though. Leaders must also understand how their network and the other networks surrounding them are arranged.

LEADERSHIP IN TEAMS

In today's world, it is common for organizations to structure work in teams. Leaders do not just manage a set of independently working employees, but instead are found in team settings. A **team** is defined as a group of individuals working collectively to accomplish shared work (O'Connor & Quinn, 2004). This section will describe the nature of leadership in team settings. One critical component of effective teams is team leader-

Team—a group of individuals working collectively to accomplish shared work

ship (Salas, Sims, & Burke, 2005). Team leadership consists of organizing a team's activities and coordinating its efforts to achieve desirable performance. Apart from the immediate team performance, a leader can serve a team more indirectly by developing the team's knowledge, skills, and abilities, as well as keeping teammates motivated by creating a positive atmosphere. As you can see, leaders may serve multiple important roles in coordinating team behavior.

LEADER CENTRALITY

Effective team leaders rely on informal power (see chapter 5); this kind of power can come from having relevant expertise or from being well liked. Leaders may gain this informal power by being central to a team's social network, as this allows them control over the flow of resources (Balkundi & Kilduff, 2006. Apart from controlling resources, being central to the team should keep the leader in the know and aware of the team's status on its work.

On the other hand, being central to the team's network may not always be a good thing. For example, if a leader is central to a network, he or she may be hesitant to punish or reprimand team members; the leader may be overly concerned with those hurting relationships. Another potential disadvantage is that the leader may think too similarly to the team members and have difficulty defining poor performance. Even though there are drawbacks to being central to a team's social network, Balkundi and Harrison (2006) provided evidence that the benefits outweigh the drawbacks. They reviewed studies about leader centrality in team networks and found that, overall, having a leader who was central to a team's network was positively related to team performance.

TEAM INFLUENCE

Leaders may help teams by setting goals and providing them with needed resources. A leader does not just influence team effectiveness; the team also influences the effectiveness of the leader (Zaccaro & Klimoski, 2002). In fact, leadership may develop in reaction to a team's operations and then can be used to increase future team performance (Marks, Mathieu, & Zaccaro, 2001). Imagine a committee that has been asked to complete a project. The committee meets and together decides who is going to be in charge of specific parts of the project. Afterwards, they split up and work on their respective tasks. If one team member has expertise in an area of the project that requires multiple team members to check with him or her, then that team member may become the informal leader. This leader emerged because of the way the work was being done.

Leadership in teams offers a unique perspective to the study of leadership. Understanding the dynamics of power helps us better understand how leaders may emerge in a team setting. Once a leader has emerged in a team setting, he or she may engage in behaviors that will directly and indirectly contribute to team performance.

DISTRIBUTED LEADERSHIP

Developed teams may have more options for how leadership should be established. This versatility includes sharing or distributing leadership responsibilities across team members. **Distributed leadership** theories propose that leadership responsibilities may be held by multiple individuals. This idea is relatively new to leadership research, where the field has traditionally focused on leaders as individual people. However, it is far more likely that leadership responsibilities, like making decisions, are shared among team members or are delegated to the best qualified team member (Yukl, 2006).

Distributed leadership— leadership where responsibilities are not held by one person, but instead are held by multiple individuals

FACILITATING CONDITIONS

Certain conditions within a team may make shared leadership a viable option, including team members having a shared purpose, social support, and voice (Carson, Tesluk, & Marrone, 2007). If team members have a **shared purpose,** then they are on the same page about their goals and are going to be more motivated, empowered, and committed to the team. Being more motivated, empowered, and committed tends to make team members more willing and open to share leadership responsibilities in the team (Avolio, Jung, & Sivasubramaniam, 1996). The second factor is social support. **Social support** exists in a team when members are there for each other by acknowledging each other's contributions. When this social support exists, team members work better together and feel responsible for the group's work (Kirkman & Rosen, 1999). The last element is **voice,** the feeling that each team member can contribute input as to how the team will carry out its work. When team members feel comfortable voicing their opinions, they will share in the influences of the group, which is related to distributed leadership. Together, these three factors facilitate an internal team environment that is conducive to shared leadership.

> **Shared purpose**—a characteristic of teams where individuals within the team have agreed upon objectives and goals
>
> **Social support**—a characteristic of teams where the individuals on the team provide consideration and acknowledgement to one another
>
> **Voice**—the feeling that each team member can contribute input as to how the team will carry out its work

In addition to these three factors critical within the team, having leadership external to the team should also help in the development of shared leadership capacities (Carson et al., 2007). The leadership external to the team should be supportive rather than intrusive or disruptive. Intrusive external leadership will stand in the way of developing the autonomy and self-management needed to share leadership responsibilities (Morgeson, 2005). Supportive leadership outside the team will tend to increase the team members' feelings of self-competence and independence within the team. When the team members feel more self-competent and independent, they may be more likely to feel comfortable and able to take on leadership responsibilities. This supportive external leader may also check the team's activities to make sure that they are in line with the organization's broader strategies (Hackman & Wageman, 2005).

OUTCOMES OF DISTRIBUTED OR SHARED LEADERSHIP

The relationship between shared leadership and team performance is not simple (Mehra, Smith, Dixon, & Robertson, 2006). Different types of distributed leadership relate differently to performance. More specifically, when the team has a distributed-coordinated leadership structure, team performance increases. **Distributed-coordinated leadership** structures represent teams that have a formal leader as well as a leader that has emerged informally. If these two leaders can acknowledge each other's leadership and work well together, then team performance will be positively influenced.

On the other hand, **distributed-fragmented leadership** teams tend to have lower performance. Like distributed-coordinated

> **Distributed-coordinated leadership**—leadership where teams have a formal leader and an informal leader, and where both leaders acknowledge and accept each other's leadership role
>
> **Distributed-fragmented leadership**—leadership where teams have both formal and informal leaders, but where the leaders do not work well together and do not recognize each other as leaders

teams, distributed-fragmented teams have both formal and informal leaders. But, when the team is fragmented, these two leaders do not work well together and do not recognize each other as leaders. The last kind of structure, the traditional **leader-centered teams** structure, represents a lack of shared or distributed leadership where there is only one formal leader. These teams tend to have lower performance than distributed-coordinated teams. You may be wondering why distributed leadership is broken down into these two categories (i.e., distributed-coordinated and distributed-fragmented), both of which distribute leadership to two team members, as opposed to many or all team members. It is very unlikely for teams to distribute leadership responsibilities to most or all of the team members, and it is far more common to see leadership distributed among just a few team members (Guetzkow & Simon, 1955).

> **Leader-centered teams—** teams that have only one individual who holds formal leadership responsibilities, with no informal leaders to share the responsibilities

In sum, distributed leadership is likely to emerge in teams that have a shared purpose, social support, and voice. When these conditions are present, a team may have the capacity to share leadership responsibilities among its members. However, this shared leadership will only increase team performance when those with leadership responsibilities recognize each other as leaders in what is called a distributed-coordinated team structure.

CROSSCULTURAL LEADERSHIP

Leaders today are often in positions where they must influence people from different cultures. Businesses are spreading to different countries, and people from different cultures are working side by side. This begs the question: Does the effectiveness of leadership vary by culture? **Crosscultural leadership** deals with the extent to which a leader's influence is specific to particular cultures and the extent to which it differs by culture.

> **Crosscultural leadership—**
> leadership across cultures;
> the extent to which a leader's
> influence is specific to par-
> ticular cultures and the extent
> to which it differs by culture

CROSSCULTURAL DIFFERENCES

Dorfman and colleagues (1997) found there were, in fact, some differences in leadership across cultures. Specifically, leader supportiveness, contingent reward (e.g., giving rewards based on high performance), and charismatic leadership were considered to be valuable in multiple countries, including Japan, South Korea, Taiwan, Mexico, and the United States. On the other hand, it was found that participative leadership, directive leadership, and contingent punishment were valued in some places but not in others. More specifically, contingent punishment, or punishing poor performance, was effective leader behavior in the United States, but not in the other four countries. In Mexico and Taiwan, it was effective to use directive leadership, where the leader was authoritarian, while in the United States and South Korea, it was effective to engage in participative leadership behavior, or giving followers more discretion and power.

Crosscultural research is not an easy area to study. Yukl (2006) proposed a number of issues confronting this area of research. For example, if one country develops a measure or questionnaire, that measure may not mean the same thing in another culture. Additionally, individuals from different cultures may have different biases in how they respond to measures. So, people from a certain culture may be more comfortable responding to questionnaires in the middle level, whereas other cultures may tend to mark high or low responses. Even if a study is well designed, there can still be problems in understanding why differences were found. Thus, a researcher may determine that a given leadership behavior is more effective in one culture than it is in another culture, but explaining why it is the case may still be impossible. These unique challenges to crosscultural research call for systematic research and careful evaluation of the methods used.

CULTURAL VALUES

One way to explain differences found in leader behavior and effectiveness is using cultural values. Cultural values have a wide-reaching influence on the norms of a culture, and they tend to be ingrained in a leader who grows up in a region (Yukl, 2006). Hofstede (1980, 1998) proposed four dimensions of cultural values: power distance, uncertainty avoidance, individualism-collectivism, and masculinity-femininity. These values may influence leadership in a number of ways (Dickson, Den Hartog, & Mitchelson, 2003). **Power distance** involves how willing individuals in a society are to accept some individuals or institutions having more power than others. When a society has a high power distance, people are more accepting of unequal power distributions and may be less comfortable disagreeing or going against a leader. If a society has a low power distance, the citizens are going to be less accepting of authority and may expect to be involved in decision making or setting goals. The second of Hofstede's (1980) cultural dimensions is **uncertainty avoidance.** This dimension represents the extent to which members of a society are comfortable with ambiguity and

> **Power distance**—the extent to which the individuals of a society are willing to accept some individuals or institutions having more power than others
> **Uncertainty avoidance**—the extent to which the individuals of a society are comfortable with ambiguity and uncertainty

225

uncertainty. When societies do not like uncertainty, they will try to avoid it or reduce it somehow, usually through rules and norms. People that do not like uncertainty will be uncomfortable taking risks and will think that cautious, predictable leaders are the most effective.

The third cultural dimension is **individualism-collectivism.** Collectivistic societies have a tight social framework, where individuals have strong loyalty and commitment to their social groups. As a result of their loyalty to the group, collectivistic societies tend to be more dedicated to a group's goals and a leader's vision of the future. Individualistic societies tend to value being unique and autonomous. People with these individualistic values may not readily buy into a group's goals or a leader's vision, but instead may respond more positively to opportunities for personal achievement and rewards. Hofstede's (1998) last cultural dimension is **masculinity-femininity.** Societies that lean toward masculine values emphasize characteristics like dominance and a focus on work, while feminine values emphasize consideration of others and supportiveness. Cultures that tend to be masculine view leaders with masculine characteristics as more effective, and cultures that tend to be feminine view leaders with feminine characteristics as more effective.

> **Individualism-collectivism—** the extent to which the individuals of a society are independent and focused on individual achievement versus identified strongly with groups and seeking group achievement
>
> **Masculinity-femininity—** the extent to which the individuals of a society value traditionally masculine traits or behaviors versus feminine traits or behaviors

These dimensions of cultural attitudes have been widely used, but they are not without criticism (e.g., Dickson et al., 2003). Such criticisms include the dimensions being too simple, the use of poor measures, and ignoring cultural differences within any given country. Additionally, cultural values change over time (Yukl, 2006), which some say has been ignored in these dimensions. Even given these criticisms, Hofstede's (1980, 1998) dimensions have had a significant effect on crosscultural research and stand as a valuable approach to considering the effect of values on leadership research.

The recent surge in crosscultural research has provided the field of leadership with new ideas and insights as to why leadership may vary by culture. Cultural values, including power distance, uncertainty avoidance, individualism-collectivism, and masculinity-femininity, have been used to explain why these differences occur. Even though cultural values help explain why differences occur, caution should be used in crosscultural research for the number of unique challenges it poses.

GENDER AND LEADERSHIP

In the 21st century, we have begun to see women in the leadership positions that were reserved for men 50 years ago. As the face of leadership changes, researchers have become interested in studying whether there are any differences between male and female leaders. Do they act differently and do they perform differently? This section will describe the current field of gender and leadership research.

DIFFERENCES BETWEEN MALE AND FEMALE LEADERS

Although the gender gap is closing, we still see more men in top leadership positions. Why have women faced a glass ceiling, where it seems difficult to climb to the highest ranks of organizations? Sex-based discrimination may be the answer (Yukl, 2006). Traditionally, the traits used to describe an effective leader—such as confidence, competitiveness, and assertiveness—were considered masculine (see chapter 4 for more traits). However, today we have a better understanding of a leader's role, and we understand that these masculine traits may not always describe the most effective leader. Another explanation for sex-based discrimination is stereotypes. In years past, the common belief was that women were not interested in leadership positions, or that they were incapable of fulfilling leadership responsibilities. Though this belief is becoming less persistent, the residual effect may still be felt today. Both of these explanations help explain why we see fewer women in leadership positions.

Some might argue that the differences we see in the number of women in leadership positions are explained by legitimate reasons, rather than sex-based discrimination. In other words, do we see fewer women in leadership positions because of real differences between male and female leaders? To answer this question, researchers have carefully studied whether men and women behave differently as leaders. Some studies have reported differences in male and female behavior (e.g., Eagly, 1995). Men are described as more aggressive, while women are described as more expressive in their emotions and compassionate. On the other hand, researchers have carefully reviewed the findings of gender and leadership behavior and have found that there are no significant differences in the behavior of male and female leaders (Eagly & Johnson, 1990). You may be surprised that differences in leadership behavior do not exist. Vecchio (2002) suggested that the organizational context in which leaders are placed imposes constraints on leadership behavior, where extreme masculine or feminine behaviors are restrained.

The question of whether men or women are more effective in leadership positions must still be considered. That is, does one gender perform better than the other in leadership positions? Researchers have reviewed findings related to leadership effectiveness (Eagly, Karau, & Makhijani, 1995), and these findings are clear: There are no differences in male and female leader effectiveness. Further, the mere fact that sex differences are reported infrequently is meaningful in itself because such differences are relatively simple to incorporate in research studies (Vecchio, 2002). However, it may be that effectiveness could differ by particular leadership positions. In other words, military leadership positions may find differences in the effectiveness of male and female leaders (Eagly et al.). More research needs to be conducted to determine if this is the case.

By and large, the research has demonstrated that male and female leaders are no different in terms of their behavior or their effectiveness. The differences that exist today in the number of men and women in leadership positions may be left over from the stereotypes and discrimination of the past. If this is the case, the gender gap should become smaller in future years.

CHAPTER SUMMARY

This chapter has provided you with just a taste of the future of leadership research. Researchers have become increasingly focused on describing leadership phenomena more comprehensively and realistically. As such, we do not simply glorify the leader as a hero with power and popularity. Instead, we understand that being a leader carries many responsibilities and difficulties. Since leaders are human, we are likely to see them be ineffective . . . and not just ineffective, but destructive. Such destructive leadership represents what we call the dark side of leadership. Researchers have realized that destructive leadership is not simply a destructive individual seizing power. Rather, destructive leadership is characterized not only by a destructive leader, but also by certain environmental and follower characteristics. Similarly, ethical leadership does not just entail an ethical and virtuous person in a leadership position. Ethical leadership, like destructive leadership, is a result of certain factors related to the environment and the organization that the leader operates within. Researchers in these areas have started to realize that many factors play into both the dark side and the ethical side of leadership. It has become clear that leaders themselves are affected by their social context.

This social context has prompted an interest in how leaders form relationships with others. A leader's relationships, and also that leader's understanding of their own and other relationship networks, are critical to leadership performance. Leaders have relationships with other people, groups, and organizations. One group a leader forms a relationship with is the team they lead. It is likely the leader will not be acting independently, but rather will be working within a team. This social context influences the leader's performance as well as the team's performance. Oftentimes, leadership in teams is shared among a few individuals. In fact, a team may be able to increase its performance by having a limited number of team members distribute or share leadership responsibilities. This distributed leadership will only work if the leaders in the team can work together and accept each other's leadership roles.

The social context is not the only context useful to consider when studying leadership. Examining the influence of cultural factors sheds light on how leadership occurs around the world. Another factor that has sparked researchers' interest is the difference between male and female leaders. Although most people can agree that men and women are different, the research mostly demonstrates they are not different in terms of their leadership behaviors or effectiveness. Thus, in the future, we are likely to see more equal numbers of women and men in leadership positions.

As you can see from reading this chapter and this book, leadership research has expanded significantly since the trait approaches of the early 1950s. We no longer try to remove the leader from their context, as we now know the context has a marked influence on the leader. As such, leadership research is ever growing and changing.

KEY TERMS AND PHRASES

- Colluder
- Conformer
- Crosscultural leadership
- Derailed leader
- Destructive leadership
- Distributed-coordinated leadership
- Distributed-fragmented leadership
- Distributed leadership
- Ego network
- Ethical context
- Ethical leadership
- Ethical role model
- Individualism-collectivism
- Interorganizational network
- Leader-centered teams
- Masculinity-femininity
- Moral reasoning
- Organizational network
- Personalized power
- Power distance
- Shared purpose
- Social capital
- Social network
- Social support
- Socialized power
- Supportive-disloyal leader
- Team
- Tyrannical leader
- Uncertainty avoidance
- Voice

REVIEW QUESTIONS

1. What personality traits are related to destructive leadership?
2. How do leaders make ethical decisions?
3. What are the types of leader networks?
4. When does distributed leadership help team performance?
5. What influence do cultural values have on crosscultural leadership?
6. How do men and women differ in leadership positions?
7. Why are there fewer women than men in leadership positions?

DISCUSSION QUESTIONS

1. Why might making ethical decisions be more difficult for leaders than for other people?
2. Have you ever been on a team where a leader was ineffective and hurt team performance? How did he or she hurt performance?
3. What is the importance of leader centrality? What are the pros and cons of leader centrality?
4. How do you think culture might shape gender differences in leadership?

INDIVIDUAL ACTIVITIES

INDIVIDUAL ACTIVITY 1

Draw your social network as a leader, current or past. What relationships are particularly useful to you and why? What relationships would help you be more effective?

INDIVIDUAL ACTIVITY 2

Select a successful leader in a foreign country. Use what you know about Hofstede's cultural dimensions to describe why and how that leader is effective in their country. Would this leader be effective in the United States? Why or why not?

GROUP ACTIVITIES

GROUP ACTIVITY 1

Give examples of famous leaders who were or are destructive (e.g., supportive-disloyal, tyrannical, or derailed). What leader behaviors demonstrate how you classified these leaders?

GROUP ACTIVITY 2

Find profiles of two or three successful female leaders. What do these women credit as the reasons for their success? How are their male counterparts different?

SUGGESTED READINGS

Borgatti, S. P., & Foster, P. C. (2003). The network paradigm in organizational research: A review and typology. *Journal of Management, 29*, 991–1013.

Burke, C. S., Stagl, K. C., Klein, C., Goodwin, G. F., Salas, E., & Halpin, S. M. (2006). What type of leadership behaviors are functional in teams? A meta-analysis. *The Leadership Quarterly, 17*, 288–307.

Ciulla, J. B. (2004). *Ethics, the heart of leadership* (2nd ed.). Westport, CT: Praeger.

House, R. J., Hanges, P., & Ruiz-Quintanila, S. A. (Eds.) (2004). *Leadership, culture, and organizations: The GLOBE study of 62 societies*. Thousand Oaks, CA: Sage Publications.

Lauterback, K. E., & Weiner, B. J. (1996). Dynamics of upward influence: How male and female managers get their way. *The Leadership Quarterly, 7,* 87–107.

Mehra, A., Smith, B. R., Dixon, A. L., & Robertson, B. (2006). Distributed leadership in teams: The network of leadership perceptions and team performance. *The Leadership Quarterly, 17,* 232–245.

Glossary

Ability to learn—the ability to recognize a learning experience and use that experience to adapt to changes in the environment

Attributions—perceptions about others' behavior

Authentic followers—individuals who follow a leader because of personal beliefs and values

Authentic leadership—leadership based on personal beliefs and values

Authoritarianism—an individual's tendency to stress authority and power

Authority—a right, or claim of legitimacy, that serves as a justification to exercise power

Big Five—a common set of personality characteristics: openness, conscientiousness, extroversion, agreeableness, neuroticism

Behavioral flexibility—the ability and the willingness to change one's behavior in response to a situation

Behavioral theory of leadership—a theory that describes leaders in terms of the actions they take rather than the traits they possess

Championing—behaviors that leaders use to create interest and excitement for new projects

Change-oriented behavior—leader behaviors that are directed at encouraging and facilitating change in organizations

Charisma—a quality of individuals that makes others perceive them as extraordinary; this perception motivates people to follow them

Charismatic leadership—a leadership style in which a leader tends to express a positive vision of the future, is highly self-confident, appears honest and generous, and attracts a wide variety of followers who are loyal to the leader rather than the leader's agenda or organization

Coercive power—power that involves a follower avoiding punishment from the person in power

Cognition—mental events where perceptions, memories, and thoughts are processed

Cognitive frameworks—the categories and their connections into which individuals place events, behaviors, objects, attributes, and concepts

Cognitive resources leadership theory—a theory that emphasizes the type of intelligence a leader uses when dealing with problems or making decisions

Cognitive theories of leadership—theories that emphasize how leaders think and make decisions in determining leader effectiveness

Cognitive traits—the characteristics of a person's ability to think or style of thinking

Cohesive—the status of a group when members are highly attracted and connected to the other members of the group

Colluder—a follower who supports a destructive leader because of shared goals and for personal gain

Confidence—a faith in one's own abilities to accomplish something

Conformer—a follower who supports a destructive leader because of unmet safety needs and/or low levels of maturity

Consideration—leader behavior that involves a leader showing concern for the well-being of his or her employees

Content analysis—a process of reviewing collected qualitative data where the information is examined for certain variables, themes, or patterns; often called content coding when numerical values are assigned to qualitative data

Contingency theory of leadership—a theory suggesting that leaders are well suited to lead in some circumstances, but that they may be ill equipped to lead in other circumstances

Control group—a group in an experiment that is given no treatment

Control variables—variables that a researcher wants to hold constant

Creative problem solving—cognitive processes that produce a novel, useful solution

Creativity interventions—training designed to enhance creative problem-solving skills

Crosscultural leadership—leadership across cultures; the extent to which a leader's influence is specific to particular cultures and the extent to which it differs by culture

Data—the pieces of information observed or obtained through research

Decision making—the process of understanding a complex situation in order to make a high-stakes decision

Dependent variables—variables that depend on, or are affected by, independent variables

Deindividuation—a situation where members become too entrenched in a group and lose their own identities

Derailed leader—a leader who ignores or acts against the best interest of both his or her followers and the organization

Destructive leadership—leader behavior that is harmful to the organization and/or the leader's followers

Directive leadership—letting subordinates know what they are expected to do, giving specific guidance, asking subordinates to follow rules and procedures, and scheduling and coordinating work

Distributed leadership—leadership where responsibilities are not held by one person, but instead are held by multiple individuals

Distributed-coordinated leadership—leadership where teams have a formal leader and an informal leader, and where both leaders acknowledge and accept each other's leadership role

Distributed-fragmented leadership—leadership where teams have both formal and informal leaders, but where the leaders do not work well together and do not recognize each other as leaders

Ego network—relationships that a leader has with other individuals

Emotional intelligence—the ability to recognize one's own feelings and the feelings of others

Emotional maturity—a realistic awareness of one's emotions and abilities

Empowering—a process by which leaders make followers feel more confident in their own abilities and their importance to the group

Energy level and stress tolerance—the abilities of remaining alert for prolonged periods of time and handling stressful situations

Ethical context—the normal practices and processes within an organization that dictate and guide ethical behavior

Ethical leadership—leadership characterized by behavior that is consistent with appropriate norms and promoting this behavior to followers

Ethical role model—an individual others can look up to who behaves in an ethical manner, learns from mistakes, and shows humility

Ethics—an individual's personal beliefs about right and wrong

Experience—active participation that leads to the accumulation of knowledge or skill

Experimental conditions—the different groupings of participants for whom different treatments of the independent variables are applied

Experimental research—research where variables of interest are isolated and studied directly by the researcher, who manipulates the independent variable of interest and controls all other variables

Expert power—power that involves a follower's beliefs that the person in power is knowledgeable and competent

Expertise—a deep understanding and knowledge of a specific area or situation

Feedback—behaviors that provide evaluation and direction for a subordinate's work

Field research—research conducted in the natural context

Followers—those individuals on whom a leader exerts influence for the purpose of achieving a collective goal

Forecasting—predicting what the world would be like if certain problems were solved

Goal-oriented activities—actions taken by a leader to set, change, clarify, or define group goals

Historiometric research—a research method where historical information is studied

Hope—a positive feeling of motivation that a task or goal can realistically be accomplished

Hypothesis—a statement that arises from a theory that states an expected relationship between variables

Ideological leadership—a leadership style in which a leader tends to express the desire to return to an idealized past state and attracts a small group of highly devoted followers with a value system similar to that of the leader

Idiosyncrasy credits—credits that a leader builds up with successful ideas over time

Implicit theories of leadership—theories that examine how peoples' beliefs and assumptions about leadership influence their perceptions of and behavior toward leadership

Impression management—the process by which leaders and followers engage in behaviors to influence how others perceive them

Impression management tactics—behaviors that influence how leaders and followers are perceived

Independent variables—variables that account for, or explain, the phenomenon of interest in research studies

Individual consideration—the process of thinking about followers as unique people and responding to their individual needs

Individualism-collectivism—the extent to which the individuals of a society are independent and focused on individual achievement versus identified strongly with groups and seeking group achievement

Influence—altering the motives or perceptions of another to accomplish a given goal

Influence attempts—actions geared toward a desired outcome

Influence processes—the processes involved in a leader influencing others, such as perceptions of the leader and the situation

Influence tactics—behaviors intended to sway the attitudes and behaviors of others

Initiating structure—a leader planning and organizing a work group's activity

Inspirational communication—emotionally powerful statements and appeals directed toward increasing follower motivation

Integrity—the extent to which a person's behavior is consistent with his or her personal values, honesty, and ethicality

Intellectual stimulation—the process of making followers aware of problems and possible solutions; getting followers to change how they think about problems

Intelligence—the capacity to acquire, store, and apply knowledge (general mental ability, verbal reasoning, analytical reasoning, etc.)

Internal standards—personal limits on how closely goals and actions must match values

Interorganizational network—relationships that the leader and individuals within the leader's organization have with others outside of the organization

Interpersonal traits—characteristics that describe the way a person treats and interacts with other people

Intuitive—the characteristic of thinking quickly, without analyzing the situation in-depth

Laboratory research—research conducted in a laboratory setting

Leader problem-solving theories—theories that explain leader performance in terms of how well a leader can solve problems and make decisions

Leader substitutes theory—a theory that suggests that in some circumstances, groups do not need a leader to function effectively

Leader-centered teams—teams that have only one individual who holds formal leadership responsibilities, with no informal leaders to share the responsibilities

Leader-member exchange (LMX) theory—theory that suggests leaders establish an in-group of followers and an out-group of followers and that they influence these two different groups of followers in different ways

Leadership—the influence of others toward a collective goal

Least preferred co-worker model (LPC contingency model)—the most accepted and applied contingency theory of leadership, which explains two types of leaders, task oriented and relationship oriented

Legitimate power—power that involves a follower's internalization of values or norms that grant rights to the person in power

Locus of control—the way a person views the causes of his or her behavior (e.g., internal or external)

Longitudinal research—research that examines a phenomenon over time by collecting data at multiple points over time

Machiavellianism—a person's tendency to deceive and manipulate others for personal gain

Manipulate—to change an independent variable so the researcher can see the impact on different groups

Masculinity-femininity—the extent to which the individuals of a society value traditionally masculine traits or behaviors versus feminine traits or behaviors

Measure—the questionnaire or test used to collect numerical data

Measurement—a number representing data collected about variables

Mediator variable—a variable that explains the relationship between the independent variable and the dependent variable

Moderator variable—a variable that influences the strength of the relationships between two other variables

Moral reasoning—the ability to understand and work through complex ethical situations

Multilevel research—research examining, in the same study, relationships among variables at multiple levels

Multiple linkage model—an integrated theory that evaluates the relationships between managerial variables, intervening variables, criterion variables, and situational variables

Mumford's theory of outstanding leadership—a theory that suggests leaders can be classified as charismatic, ideological, or pragmatic as defined by the way they approach leading their group

Need for achievement—a characteristic of individuals who are motivated by the satisfaction they feel when they complete a difficult task

Need for affiliation—a characteristic of individuals who are motivated by feeling liked and accepted by others

Need for power—a characteristic of individuals who are motivated by their ability to influence and control other people

Needs or motives—the impulses that motivate a person to act in a particular manner

Neutralizers—the aspects of a situation that make a leader ineffective, such as a leader's lack of authority or a follower's lack of interest

Nonexperimental research—research that involves relationships between variables of interest that are studied by observing or measuring them as they naturally occur

Novice—a person who is new to a field or activity (i.e., a beginner)

Optimism—an expectation that events or actions will work out in a positive way

Organizational network—relationships that exist within an individual's organization

Participative leadership—leader behavior that involves a leader involving his or her subordinates in making important decisions and doing supervisor-type tasks

Path-goal theory—a theory that emphasizes the role of a leader as setting, defining, and clarifying goals; motivating followers to achieve those goals; and helping followers see a clear path toward goal attainment

Path-oriented activities—actions taken by a leader to shape the way a group pursues its goals, such as providing guidance or obtaining materials

Personality traits—relatively stable characteristics that influence the way a person acts in certain situations

Personalized power—power that is used to serve selfish needs and desires while ignoring or even acting against the needs and desires of others

Person-focused definition of leadership—a mind-set that defines leadership by the traits or skills that make someone a leader

Planning—the ability to forecast, and predict, potential actions and their consequences in order to determine the best course of action

Political tactics—behaviors intended to affect broad organizational decisions, or how such decisions can benefit the individual or his or her group

Power—the capacity of one person to influence the behavior or attitudes of others

Power distance—the extent to which the individuals of a society are willing to accept some individuals or institutions having more power than others

Pragmatic leadership—a leadership style in which a leader emphasizes knowledge management, expertise, problem solving, and consensus building rather than a loyal following or adherence to an ideological stance

Proactive influence attempt—a single request from one person to another

Proactive influence tactics—behaviors geared toward achieving a particular outcome

Problem solving—the process of understanding many aspects of a complex problem in order to solve that problem

Process-focused definition of leadership—a mind-set that defines leadership as an influence process that occurs between individuals

Qualitative research—research that collects data by observing leader behavior or interviewing leaders and/or followers and taking detailed notes

Quantitative research—research that measures variables when specific hypotheses are to be tested

Questioning assumptions—the process of challenging beliefs about a problem

Random assignment—the act of putting research participants into different experimental groups at random

Recombination of existing knowledge—the process of restructuring or reorganizing existing concepts to provide new understandings that can serve as the basis for generating alternative solutions

Referent power—power that involves a follower liking or admiring the person in power

Reframing—the act of putting a problem in a different context, or viewing it in a different way

Relational leadership theories—theories that emphasize relationship building as the main method of a leader exerting influence on his or her followers

Relations-oriented behaviors—behaviors that revolve around building relationships and motivating followers

Research—a formal, systematic process that utilizes observation and/or experimentation to collect information about a phenomenon of interest in order to draw conclusions that contribute to broader knowledge about the topic

Research design—the final plan consisting of the research methods and procedures that will be used in a study

Research methods—the techniques, or procedures, used to collect information about leadership

Research subjects (or participants)—the people that data are collected about in a research study

Resilience—the ability to deal with setbacks or negative outcomes

Reward power—power that involves a follower seeking rewards provided by the person in power

Role modeling—behaviors that a leader uses to set a work climate

Role-focused definition of leadership—a mind-set that defines leadership as a set of behaviors or actions that someone acting as a leader engages in

Self-awareness—an awareness of one's own values, identity, emotions, and motives

Self-confidence—a belief in one's ability to accomplish difficult tasks

Self-efficacy—the extent to which an individual feels they are qualified to perform a given activity

Self-regulation—a process through which an individual matches values with goals and actions

Shared purpose—a characteristic of teams where individuals within the team have agreed upon objectives and goals

Situational theory of leadership—a theory of leadership suggesting that leaders should be able to recognize the circumstances they are facing and adjust their leadership style to match that situation

Skill—the ability to do something well, in both general and specific ways

Social capital—the idea that relationships are a valuable resource, and that knowing the right people can help leaders in a number of ways (e.g., providing information, getting permission, obtaining funding)

Social exchange theory—a theory that defines changes in power in terms of the relationship between leaders and followers over time

Social intelligence—the ability to recognize and choose the best way to address interpersonal situations

Social judgment skills—the ability to understand and monitor social dynamics within the problem domain and integrate potential solutions with the practical demands of an organization

Social network—a set of relationships that a leader has with other individuals, groups, and organizations

Social perceptiveness—the ability to recognize the needs, the potential problems, and the potential opportunities for an organization

Social support—a characteristic of teams where the individuals on the team provide consideration and acknowledgement to one another

Socialized power—power that acts for the good of others and not solely for oneself

Statistics—a set of concepts, rules, and procedures that helps researchers organize, understand, and draw conclusions from quantitative data

Strategic contingencies theory—a theory that attempts to describe how power is distributed among various subunits, or departments, in an organization

Substitutes—the aspects of a task, a group of followers, or an organization that replace leadership, making it unnecessary

Support—leader behaviors that allow employees to have enough time and resources to complete their tasks

Supportive-disloyal leader—a leader who acts in the best interest of his or her followers, while ignoring or acting against the organization's best interest

Survey—a set of questions with numerical scales that research participants can use to choose their responses

Survey research—a research method where surveys are administered to a sample of participants in order to collect data

Task-oriented behaviors—behaviors that involve a leader planning and organizing a work group's activity

Team—a group of individuals working collectively to accomplish shared work

Theory—a set of concepts (or ideas) that presents a possible explanation for a particular phenomenon

Trait theory of leadership—a theory that says leaders have unique traits that enable them to be leaders

Traits—characteristics of a person that describe the person's thinking, personality, motivation, or how they deal with people

Transformational leaders—leaders who are able to motivate their followers to achieve above and beyond their followers' own expectations

Transformational leadership theory—a theory that attempts to explain leader effectiveness by how a leader is able to mold and shape the way his or her followers perceive themselves, their world, and their place in the world

Tyrannical leader—a leader who acts in the best interest of the organization, while ignoring or acting against his or her followers' best interest

Uncertainty avoidance—the extent to which the individuals of a society are comfortable with ambiguity and uncertainty

Unconventional methods—the use of methods for solving a problem that are not normally associated with the type of problem

Values—personal opinions about what is desirable in a given situation

Variable—any factor, trait, or condition that can exist in differing amounts or types

Vision—a set of beliefs about how people should act, and interact, to achieve some ideal future

Voice—the feeling that each team member can contribute input as to how the team will carry out its work

Wisdom—the successful use of intelligence, creativity, and experience to reach a common good

References

Amabile, T. M., Schatzer, E. A., Moneta, G. B., & Kramer, S. J. (2004). Leader behaviors and work environment for creativity: Perceived leader support. *The Leadership Quarterly, 15*, 5–32.

Ancona, D., & Caldwell, D. (1992). Demography and design: Predictors of new product team performance. *Organization Science, 3*, 321–341.

Anderson, L. R. (1966). Leader behavior, member attitudes, and task performance of intercultural discussion groups. *Journal of Social Psychology, 69*, 305–391.

Antes, A. L., & Mumford, M. D. (in press). Effects of time frame on creative thought: Process versus problem-solving effects. *Creativity Research Journal.*

Ashour, A. S. (1973). The contingency model of leadership effectiveness: An evaluation. *Organizational Behavior and Human Performance, 9*, 336–355.

Avolio, B. J., & Bass, B. M. (1995). Individual consideration viewed at multiple levels of analysis: A multi-level framework for examining the diffusion of transformational leadership. *The Leadership Quarterly, 6*, 199–218.

Avolio, B. J., & Gardner, W. (2005). Authentic leadership development: Getting to the root of positive forms of leadership. *The Leadership Quarterly, 16*, 315–338.

Avolio, B. J., Jung, D. I., & Sivasubramaniam, N. (1996). Building highly developed teams: Focusing on shared leadership processes, efficacy, trust, and performance. In M. M. Beyerlein & D. A. Johnson (Eds.), *Advances in interdisciplinary study of work teams: Vol. 3. Team leadership* (pp. 173–209). Greenwich, CT: JAI Press.

Avolio, B. J., Gardner, W., Walumbwa, F., Luthans, F., & May, D. (2004). Unlocking the mask: A look at the process by which authentic leaders impact follower attitudes and behaviors. *The Leadership Quarterly, 15,* 801–823.

Balkundi, P., & Harrison, D. (2006). Ties, leaders, and time in teams: Strong inference about network structure's effects on team viability and performance. *Academy of Management Journal, 49,* 49–68.

Balkundi, P., & Kilduff, M. (2006). The ties that lead: A social network approach to leadership. *The Leadership Quarterly, 17,* 419–439.

Bandura, A. (1997). *Self-efficacy: The exercise of control.* New York: W. H. Freeman/Times Books/Henry Holt & Co.

Barreto, M., Spears, R., Ellemers, N., & Shahinper, K. (2003). Who wants to know? The effect of audience on identity expression among minority group members. *British Journal of Social Psychology, 42,* 299–318.

Barrow, J. C. (1977). The variables of leadership: A review and conceptual framework. *Academy of Management Review, 2,* 231–251.

Bass, B. M. (1960). *Leadership, psychology, and organizational behavior.* New York: Harper.

Bass, B. M. (1985a). *Leadership and performance beyond expectations.* New York: Free Press.

Bass, B. M. (1985b). Leadership: Good, better, best. *Organizational Dynamics, 13,* 26–40.

Bass, B. M. (1990). *Bass & Stogdill's handbook of leadership: Theory, research, and managerial application* (3rd ed.). New York: Free Press.

Bass, B. M. (1999). Current developments in transformational leadership: Research and applications. *Psychologist-Manager Journal, 3,* 5–21.

Bass, B. M., & Avolio, B. J. (1990). The implications of transactional and transformational leadership for individual, team, and organizational development. In W. Pasmore & R. W. Woodman (Eds.), *Research in organizational change and development: Vol. 4* (pp. 231–272). Greenwich, CT: JAI Press.

Bass, B. M., & Avolio, B. J. (1993). Transformational leadership: A response to critiques. *Leadership theory and research: Perspectives and directions* (pp. 49–80). San Diego, CA: Academic Press.

Bass, B. M., & Avolio, B. J. (1994). *Improving organizational effectiveness through transformational leadership.* Thousand Oaks, CA: Sage Publications.

Bass, B. M., & Avolio, B. J. (1995). *Manual for the multifactor leadership questionnaire: Rater form (5X short)*. Palo Alto, CA: Mind Garden.

Bass, B. M., & Riggio, R. (2006). *Transformational leadership* (2nd ed.). Mahwah, NJ: Lawrence Erlbaum Associates.

Bennis, W., & Nanus, B. (1985). *Leaders: The strategies of taking charge.* San Francisco: Harper-Collins.

Berson, Y., Shamir, B., Avolio, B. J., & Popper, M. (2001). The relationship between vision strength, leadership style, and context. *The Leadership Quarterly, 12,* 53–73.

Beyer, J., & Browning, L. (1999). Transforming an industry in crisis: Charisma, routinization, and supportive cultural leadership. *The Leadership Quarterly, 10,* 483–520.

Blank, W., Weitzel, J. R., & Green, S. G. (1999). A test of situational leadership theory. *Personnel Psychology, 43,* 579–597.

Bliese, P. D., Halverson, R. R., & Schriesheim, C. A. (2002). Benchmarking multilevel methods in leadership: The articles, the model, and the data set. *The Leadership Quarterly, 13,* 3–14.

Borden, D. F. (1980). *Leader-boss, stress, personality, job satisfaction, and performance: Another look at the interrelationship of some old constructs in the modern large bureaucracy.* Doctoral dissertation, University of Washington, Seattle.

Brown, D. J., & Keeping, L. M. (2005). Elaborating the construct of transformational leadership: The role of affect. *The Leadership Quarterly, 16,* 245–272.

Brown, M. E., & Trevino, L. K. (2006). Ethical leadership: A review and future directions. *The Leadership Quarterly, 17,* 595–616.

Brown, M. E., Trevino, L. K., & Harrison, D. (2005). Ethical leadership: A social learning perspective for construct development and testing. *Organizational Behavior and Human Decision Processes, 97,* 117–134.

Bryman, A. (2004). Qualitative research on leadership: A critical but appreciative review. *The Leadership Quarterly, 15,* 729–769.

Burke, W. (1986). Leadership as empowering others. In S. Srivastra (Ed.), *Executive power* (pp. 51–77). San Francisco: Jossey-Bass.

Burns, J. M. (1978). *Leadership.* New York: Harper & Row.

Cantoni, L. J. (1955). Emotional maturity needed for success in business. *Personnel Journal, 34,* 173–176.

Carson, J. B., Tesluk, P. E., & Marrone, J. A. (2007). Shared leadership in teams: An investigation of antecedent conditions and performance. *Academy of Management Journal, 50,* 1217–1234.

Coch, L., & French, J. R. P., Jr. (1948). Overcoming resistance to change. *Human Relations, 1*, 512–532.

Conger, J. (1989). *The charismatic leader: Behind the mystique of exceptional leadership.* San Francisco, CA: Jossey-Bass.

Conger, J. (1993). Max Weber's conceptualization of charismatic authority: Its influence on organizational research. *The Leadership Quarterly, 4*, 277–288.

Conger, J. (1999). Charismatic and transformational leadership in organizations: An insider's perspective on these developing streams of research. *The Leadership Quarterly, 10*, 145–179.

Conger, J., & Kanungo, R. (1987). Toward a behavioral theory of charismatic leadership in organizational settings. *Academy of Management Review, 12*, 637–647.

Conger, J., & Kanungo, R. (1988). *Charismatic leadership: The elusive factor in organizational effectiveness.* San Francisco, CA: Jossey-Bass.

Conger, J., & Kanungo, R. (1998). *Charismatic leadership in organizations.* Thousand Oaks, CA: Sage Publications.

Connelly, M. S., Gilbert, J. A., Zaccaro, S. J., Threlfall, K. V., Marks, M. A., & Mumford, M. D. (2000). Exploring the relationship of leader skills and knowledge to leader performance. *The Leadership Quarterly, 11*, 65–86.

Dickson, M. W., Den Hartog, D. N., & Mitchelson, J. K. (2003). Research on leadership in a cross-cultural context: Making progress, and raising new questions. *The Leadership Quarterly, 14*, 729–768.

Dorfman, P. W., Howell, J. P., Hibino, S., Lee, J. K., Tate, U., & Bautista, A. (1997). Leadership in Western and Asian countries: Commonalities and differences in effective leadership processes across cultures. *The Leadership Quarterly, 8*, 233–274.

Eagly, A. H. (1995). The science and politics of comparing women and men. *American Psychologist, 50*, 145–158.

Eagly, A. H., & Johnson, B. T. (1990). Gender and leadership-style: A meta-analysis. *Psychological Bulletin, 108*, 233–256.

Eagly, A. H., Karau, S. J., & Makhijani, M. G. (1995). Gender and the effectiveness of leaders: A meta-analysis. *Psychological Bulletin, 117*, 125–145.

Eden, D., & Leviatan, U. (1975). Implicit leadership theory as a determinant of the factor structure underlying supervisory behavior scales. *Journal of Applied Psychology, 60*, 736–741.

Einarsen, S., Aasland, M. S., & Skogstad, A. (2007). Destructive leadership behavior: A definition and conceptual model. *The Leadership Quarterly, 18*, 207–216.

Ekvall, G., & Ryhammer, L. (1999). The creative climate: Its determination and effects at a Swedish University. *Creativity Research Journal, 12*, 303–310.

Fernandez, C. F., & Vecchio, R. P. (1997). Situational leadership theory revisited: A test of an across-jobs perspective. *The Leadership Quarterly, 8*, 67–84.

Ferris, G. R., Zinko, R., Brouer, R. L., Buckley, M. R., & Harvey, M. G. (2007). Strategic bullying as a supplementary, balanced perspective on destructive leadership. *The Leadership Quarterly, 18*, 195–206.

Fiedler, F. E. (1967). *A theory of leadership effectiveness.* New York: McGraw-Hill.

Fiedler, F. E. (1970). *Personality, motivational systems, and behavior of high and low LPC persons* (Tech. Rep. No. 70–12). Seattle: University of Washington, Department of Psychology.

Fiedler, F. E. (1973). The contingency model: A reply to Ashour. *Organizational Behavior and Human Performance, 9*, 356–368.

Fiedler, F. E. (1977). A rejoinder to Schriesheim and Kerr's premature obituary of the contingency model. In J. G. Hunt & L. L. Larson (Eds.), *Leadership: The cutting edge.* Carbondale: Southern Illinois University Press.

Fiedler, F. E. (1986). The contribution of cognitive resources and leader behavior to organizational performance. *Journal of Applied Social Psychology, 16*, 532–548.

Fiedler, F. E., & Garcia, J. E. (1987). *New approaches to effective leadership: Cognitive resources and organizational performance.* New York: Wiley.

Fiedler, F. E., & Leister, A. F. (1977). Leader intelligence and task performance: A test of a multiple screen model. *Organizational Behavior and Human Performance, 20*, 1–14.

Fiedler, F. E., Potter, E. H., III, Zais, M. M., & Knowlton, W. A., Jr. (1979). Organizational stress and the use and misuse of managerial intelligence and experience. *Journal of Applied Psychology, 64*, 635–647.

Fleishman, E. A. (1951). *Leadership climate and supervisory behavior* (Personnel Research Board). Columbus: Ohio State University.

Fleishman, E. A. (1953). The description of supervisory behavior. *Journal of Applied Psychology, 37*, 1–6.

Fleishman, E. A. (1973). Twenty years of consideration and structure. In E. A. Fleishman & J. G. Hunt (Eds.), *Current developments in the study of leadership.* Carbondale: Southern Illinois University Press.

Foundation for Research on Human Behavior. (1954). *Leadership patterns and organizational effectiveness*. Report of a seminar conducted by the Foundation for Research on Human Behavior, March 12–13, 1954, at Corning, NY; April 23–24, 1954, at Ann Arbor, MI; and May 14–15, 1954, at Pocono Manor, PA.

French, J., & Raven, B. H. (1959). The bases of social power. In D. Cartwright (Ed.), *Studies of social power* (pp. 150–167). Ann Arbor, MI: Institute for Social Research.

Friedlander, F., & Walton, E. (1964). Positive and negative motivations toward work. *Administrative Science Quarterly, 9*, 194–207.

Frost, D. E. (1983). Role perceptions and behavior of the immediate supervisor: Moderating effects on the prediction of leadership effectiveness. *Organizational Behavior and Human Performance, 31*, 123–142.

Gabler, N. (2006). *Walt Disney: The triumph of the American imagination*. New York: Vintage.

Gardner, W., Avolio, B. J., Luthans, F., May, D., & Walumbwa, F. (2005). Can you see the real me? A self-based model of authentic leader and follower development. *The Leadership Quarterly, 16*, 343–372.

George, W. (2003). *Authentic leadership: Rediscovering the secrets to creating lasting value*. San Francisco: Jossey-Bass.

Gibson, F. W., Fiedler, F. E., & Barrett, K. M. (1993). Stress, babble, and the utilization of the leader's intellectual abilities. *The Leadership Quarterly, 4*, 189–208.

Goldberg, L. R. (1999). A broad-bandwidth, public domain, personality inventory measuring the lower-level facets of several five-factor models. In I. Mervielde, I. Deary, F. De Fruyt, & F. Ostendorf (Eds.), *Personality psychology in Europe: Vol. 7, Selected papers from the Eighth European Conference on Personality held in Ghent, Belgium, July 1996* (pp. 7–28). Tilburg, The Netherlands: Tilburg University Press.

Goleman, D. (1995). *Emotional intelligence*. New York: Bantam Books.

Graef, C. L. (1983). The situational leadership theory: A critical review. *Academy of Management Review, 8*, 285–296.

Graen, G. B. (1976). Role making processes within complex organizations. In M. D. Dunnette (Ed.), *Handbook of industrial and organizational psychology*. Chicago: Rand McNally.

Graen, G. B., Alvares, K. M., Orris, J. B., & Martella, J. A. (1970). Contingency model of leadership effectiveness: Antecedent and evidential results. *Psychological Bulletin, 74*, 285–296.

Graen, G. B., & Cashman, J. F. (1975). A role-making model of leadership in formal organizations: A developmental approach. In J. G. Hunt & L. L. Larson (Eds.), *Leadership frontiers.* Kent, OH: Kent State University Press.

Graen, G. B., Novak, M., & Sommerkamp, P. (1982). The effects of leader-member exchange and job design on productivity and satisfaction: Testing a dual attachment model. *Organizational Behavior and Human Performance, 30,* 109–131.

Graen, G. B., & Uhl-Bien, M. (1995). Relationship-based approach to leadership: Development of leader-member exchange (LMX) theory of leadership over 25 years: Applying a multi-level multi-domain approach. *The Leadership Quarterly, 6,* 219–247.

Graziano, A. M., & Raulin, M. L. (2004). *Research methods: A process of inquiry* (5th ed.). Boston: Pearson Education.

Green, S. G., & Mitchell, T. R. (1979). Attributional processes of leaders in leader-member exchanges. *Organizational Behavior and Human Performance, 23,* 429–458.

Guetzkow, H., & Simon, H. (1955). The impact of certain communication nets upon organization and performance in task-oriented groups. *Management Science, 1,* 233–250.

Hackman, J. R., & Wageman, R. (2005). A theory of team coaching. *Academy of Management Review, 30,* 269–287.

Hackman, J. R., Brousseau, K. R., & Weiss, J. A. (1976). The interaction of task design and group performance strategies in determining group effectiveness. *Organizational Behavior and Human Performance, 16,* 350–365.

Halpin, A. W., & Winer, B. J. (1957). A factorial study of the leader behavior descriptions. In R. M. Stogdill & A. E. Coons (Eds.), *Leader behavior: Its description and measurement.* Columbus: Ohio State University, Bureau of Business Research.

Hersey, P., & Blanchard, K. H. (1969). Life cycle theory of leadership. *Training & Development Journal, 23,* 26–34.

Hersey, P., & Blanchard, K. H. (1972). The management of change: Change and the use of power. *Training & Development Journal, 26*(1), 6–10.

Hersey, P., & Blanchard, K. H. (1993). *Management of organizational behavior: Utilizing human resources* (6th ed.). Englewood Cliffs, NJ: Prentice Hall.

Hofstede, G. (1980). *Culture's consequences: International differences in work-related values* (Abridged ed.). Newbury Park, CA: Sage Publications.

Hofstede, G. (1998). Attitudes, values, and organizational culture: Disentangling the concepts. *Organization Studies, 19*, 477–493.

Hogan, R., Curphy, G. J., & Hogan, J. (1994). What we know about leadership: Effectiveness and personality. *American Psychologist, 49*, 493–504.

Hollander, E. P. (1958). Conformity, status, and idiosyncrasy credit. *Psychological Review, 65*, 117–127.

Hollander, E. P. (1978). *Leadership dynamics: A practical guide to effective relationships*. New York: Free Press.

House, R. J. (1971). A path goal theory of leader effectiveness. *Administrative Science Quarterly, 16*, 321–338.

House, R. J., Hanges, P., & Ruiz-Quintanila, S. A. (Eds.) (2004). *Leadership, culture, and organizations: The GLOBE study of 62 societies*. Thousand Oaks, CA: Sage Publications.

House, R. J., & Mitchell, T. R. (1974). Path-goal theory of leadership. *Journal of Contemporary Business, 3*, 81–97.

House, R. J., & Podsakoff, P. (1994). Leadership effectiveness: Past perspectives and future directions for research. In J. Greenberg (Ed.), *Organizational behavior: The state of the science* (pp. 45–82). Hillsdale, NJ: Lawrence Erlbaum Associates.

House, R. J., & Shamir, B. (1993). Toward the integration of transformational, charismatic, and visionary theories. In M. M. Chemers & R. Ayman (Eds.), *Leadership theory and research: Perspectives and directions* (pp. 81–108). San Diego, CA: Academic Press.

Howell, J. M., & Boies, K. (2004). Champions of technological innovation: The influence of contextual knowledge, role orientation, idea generation, and idea promotion on champion emergence. *The Leadership Quarterly, 15*, 123–143.

Howell, J. P., Dorfman, P. W., & Kerr, S. (1986). Moderator variables in leadership research. *Academy of Management Review, 11*, 88–102.

Hunt, J. G., Boal, K. B., & Dodge, G. E. (1999). The effects of visionary and crisis-responsive charisma on followers: An experimental examination of two kinds of charismatic leadership. *The Leadership Quarterly, 10*, 423–448.

Hunter, S. T., Bedell-Avers, K. E., & Mumford, M. D. (2007). The typical leadership study: Assumptions, implications, and potential remedies. *The Leadership Quarterly, 18*, 435–446.

Ilies, R., Morgeson, F., & Nahrgang, J. (2005). Authentic leadership and eudaemonic well-being: Understanding leader-follower outcomes. *The Leadership Quarterly, 16*, 373–394.

Jaussi, K. S., & Dionne, S. D. (2003). Leading for creativity: The role of unconventional leader behavior. *The Leadership Quarterly, 14*, 475–498.

Jelinek, M., & Schoonhoven, C. B. (1990). *The innovation marathon: Lessons learned from high technology firms*. Oxford, England: Blackwell.

Johnson, S. K. (2008). I second that emotion: Effects of emotional contagion and affect at work on leader and follower outcomes. *The Leadership Quarterly, 19*, 1–19.

Kanter, R. M. (1983). *The change masters*. New York: Simon & Schuster.

Katz, D., Maccoby, N., Gurin, G., & Floor, L. (1951). *Productivity, supervision, and morale in an office situation*. Ann Arbor, MI: Institute for Social Research.

Keane, M. (1996). On adaptation in analogy: Tests of pragmatic importance and adaptability in analogical problem solving. *The Quarterly Journal of Experimental Psychology, 49A*, 1062–1085.

Kerr, S. (1977). Substitutes for leadership: Some implications for organizational design. *Organization and Administrative Sciences, 8*, 135–146.

Kerr, S., & Jermier, J. (1978). Substitutes for leadership: Their meaning and measurement. *Organizational Behavior and Human Performance, 22*, 374–403.

Kilduff, M., Tsai, W., & Hanke, R. (2006). A paradigm too far? A dynamic stability reconsideration of the social network research program. *Academy of Management Review, 31*, 1031–1048.

Kirkman, B. L., & Rosen, B. (1999). Beyond self-management: Antecedents and consequences of team empowerment. *Academy of Management Journal, 42*, 58–74.

Knowlton, W. (1979). *The effects of stress, experience, and intelligence on dyadic leadership performance*. Doctoral dissertation, University of Washington, Seattle.

Kotter, J. P. (1990). *A force for change: How leadership differs from management*. New York: Free Press.

Kouzes, J. M., & Posner, B. Z. (1987). *The leadership challenge: How to get extraordinary things done in organizations*. San Francisco: Jossey-Bass.

Latham, G. P., Erez, M., & Locke, E. A. (1988). Resolving scientific disputes by the joint design of crucial experiments: Application to the Erez-Latham dispute regarding participation in goal setting. *Journal of Applied Psychology, 73*, 753–777.

Leana, C. R., Locke, E. A., & Schweiger, D. M. (1990). Fact and fiction in analyzing research on participative decision making: A critique of Cotton, Vollrath, Froggatt, Lengnick-Hall, and Jennings. *Academy of Management Review, 15*, 137–146.

Levay, C. (in press). Charismatic leadership in resistance to change. *The Leadership Quarterly*.

Lewin, K., Lippitt, R., & White, R. K. (1939). Patterns of aggressive behavior in experimentally created social climates. *Journal of Social Psychology, 10*, 271–301.

Liden, R. C., & Maslyn, J. M. (1998). Multidimensionality of leader-member exchange: An empirical assessment through scale development. *Journal of Management, 24*, 43–72.

Likert, R. (1967). *The human organization: Its management and value.* New York: McGraw-Hill.

Lord, R. G., Brown, D. J., Harvey, J. L., & Hall, R. J. (2001). Contextual constraints on prototype generation and their multilevel consequences for leadership perceptions. *The Leadership Quarterly, 12*, 311–338.

Lord, R. G., & Hall, R. J. (2005). Identity, deep structure, and the development of leadership skill. *The Leadership Quarterly, 16*, 591–615.

Lord, R. G., & Maher, K. J. (1991). *Leadership and information processing: Linking perceptions and performance.* Boston: Unwin-Hyman.

Luthans, F., & Avolio, B. J. (2003). Authentic leadership: A positive development approach. In K. S. Cameron, J. E. Dutton, & R. E. Quinn (Eds.), *Positive organizational scholarship* (pp. 241–258). San Francisco: Berrett-Koehler.

Maney, K. (2003). *The maverick and his machine: Thomas Watson, Sr. and the making of IBM.* Hoboken, NJ: Wiley.

Marcy, R. A. & Mumford, M. D. (in press). Leader cognition: Improving leader performance through causal analysis. *The Leadership Quarterly*.

Marks, M. A., Mathieu, J. E., & Zaccaro, S. J. (2001). A temporally based framework and taxonomy of team processes. *Academy of Management Review, 26*, 356–376.

Marta, S., Lertiz, L. E., & Mumford, M. D. (2005). Leadership skills and the group performance: Situational demands, behavioral requirements, and planning. *The Leadership Quarterly, 16*, 97–120.

McCall, M., & Lombardo, M. (1983). *Off the track: Why and how successful executives get derailed* (Tech. Rep. No. 21). Greensboro, NC: Center for Creative Leadership.

McClelland, D. C. (1970). The two faces of power. *Journal of International Affairs, 24*, 29–47.

McClelland, D. C. (1975). *Power: The inner experience*. New York: Irvington.

McClelland, D. C. (1985). How motives, skills, and values determine what people do. *American Psychologist, 40*, 812–825.

McGrath, J. E. (1984). *Groups: Interaction and performance*. Englewood Cliffs, NJ: Prentice-Hall.

McIntosh, N. J. (1988, August). *Substitutes for leadership: Review, critique, and suggestions*. Paper presented at the Academy of Management Annual Meeting, Los Angeles.

McMahon, J. T. (1972). The contingency theory: Logic and method revisited. *Personnel Psychology, 25*, 697–711.

McPherson, M., Smith-Lovin, L., & Cook, J. M. (2001). Birds of a feather: Homophily in social networks. *Annual Review of Sociology, 27*, 415–444.

Mehra, A., Smith, B. R., Dixon, A. L., & Robertson, B. (2006). Distributed leadership in teams: The network perceptions and team performance. *The Leadership Quarterly, 17*, 232–245.

Mitchell, T. R., & Kalb, L. S. (1982). Effects of job experience on supervisor attributions for a subordinate's peer performance. *Journal of Applied Psychology, 67*, 181–188.

Morgeson, F. P. (2005). The external leadership of self-managing teams: Intervening in the context of novel and disruptive events. *Journal of Applied Psychology, 90*, 497–508.

Mumford, M. D. (2006). *Pathways to outstanding leadership: A comparative analysis of charismatic, ideological, and pragmatic leaders*. Mahwah, NJ: Lawrence Erlbaum Associates.

Mumford, M. D., Antes, A. L., Caughron, J. J., & Friedrich, T. L. (2008). Charismatic, ideological, and pragmatic leadership: Multi-level influences on emergence and performance. *The Leadership Quarterly, 19*, 144–160.

Mumford, M. D., & Connelly, M. S. (1991). Leaders as creators: Leader performance and problem solving in ill-defined domains. *The Leadership Quarterly, 2*, 289–315.

Mumford, M. D., Connelly, M. S., Brown, R. P., Murphy, S. T., Hill, J. H., Antes, A. L., Waples, E. P., & Devenport, L. D. (2008). A sensemaking approach to ethics training for scientists: Preliminary evidence of training effectiveness. *Ethics and Behavior, 18*, 315–339.

Mumford, M. D., Connelly, M. S., & Gaddis, B. (2003). How creative leaders think: Experimental findings and cases. *The Leadership Quarterly, 14*, 411–432.

Mumford, M. D., Espejo, J., Hunter, S. T., Bedell-Avers, K. E., Eubanks, D. L., & Connelly, S. (2007). The sources of leader violence: A comparison of ideological and non-ideological leaders. *The Leadership Quarterly, 18*, 217–235.

Mumford, M. D., Eubanks, D. L., & Murphy, S. T. (2007). Creating the conditions for success: Best practices in leading for innovation. In J. A. Conger & R. E. Riggio (Eds.), *The practice of leadership: Developing the next generation of leaders* (pp. 129–149). San Francisco: Jossey-Bass.

Mumford, M. D., Friedrich, T. L., Caughron, J. J., & Antes, A. L. (in press a). Leadership development and assessment. In K. A. Ericsson (Ed.), *The development of professional performance*.

Mumford, M. D., Friedrich, T. L., Caughron, J. J., & Antes, A. L. (in press b). Leadership research: Traditions, developments and current directions. In D. A. Buchanan & A. Bryman (Eds.), *Handbook of organizational research methods*.

Mumford, M. D., Friedrich, T. L., Caughron, J. J., & Byrne, C. L. (2007). Leader cognition in real-world settings: How do leaders think about crises? *The Leadership Quarterly, 18*, 515–543.

Mumford, M. D., Gessner, T. E., Connelly, M. S., O'Connor, J. A., & Clifton, T. C. (1993). Leadership and destructive acts: Individual and situational influences. *The Leadership Quarterly, 4*, 115–147.

Mumford, M. D., Hunter, S. T., Eubanks, D. L., Bedell, K. T., & Murphy, S. T. (2007). Developing leaders for creative efforts: A domain-based approach to leadership development. *Human Resource Management Review, 17*, 402–417.

Mumford, M. D., Licuanan, B. (2004). Leading for innovation: Conclusions, issues, and directions. *The Leadership Quarterly, 15*, 217–221.

Mumford, M. D., Marks, M. A., Connelly, M. S., Zaccaro, S. T., & Reiter-Palmon, R. (2000). Development of leadership skills: Experience and training. *The Leadership Quarterly, 11*, 87–114.

Mumford, M. D., Schultz, R. A., & Osburn, H. K. (2002). Planning in organizations: Performance as a multi-level phenomenon. In F. J. Yammarino & F. Dansereau (Eds.), *Research in multi-level issues: The many faces of multi-level issues* (pp. 3–35). Oxford, England: Elsevier Science.

Mumford, M. D., Schultz, R. A., & Van Doorn, J. R. (2001). Performance in planning: Processes, requirements, and errors. *Review of General Psychology, 5*, 213–240.

Mumford, M. D., Scott, G. M., Gaddis, B., & Strange, J. M. (2002). Leading creative people: Orchestrating expertise and relationships. *The Leadership Quarterly, 13*, 705–750.

Mumford, M. D., Scott, G., & Hunter, S. (2006). Charismatic, ideological, and pragmatic leaders: How do they lead, why do they lead, and who do they lead? In M. D. Mumford (Ed.), *Pathways to outstanding leadership* (pp. 25–50). Mahwah, NJ: Lawrence Erlbaum Associates.

Mumford, M. D., Strange, J., & Bedell, K. (2006). Charismatic, ideological, and pragmatic leaders: Are they really different? In M. D. Mumford (Ed.), *Pathways to outstanding leadership* (pp. 3–24). Mahwah, NJ: Lawrence Erlbaum Associates.

Mumford, M. D., Strange, J., Scott, G., & Gaddis, E. (2006). What history remembers and predicts for outstanding leaders. In M. D. Mumford (Ed.), *Pathways to outstanding leadership* (pp. 51–80). Mahwah, NJ: Lawrence Erlbaum Associates.

Mumford, M. D., Van Doorn, J. (2001). The leadership of pragmatism: Reconsidering Franklin in the age of charisma. *The Leadership Quarterly, 12*, 279–309.

Mumford, M. D., Zaccaro, S. J., Connelly, M. S., & Marks, M. A. (2000). Leadership skills: Conclusions and future directions. *The Leadership Quarterly, 11*, 155–170.

Mumford, M. D., Zaccaro, S. J., Harding, F. D., Jacobs, T. O., & Fleishman, E. A. (2000). Leadership skills for a changing world: Solving complex social problems. *The Leadership Quarterly, 11*, 11–35.

Murphy, S. E., & Ensher, E. A. (2008). A qualitative analysis of charismatic leadership in Teams: The case of television directors. *The Leadership Quarterly, 19*, 335–352.

Norris, W. R., & Vecchio, R. P. (1992). Situational leadership theory: A replication. *Group and Organization Management, 17*, 331–342.

Northouse, P. G. (2007). *Leadership: Theory and practice*. Thousand Oaks, CA: Sage Publications.

O'Connor, J., Mumford, M. D., Clifton, T. C., Gessner, T. L., & Connelly, M. S. (1995). Charismatic leaders and destructiveness: An historiometric study. *The Leadership Quarterly, 6*, 529–555.

O'Connor, P. M. G., & Quinn, L. (2004). Organizational capacity for leadership. In C. D. McCauley & E. Van Velsor (Eds.), *The Center for Creative Leadership handbook of leadership development* (2nd ed., pp. 417–437). San Francisco: Jossey-Bass.

Padilla, A., Hogan, R., & Kaiser, R. B. (2007). The toxic triangle: Destructive leaders, susceptible followers, and conducive environments. *The Leadership Quarterly, 18,* 176–194.

Peters, L. H., Hartke, D. D., & Pohlmann, J. T. (1985). Fiedler's contingency theory of leadership: An application of the meta-analysis procedures of Schmidt and Hunter. *Psychological Bulletin, 97,* 274–285.

Peters, T. J., & Waterman, R. H., Jr. (1982). *In search of excellence: Lessons from America's best-run companies.* New York: Harper & Row.

Petty, R., & Cacioppo, J. (1981). *Attitudes and persuasion: Classic and contemporary approaches.* Dubuque, IA: Brown.

Podsakoff, P. M., MacKenzie, S. B., Ahearne, M., & Bommer, W. H. (1995). Searching for a needle in a haystack: Trying to identify the illusive moderators of leadership behaviors. *Journal of Management, 21,* 423–470.

Podsakoff, P. M., Niehoff, B. P., MacKenzie, S., & Williams, M. L. (1993). Do substitutes for leadership really substitute for leadership? An examination of Kerr and Jermier's situational leadership model. *Organizational Behavior and Human Decision Processes, 54,* 1–44.

Porter, L. W., & Lawler, E. E. (1968). *Managerial attitudes and performance.* Homewood, IL: Irwin-Dorsey.

Post, J., Ruby, K., & Shaw, E. (2002). The radical group in context: 1. An integrated framework for the analysis of group risk for terrorism. *Studies in Conflict & Terrorism, 25,* 73–100.

Potter, E. H. (1978). *The contribution of intelligence and experience to the performance of staff personnel.* Doctoral dissertation, University of Washington, Seattle.

Rafferty, A., & Griffin, M. (2004). Dimensions of transformational leadership: Conceptual and empirical extensions. *The Leadership Quarterly, 15,* 329–354.

Roberts, N., & Bradley, R. (1988). Limits of charisma. In J. Conger & R. Kanungo (Eds.), *Charismatic leadership: The elusive factor in organizational effectiveness* (pp. 253–275). San Francisco: Jossey-Bass.

Rosenthal, S. A., & Pittinsky, T. L. (2006). Narcissistic leadership. *The Leadership Quarterly, 17,* 617–633.

Rotter, J. B. (1966). Generalized expectancies for internal versus external control of reinforcement. *Psychological Monographs: General & Applied, 80,* 1–28.

Sagie, A., & Koslowsky, M. (2000). *Participation and empowerment in organizations*. Thousand Oaks, CA: Sage Publications.

Salas, E., Sims, D. E., & Burke, C. S. (2005). Is there a "Big Five" in teamwork? *Small Group Research, 36*, 555–599.

Scandura, T. A., & Graen, G. B. (1984). Moderating effects of initial leader-member exchange status on the effects of leadership intervention. *Journal of Applied Psychology, 69*, 428–436.

Schriesheim, C. A., Neider, L. L., Scandura, T. A., & Tepper, B. J. (1992). Development and preliminary validation of a new scale (LMX-6) to measure leader-member exchange in organizations. *Educational and Psychological Measurement, 52*, 135–147.

Schwartz, S. (1999). A theory of cultural values and some implications for work. *Applied Psychology: An International Review, 48*, 23–47.

Seligman, M. (1998). *Learned optimism*. New York: Pocket Books.

Shamir, B., & Eilam, G. (2005). What's your story? A life-stories approach to authentic leadership development. *The Leadership Quarterly, 16*, 395–417.

Shamir, B., House, R., & Arthur, M. (1993). The motivational effects of charismatic leadership: A self-concept based theory. *Organization Science, 4*, 577–594.

Shea, C., & Howell, J. (1999). Charismatic leadership and task feedback: A laboratory study of their effects on self-efficacy and task performance. *The Leadership Quarterly, 10*, 375–396.

Shiflett, S. C. (1973). The contingency model of leadership effectiveness: Some implications of its statistical and methodological properties. *Behavioral Science, 18*, 429–440.

Sosik, J., Kahai, S., & Avolio, B. J. (1999). Leadership style, anonymity, and creativity in group decision support systems: The mediating role of optimal flow. *Journal of Creative Behavior, 33*, 227–256.

Sparrowe, R. T., & Liden, R. C. (2005). Two routes to influence: Integrating leader-member exchange and network perspectives. *Administrative Science Quarterly, 50*, 505–535.

Sparrowe, R., Liden, R. C., Wayne, S. J., & Kraimer, M. L. (2001). Social networks and the performance of individuals and groups. *Academy of Management Journal, 44*, 316–325.

Spectors, P. E. (1986). Perceived control by employees: A meta-analysis of studies concerning autonomy and participation at work. *Human Relations, 39*, 1005–1016.

Stajkovic, A., & Luthans, F. (1998). Social cognitive theory and self-efficacy: Going beyond traditional motivational and behavioral approaches. *Organizational Dynamics, 26*, 62–74.

Sternberg, R. J. (2007). A systems model of leadership: WICS. *American Psychologist, 62*, 34–42.

Stogdill, R. M. (1948). Personal factors associated with leadership: A survey of the literature. *Journal of Psychology, 25*, 35–71.

Strange, J. M., & Mumford, M. D. (2002). The origins of vision: Charismatic versus ideological leadership. *The Leadership Quarterly, 13*, 343–377.

Strauss, G. (1977). Managerial practices. In J. R. Hackman & J. L. Suttle (Eds.), *Improving life at work: Behavioral science approaches to organizational change* (pp. 297–363). Santa Monica, CA: Goodyear.

Strube, M. J., & Garcia, J. E. (1981). A meta-analytic investigation of Fielder's contingency model of leadership effectiveness. *Psychological Bulletin, 90*, 307–321.

Tannenbaum, R., & Schmidt, W. H. (1958). How to choose a leadership pattern. *Harvard Business Review, 36* (March–April), 95–101.

Tepper, B. J. (2000). Consequences of abusive supervision. *Academy of Management Journal, 43*, 178–190.

Thomas, J., & McDaniel, R. (1990). Interpreting strategic issues: Effects of strategy and the information-processing structure of top management teams. *Academy of Management Journal, 33*, 286–306.

Thomas, K., & Velthouse, B. (1990). Cognitive elements of empowerment: An "interpretive" model of intrinsic task motivation. *Academy of Management Review, 15*, 666–681.

Treviño, L. K., Hartman, L. P., & Brown, M. (2000). Moral person and moral manager: How executives develop a reputation for ethical leadership. *California Management Review, 42*, 128–142.

Treviño, L. K., Weaver, G. R., Gibson, D. G., & Toffler, B. L. (1999). Managing ethics and legal compliance: What hurts and what works. *California Management Review, 41*, 131–151.

Vecchio, R. P. (1983). Assessing the validity of Fiedler's contingency model of leadership effectiveness: A closer look at Strube and Garcia. *Psychological Bulletin, 93*, 404–408.

Vecchio, R. P. (2002). Leadership and gender advantage. *The Leadership Quarterly, 13*, 643–671.

Victor, B., & Cullen, J. B. (1988). The organizational bases of ethical work climates. *Administrative Science Quarterly, 33*, 101–125.

Vroom, V. H., & Jago, A. G. (2007). The role of the situation in leadership. *American Psychologist, 62,* 17–24.

Vroom, V. H., & Yetton, P. W. (1973). *Leadership and decision making.* Pittsburgh, PA: University of Pittsburgh Press.

Walster, E., Aronson, E., & Abrahams, D. (1966). On increasing the persuasiveness of a low prestige communicator. *Journal of Experimental Social Psychology, 2,* 325–342.

Weber, M. (1947). *The theory of social and economic organization* (Trans. T. Parsons). New York: Free Press.

Wofford, J. C., & Liska, L. Z. (1993). Path-goal theories of leadership: A meta-analysis. *Journal of Management, 19,* 858–876.

Yukl, G. (1970). Leader LPC scores: Attitude dimensions and behavioral correlates. *Journal of Social Psychology, 80,* 207–212.

Yukl, G. (2006). *Leadership in organizations* (6th ed.). Upper Saddle River, NJ: Prentice Hall.

Yukl, G., & Chavez, C. (2002). Influence tactics and leader effectiveness. In L. L. Neider & C. A. Schriesheim (Eds.), *Leadership* (pp. 139–165). Greenwich, CT: New Information Age Publishing.

Yukl, G., & Falbe, C. M. (1991). The importance of different power sources in downward and lateral relations. *Journal of Applied Psychology, 76,* 416–423.

Yukl, G., & Tracey, B. (1992). Consequences of influence tactics used with subordinates, peers, and the boss. *Journal of Applied Psychology, 77,* 525–535.

Zaccaro, S. J., Gilbert, J. A., Thor, K. K., & Mumford, M. D. (1991). Leadership and social intelligence: Linking social perspectives and behavioral flexibility to leader effectiveness. *The Leadership Quarterly, 2,* 317–342.

Zaccaro, S. J., & Klimoski, R. (2002). The interface of leadership and team processes. *Group Organization Management, 27,* 4–13.

Zaccaro, S. J., Mumford, M. D., Connelly, M. S., Marks, M. A., & Gilbert, J. A. (2000). Assessment of leader problem-solving capabilities. *The Leadership Quarterly, 11,* 37–64.

Zais, M. M. (1979). *The impact of intelligence and experience on the performance of army line and staff officers.* Master's thesis, University of Washington, Seattle.

Zellars, K. L., Tepper, B. J., & Duffy, M. K. (2002). Abusive supervision and subordinates' organizational citizenship behavior. *Journal of Applied Psychology, 87,* 1068–1076.

Index